LEADERSHIP AND T
REFORM OF EDUC/

Helen M. Gunter

First published in Great Britain in 2012 by

The Policy Press
University of Bristol
Fourth Floor
Beacon House
Queen's Road
Bristol BS8 1QU
UK

Tel +44 (0)117 331 4054
Fax +44 (0)117 331 4093
e-mail tpp-info@bristol.ac.uk
www.policypress.co.uk

North American office:
The Policy Press
c/o The University of Chicago Press
1427 East 60th Street
Chicago, IL 60637, USA
t: +1 773 702 7700
f: +1 773-702-9756
e:sales@press.uchicago.edu
www.press.uchicago.edu

British Library Cataloguing in Publication Data
A catalogue record for this book is available from the British Library.

Library of Congress Cataloging-in-Publication Data
A catalog record for this book has been requested.

ISBN 978 1 84742 766 3 paperback
ISBN 978 1 84742 767 0 hardcover

Cover design by The Policy Press
Front cover: image kindly supplied by www.istock.com
Printed and bound in Great Britain by TJ International,
Padstow
The Policy Press uses environmentally responsible print
partners.

Contents

Acknowledgements   iv
Abbreviations   vi

one   New Labour and leadership   1

two   The leadership of schools   17

three   New Labour and intellectual work   37

four   Institutionalised governance   53

five   Regimes of practice   75

six   Professional practice   95

seven   Regime practices   117

eight   New games?   133

Appendix   153
References   155
Index   191

Acknowledgements

This book has a long antecedence. It is located in my first degree in modern history and politics when I did an assignment on the Fulton Report and became interested in the interrelationship within policymaking between elected representatives, the permanent civil service and experts brought in to advise and deliver. Ten years on from this assignment, I was studying for a Masters in Educational Management and became very interested in the origins of the field's knowledge claims, particularly the seemingly unreflexive adoption of business models as best practice. I was able to take this forward in my PhD where I undertook an intellectual history of the field of educational management through the biographies and outputs of field members in higher education. In the late 1980s, there was a TV programme based on Pete Frame's (1993) *Rock Family Trees* (London: Omnibus Press) research where he charted the formation and repositioning of musicians. This genealogical approach to social practice and the development of rock bands over time has been inspirational. I have not yet begun this detailed process, but it is something that remains an ambition.

Examining the working lives of academics through my doctorate is where I first met Pierre Bourdieu and began an intellectual journey through using his thinking tools to understand the way power works. It is interesting that hardly anyone I interviewed in the mid-1990s for my PhD mentioned leadership: this is because management was seen to be the most important process for the running of a school. I watched the rapid growth in leadership with interest, and I was able to reach back to my first degree work on Fulton and connect it with New Labour's investment in education through studying the relationship between the state, public policy and knowledge production. The Knowledge Production in Educational Leadership (KPEL) project is therefore the current stage in my research and it has enabled me to make a contribution to understanding and explaining policy processes.

This book is a culmination of a body of writing regarding the field of educational leadership, and I am deeply indebted to colleagues whom I have worked and talked with over the past two decades for helping me to think. In particular, I would like to thank the Economic and Social Research Council (ESRC) for funding the project, the KPEL Project Advisory Group for their superb contribution and Gillian Forrester who, as the research assistant, travelled and interviewed people with great professionalism. While the text is mainly a new contribution, I have drawn on some preliminary thinking about institutionalised governance (Gunter and Forrester, 2009a), and with permission from Taylor and Francis Ltd, I have used some text and a reworking of the diagram on regimes of practice (Gunter and Forrester, 2009b).

There are a number of people to thank. Stewart Ranson helped me to shape my ideas for what eventually became the KPEL project, and supported my intellectual development through reading and dialogue. Thanks also go to Tanya Fitzgerald and Pat Thomson who are always stimulating to work with and great fun in playing with ideas and working on collaborative projects. Tanya Fitzgerald and Colin Mills read and commented on the text, and I am deeply grateful for their taking time in their busy lives to read the draft and for their feedback. Of course, I take full responsibility for the text, there is so much that I have had to leave out and so there is much more still to write.

Abbreviations

AAA	Anti-Academies Alliance
ACEL	Australian Council for Educational Leaders
ARK	Absolute Return for Kids
BECTA	British Educational Communications and Technology Agency
BELMAS	British Educational Leadership Management and Administration Society
BERA	British Educational Research Association
BME	Black and minority ethnic
BSF	Building Schools for the Future
CASEA	Canadian Association for Studies in Educational Administration
CCEAM	Commonwealth Council for Educational Administration and Management
CMR	Conservative Market Regime
CTC	City Technology College
CVA	Contextual Value Added
CWDC	Children's Workforce Development Council
DCSF	Department for Children, Schools and Families
DES	Department of Education and Science
DfE	Department for Education
DfEE	Department for Education and Employment
DfES	Department for Education and Skills
EAZ	Education Action Zones
ECM	Every Child Matters
EiC	Excellence in Cities
ESDS	Economic and Social Data Service
ESRC	Economic and Social Research Council
FOIA	Freedom of Information Act
GMS	Grant-maintained status
GTCE	General Teaching Council for England
HEADLAMP	Headteacher Leadership and Management Programme
HEI	Higher Education Institution
HTI	Headteachers into Industry
ICSEI	International Congress for School Effectiveness and Improvement
IPPR	Institute of Public Policy Research

IQEA	Improving the Quality of Education for All
KPEL	Knowledge Production in Educational Leadership
LIG	Leadership Incentive Grant
LMS	Local Management of Schools
LPSH	Leadership Programme for Serving Headteachers
NAHT	National Association of Headteachers
NASUWT	National Association of Schoolmasters Union of Women Teachers
NCLB	No Child Left Behind
NCSL	National College for School Leadership (from 2009, the National College for Leadership of Schools and Children's Services [NCLSCS])
NDC	National Development Centre
NDPB	Non-Departmental Public Body
NESSRT	National Evaluation of Sure Start Research Team
NET	National Education Trust
NLE	National Leaders of Education
NLPR	New Labour Policy Regime
NPQH	National Professional Qualification for Headship
NRT	National Remodelling Team
NSN	New Schools Network
NZEALS	New Zealand Educational Administration and Leadership Society
OECD	Organisation for Economic Co-operation and Development
Ofsted	Office for Standards in Education
PANDA	Performance and Assessment
PFI	Private Finance Initiative
PISA	Programme for International Student Assessment
PIU	Performance and Innovation Unit
PRR	Policy Research Regime
PwC	PricewaterhouseCoopers
QCA	Qualifications and Curriculum Authority
QTS	Qualified Teacher Status
RAE	Research Assessment Exercise
SATs	Standard Attainment Tests
SEF	School Evaluation Form
SESI	School Effectiveness, School Improvement
SEU	Standards and Effectiveness Unit
SHA	Secondary Heads Association
SIP	School Improvement Partner
SLR	School Leadership Regime

SMTF	School Management Task Force
SQH	Scottish Qualification for Headship
SSAT	Specialist Schools and Academies Trust
STRB	School Teachers' Review Body
TDA	Training and Development Agency
TIMSS	Trends in International Mathematics and Science Study
TTA	Teacher Training Agency
UCEA	University Council for Educational Administration
UCET	Universities' Council for the Education of Teachers
UPG	University Partnership Group
WAMG	Workforce Agreement Monitoring Group

KPEL project interviewees

Ac	academic
CS	civil servant
Hd	headteacher
Min	minister
PC	private-sector consultant

ONE

New Labour and leadership

Introduction

The front page of the right-of-centre newspaper *The Mail on Sunday* on 10 November 1991 had the following headline, 'Back to the blackboard', with a story about how Kenneth Clarke, the then Education Secretary, planned 'a radical overhaul of state primary schools' (Lightfoot, 1991, p 1). The approach to be adopted was to return to whole-class teaching and subject-based learning. When New Labour took office in 1997, they said in *Excellence in Schools* (DfEE, 1997, p 10) that 'in the 1996 national tests only 6 in 10 of 11 year olds reached the standard in maths and English expected for their age', and the solution was 'at least an hour each day devoted to both literacy and numeracy in every primary school' (p 5). Nearly 20 years after the Clarke intervention and over 10 years after the New Labour National Literacy and Numeracy Strategies, the *Mail Online* applauded the 2010 Conservative-led government for pledging a return to 'traditional lessons in English and maths after warning that achievement had "flatlined" for much of Labour's time in office' (Clark, L., 2010).

The issue of standards is an international discourse. For example, in 1983 *A Nation at Risk* (National Commission on Excellence in Education, 1983) was published in the USA where 'its conclusions were alarming, and its language was blunt to the point of being incendiary' (Ravitch, 2010, p 24); and in 1988 the publication of *Tomorrow's Schools* (Government of New Zealand, 1988) led to decentralisation in New Zealand as a means of improving learning outcomes, whereby, in Codd's terms, teachers became '"managed professionals" in a global industry' (2005, p 193). It seems that functional and measured standards in publicly funded schools are *the* problem,[1] and, following Bacchi (2009), the approach I intend to take to understanding how this is framed and the solutions generated during New Labour's time in office (1997–2010)[2] is about 'the ways in which particular representations of "problems" play a central role in how we are governed' (p xi).

The aim of this book is to describe and explain how the problem of standards has been represented through creating solutions for identified workforce deficiencies, and how New Labour constructed and deployed leaders, leading and leadership as the solution. This emphasis on what O'Reilly and Reed (2010, p 960) call 'leaderism' is evident across the public services, and internationally it was promoted as integral to good government and service provision (OECD, 2001). In Bourdieu's[3] (1990) terms, leadership was *codified* by New Labour as the dominant *game* to play where speeches, policies, research and training brought recognition and acclaim. Playing happens when 'a set of people take part in rule-bound activity, an activity which, without necessarily being the product of obedience to rules, *obeys certain regularities*' (Bourdieu, 1990, p 64, emphasis in original). The players were ministers,[4] civil servants, private-sector consultants, private philanthropists, think tanks, headteachers and professors who 'have a feel for the necessity and the logic of the game' (Bourdieu, 1990, p 64), and so they staked their interests, ideas and careers in the *game* through the regularities of a harmonised *disposition* towards the importance and legitimacy of leadership.

The approach taken is to explore the relationship between the state, public policy and knowledge, with a specific focus on: what type of knowledge was used and why? What forms of knowing were deemed legitimate and why? Who were regarded as knowers and why? New Labour drew on functional approaches to knowledge where the purposes of knowing were to remove dysfunctions from the system, and so the rationales were about outcomes and the narratives about targets, plans and data (Raffo and Gunter, 2008). I examine this by focusing on New Labour's investment in the *leadership of schools* as the strategy for delivering national reforms locally. This was a centrally designed and regulated form of leadership where policy strategy was held by the London government, with headteachers left with tactical options about efficient and effective implementation. Notably, the role of the single 'transformational' leader dominated policy statements and interventions in professional identity and practice. Distributed leadership, as hybridised delegation, enabled a totalising reform strategy where all could be responsible and accountable for standards. While the language of transformation and social justice was used, policymakers did not draw on socially critical models of leadership where the purposes are about revealing oppression and working for rights, the rationales are about equity, and the narratives are about giving recognition and enabling participation (Raffo and Gunter, 2008). While the language of education was used, the form of school leadership was not necessarily educational: children and teachers were presented as the objects that leaders and leadership impact upon, and the effective leader could be appointed from the public, private or voluntary sectors.

—

I explain the development of the leadership of schools *game* through conceptualising *institutionalised governance* as the space where public institutions controlled policy ideas and agenda setting by working with and generating a leadership industry. Trusted knowledge workers were contracted to advise and deliver policy outcomes, and, using Bourdieu's (2000) thinking tools, I reveal a New Labour *habitus* or *disposition* to think and practise in complementary ways, combined with a *doxa* of self-evident leadership truths that spoke to those who staked their professional practice as *capital* in the *field* (Bourdieu, 2000). I identify a *logic of practice* within which knowledge producers in companies, schools, think tanks and universities at home and abroad located themselves within *regimes of practice* as structured positions in the *field*. A study of the New Labour Policy Regime (NLPR) shows that those who positioned themselves here (ministers, civil servants, advisers, private consultants, researchers and some headteachers) sought to dominate but were dominated by the demands of the market and the role of the private sector in educational provision. Headteachers were officially positioned in the NLPR, but in reality only a few were comfortable there; heads tended to focus on teaching and learning and were critical of speedy reforms that did not engage with professional values and context. The Policy Research Regime (PRR) was (and is) a preferred location for social science researchers and some headteachers with a focus on scholarly critical analysis of policy and the identification of alternative approaches to reform.

In mapping and examining these regimes, I intend to draw on over 20 years of research and study, including my doctoral thesis on the history of the field (Gunter, 1999) and, more recently, the Economic and Social Research Council (ESRC)-funded Knowledge Production in Educational Leadership (KPEL) project (see Appendix). The chapters in this book present the intellectual work and data from this project, where I focus specifically on how and why New Labour established and used the National College[5] from 2000 as the means to radically change professional identities and practice.

Leaders, leading and leadership

The New Labour time in office (1997–2010) was a period of rampant adjectival leadership, variously: 'transformational', 'middle', 'teacher', 'distributed', 'instructional' and so on. Role titles such as headteacher or head of department were redesigned as 'leaders'; the right type of thinking, behaviours, skills and knowledge was known as 'leading'; and the power relationship to secure commitment to reforms was known as 'leadership'. Leadership was inherently a good thing, it was necessary as a practice and as a rhetorical device to enable 'improvement', 'modernisation', 'transformation', 'effectiveness' and the delivery of predetermined outcomes. Leaders, leading and leadership could be known, understood, trained, practised and evaluated in such a way as to be meaningful to the person doing it and to those who are deemed to be followers.

Major interventions took place: first, a workforce reform designed to eradicate professional educational knowledge and knowing, and replace it with the leadership behaviours, skills and know-how required for running a school as an effective and efficient business; second, a school system reform based on leaders rectifying failure (eg Fresh Start Schools; Executive Heads; Federations)[6] and working with powerful private interests (eg the Academies Programme);[7] third, the control of professional training and licensing both as remediation to secure local reform delivery, and as developmental through producing a pool of reform-ready leaders; and, fourth, the control of practice through direct interventions into teaching and learning (eg the Literacy and Numeracy Strategies)[8] together with performance structures and cultures where enthusiasm for compliance was a requirement, and which were secured by data generation and external validation (eg Ofsted, School Improvement Partners).[9]

Leadership was and remains a political and ideological project. Permanent revolution of change – with Hansard reporting 350 policy targets sent out to schools in 2001 alone (Jenkins, 2010) – required implementation and data generation in ways that enabled government to defend the mandate and people to be governable. Education policy was run directly out of Number 10 (Beckett and Hencke, 2004), where the model of change was calculable and linear, or what Barber (2007, p 70) identified as 'deliverology', where what was in the minister's mind in London would happen through a 'delivery chain' (p 85) to the child in the classroom. So leadership was the means by which the reform agenda was configured and secured, particularly through using rational claims combined with emotional seduction to restructure, reculture and reimagine identities and practice (Gewirtz, 2001; Pollitt, 2007). Reforms directly related to the learning needs and welfare of children spoke to the profession, even if the profession realised reform was problematic. The speed and contradictory situations created by certain reforms meant that professional practice was turned into handling 'assemblages' or 'the idea that the institutionalisation of specific projects involves the work of assembling diverse elements into an apparently coherent form' (Newman and Clarke, 2009, p 9).

So leadership was constructed and promoted as the means of suturing together a vast array of interventions in the curriculum, staffing, lesson planning and assessment, and to evidence success or be accountable for failure. It was about risk management by a government determined to be radical: in return for delivering national reforms locally, the elite and highly conservative project of the headteacher as leader with improved status, and pay parity with the private sector, would ensure that reforms happened.

No other way of being in the professional world was thinkable let alone doable. It was a period of belief-based policymaking that impacted on how research evidence was read and used. It was also part of a wider cultural turn towards celebrity with particular headteachers lauded for their leadership, and where honours and recognition were plentiful, and saying that something is the case made it somehow true. New Labour used leadership training colleges to regulate public-sector workers and knowledge production,[10] and, in education, the National College was established in 2000 as a Non-Departmental Public Body (NDPB) with a remit to lead knowledge production and training, and with a 'signature pedagogy' where they:

> implicitly define what counts as knowledge in the field and how things become known. They define how knowledge is analyzed, criticized, accepted, or discarded. They define the functions of expertise in a field, the locus of authority, and the privileges of rank and standing ... these pedagogies even determine the architectural design of educational institutions, which in turn serves to perpetuate these approaches. (Shulman, 2005, p 54)

New Labour through the National College worked with and boosted a leadership industry and so determined what is to be known about professional practice, what could be said, what words and tone could be used, and what *dispositions* could be displayed. This again fitted the cultural predilection for makeovers with trusted experts designing the rules of leadership and securing compliance to participate and conform to the required identity (Gunter and Thomson, 2009). Functional approaches to knowledge and knowledge production were preferred, mainly from school improvement and effectiveness research, where models of effective and efficient leadership could be identified, packaged and trained (Raffo and Gunter, 2008). The emphasis on what Ball (1995) identifies as 'policy science' (Has it worked and, if so, how can it be scaled up?) and 'policy entrepreneurship' (Does it sell?)

means that 'the academy is tamed' (p 259) with the sites for debate through 'policy scholarship' under threat. So the state drew on particular forms of knowledge, knowing and knowers in order to frame policy, and 'knowledge structures the field of possible action' (Popkewitz and Lindblad, 2004, p 243), so professional practice was colonised.

The leadership industry

New Labour worked with and invested in a leadership industry or 'edu-business' (Mahony et al, 2004, p 277). As Hatcher (2001) has shown in England (and Burch [2009] in the USA), there has been both 'endogenous' and 'exogenous' privatisation, with the former being the business agenda of schools in the marketplace, and the latter describing how schools design and trade products and services as businesses.

The interconnection of business practice within and outside of the school can be illuminated through data design and production. In explaining the knowledge production problems within school effectiveness, Gorard (2010, p 756) is intrigued by the question: 'why ... do so many analysts, policy-makers, users and practitioners seem to believe that school effectiveness yields useful and practical information?'. His answer is:

> In England, school effectiveness has become an industry, employing civil servants at DCSF [Department for Children, Schools and Families] and elsewhere, producing incentives for teachers deemed CVA [Contextual Value Added] experts in schools, creating companies and consultants to provide data analysis, paying royalties to software authors and funding for academics from the taxpayer. A cynical view would be that most people in England do not understand CVA, but a high proportion of those who do stand to gain from its use in some way. (Gorard, 2010, pp 756–7)

Similarly, Rowan (2002) has shown how textbook and test publishers, professional development trainers, and research and consultancy firms operate as a 'school improvement industry' in the US where 'the renowned "faddishness" ... [or] the constant swirl of innovation and reform' is caused by the culture of short-term quick fixes 'because the organizations providing ... resources either come or go quite rapidly or change directions on a dime' (p 286).

Explaining the privatisation of education in England requires a theory of power, and following Thomson's (2005) deployment of Bourdieu's arguments about *field*, I would agree that 'the changes in the field of education made by the political field as direct interventions via policy ... were the result of a synchrony of crises within the economic, political and educational fields' (p 750). *Symbolic capital exchange* took place where the economic *field* needed to expand its markets through entry into the public services, and the political *field* needed the modernising status of the private sector. So actors from the dominant economic and political *fields* ruptured the borders of education as a dominated *field*:

> agents in the superior field use administrative mechanisms, both policy and enacted policy via new regulations, jobs, procedures etc., to effect significant changes in other fields. After this crisis the relative autonomies of each field are reassumed, the field of education operates through the play of its new games and remains in a position vulnerable to further intervention. (Thomson, 2005, p 752)

So, while educational professionals may play the leadership *game* in ways that could be read as politically neutral, '*misrecognition*' (Bourdieu, 2000, p 142) of how practice is constructed by the *game* may be part of the *game*. The *logic of practice* within the workings of the leadership industry is that this is a *game* worth playing, indeed, the *only game* worth playing.

A leadership industry grew rapidly, from individual England-based entrepreneurs through to large-scale international companies. It was and remains a complex business that is difficult to track and disentangle, but those who played the leadership *game* located their practice in for-profit companies as well as in public-sector organisations such as schools and universities. This business pre-dated New Labour, was generated by New Labour, and business growth contributed to the need for New Labour to control and regulate the market and product development. Grace (1995) shows how Thatcherism created the chief executive, secularised, entrepreneurial headteacher in order to make site-based management work, with the school as a business, often outside of local authority control, within a marketised system. For example, City Technology Colleges (CTCs) were planned from 1986 as 'state-independent schools' in industrial areas, sponsored by business and with an emphasis on practical and technical education (Whitty et al, 1993). The Education Reform Act 1988 introduced both Local Management of Schools (LMS) – where a school remained within the local authority, but funding was based on pupil enrolment and the exercise of a preference to attend a particular school – and Grant Maintained Status (GMS) – where a school was set up following a ballot to opt out of local authority control and was funded directly on a per pupil basis, in addition to the funds that had previously been top-sliced by the local authority. A central feature of these schemes was that budget strategy and management was relocated to the school where the composition and number of staff would be decided locally with the right to hire and fire. While a national curriculum was introduced, the school could commodify its particular specialisation, and so offer diversity and choice to parents.

A leadership industry grew rapidly as it helped to both create and develop site-based management. The state became directly involved in training initiatives, for example: the coordination of training through the National Development Centre from 1983 to 1988 (Bolam, 2004); the funding of training such as the Headteacher Leadership and Management Programme (HEADLAMP) from 1995 (see Bolam, 2003); and the provision of training with the introduction of the National Professional Qualification for Headship (NPQH) from 1995 (see Bolam, 2003; Tomlinson, 2003). The publishing industry responded with academics, consultants and practitioners producing 'how to do it' books and ring binders that provided effective and efficient ways of managing a budget, sacking incompetent staff, marketing the school and planning for change (Gunter, 1997). Peters and Waterman (1982) had led the way in identifying the key features of an effective business, using their list of catchy aphorisms that sound business practice should 'stick to the knitting' (p 292) and be 'hands-on, values driven' (p 278). The industry could both prevent and deal with failure through the adoption of managerial processes based on contractual audit and performance measures. Rational lists of what makes an effective school, head and teacher together with models of change could easily be communicated through consultancy meetings and training sessions, particularly through the development of electronic computer-based presentation software. Furthermore, it could show itself to be modern, as where Coopers and Lybrand (1988) framed LMS as a modernising and liberating opportunity that should not be thwarted by out-of-date *dispositions* and notions. So business could lead the way as high-status knowers, particularly in comparison to local authorities which seemed out of date and universities which seemed out of touch. Comparisons between the presentation of *Better Schools* (DES, 1985) and Coopers and Lybrand's (1988) *Local Management of Schools* demonstrated that branding and communication seemed to matter more than educational values in capturing hearts and minds and persuading them to buy into the reform agenda.

So the leadership industry was in business prior to 1997: the map of what is to be known, why, and who knows, about leadership had been drafted in a particular way, and New Labour did not radically alter this.[11] England has a leader-centric culture, and so the headteacher as a leader is readily accepted, but how this leadership is constructed is what needed scrutiny: under Thatcher the head was meant to become a market entrepreneur, and under New Labour this was reworked as a regulated and licensed reform deliverer. Thatcherism had created the conditions in which a leadership industry could flourish and New Labour directly intervened and became an investor and provider in this industry. So when New Labour took office in 1997, research evidence presented the problematic realities of the impact of Thatcherism on schools and the profession (Whitty et al, 1998) and showed that, beyond a belief in the normality of the leader, there was no clear evidence that headteachers made a difference to learning (Hall and Southworth, 1997). However, there was more a continuity than a break with the previous policies. While researchers were engaged in an ESRC seminar series to examine the state of the *field* (Bush et al, 1999), policymakers seemed to be impatient with debate and sought to nationalise training preparation and colonise the *field* regarding what is to be known and worth knowing by establishing a National College.

New Labour and the Thatcher legacy

The leadership of schools *game* can only be understood and explained through examining the underlying thinking about the borders between the state, markets and civil society, and how this is manifest in debates about the purposes of schools. For the Thatcherite governments (1979–97), the enduring question of government, or how is one to 'conduct conduct' (Miller and Rose, 2008, p 14), was to construct the problem of an overloaded state with too many 'dependency relationships' (King, 1976, p 19). Ranson (1994, p 241) quotes a Department official saying that: 'if we have a highly educated and idle population we may possibly anticipate more serious social conflict. People must be educated once more to know their place.' This illustrates what I have elsewhere called a neoliberal position (Gunter et al, 2010; Gunter, 2011), where investment in a public service is about servicing the economy and protecting capital accumulation, particularly through generating entrepreneurial aspirations and protecting private property. All activity is to be costed, with value-for-money measurements dominating organisational processes and practices. Social cohesion is constructed through accepted dominant moral values (or neo-conservatism) regarding behaviour, and so schools had to produce the right type of human capital, where school-leavers could do the work and operate in a hierarchy.

This neoliberal position produced projects that generated debates and reforms, and a particular emphasis was put on public institutions such as local authorities with public-sector professionals and trade unions identified as *the* problem and 'branded as inefficient, self-interested and guilty of fostering welfare dependency and undermining the self-reliance of their clients' (Gewirtz, 2002, p 3). This attacked the civic position that had produced the welfare state and projects such as comprehensive schools from the 1950s, and so the place of the school in social democratic development and the securing of social justice opportunities faced ridicule and restructuring (Gunter et al, 2010; Gunter, 2011). However, tracking the antecedence of the relationship between ideas and policies is not easy because the neoliberal position has not generated a set of coherent ideas and policy prescriptions. Rizvi (2006) talks about a 'neo-liberal imaginary' that has become 'globally convergent', with 'an unmistakable trend towards an acceptance of a similar set of policy solutions to educational problems by a wide variety of nation states that otherwise have very different social, historical and economic characteristics' (p 200). Plant (2010, p 270) argues that 'there is no stable doctrinal place' for neoliberalism, and Shamir (2008, p 3) frames it as 'a complex, often incoherent, unstable and even contradictory set of practices'. As Gray (2010) has shown, such challenges mean that to understand and critique neoliberalism, 'one must first reconstruct it' (p 52). Such incoherence, combined with the action imperative of a new government from 1997, meant that New Labour could build a Third Way (Giddens, 2000) that rejected Labour's old ways of class divide and the Conservatives' protection of elite class interests in favour of 'a discursive strategy that aimed to build new coalitions and establish a consensus around new Labour as a political party and government' (Newman, 2001, p 46). For New Labour, this meant working through structures and groups that had a delivery *disposition*, where, in Shamir's (2008, p 3) terms, the border between society and the market 'dissolves' and all 'become "the business of market actors"'.

Thatcherism, and the Blairite hybrid, drew on the following neoliberal ideas, which challenged the legitimacy of public institutions and professional practices: first, 'economic deregulation' for securing efficient public services; second, 'welfare state devolution, retraction and recomposition' to open up to the market and retrain the public regarding the required behaviours of those in receipt of welfare wages; third, 'the cultural trope of individual responsibility' with the self as entrepreneurial income generator, family welfare protector and consumer; and, fourth, 'an expansive, intrusive, and proactive penal apparatus' deemed necessary 'to contain the disorders and disarray generated by diffusing social insecurity and deepening inequality' (Wacquant, 2009, p 307). While the purposes of change based on market development, rationales based on efficiency and effectiveness, and narratives steeped in notions of self-reliance and liberty were presented as rational common sense, in reality change was not a clearly ordered agenda. Furthermore, as Wacquant (2009, p 308) has shown in the US, 'the soft touch of libertarian proclivities favoring the upper class gives way to the hard edge of authoritarian oversight, as it endeavors to direct, nay dictate, the behaviour of the lower class'. Indeed, in reviewing recent school restructuring in England, Gleeson (2011, p 209) makes the point that 'the irony is not in the gap between rhetoric and reality but the inefficiency of the neoliberal project to implement market policies without recourse to the use of highly centralist powers that generate far greater costs and controls than those they seek to replace'.

While investment by New Labour from 1997 meant that headteachers were upgraded, new posts were created and pay was increased, in reality the school as a publicly funded business became, in Wacquant's (2009) terms, prison-like. Teachers continued to be mistrusted as 'offenders' for their lack of entrepreneurial spirit, their clear inability to hack it in the real world of risk and reward, and their proclivities towards professional rather than consumer goals. And so regulation combined with punishments, such as relentless targets and grading, became a key feature of the way the UK state has operated in England. While forms of devolution have been granted to three home nations, it is in England that the conduct of the conduct of the public-sector workforce (teacher, headteacher, professor, local authority officer) has had punishment as a central feature. Notions and practices of professional care, knowledge, regulation and standards were undermined, overlaid with and overtaken by business relationships and interests. Those dependent on a public wage (like the unemployed, old and sick) had to be audited and, if necessary, redesigned to secure predetermined standards and eliminate failure.

When New Labour came to power in 1997, it inherited a commitment from previous Conservative governments to improve standards and tackle school failure (Joseph, 1984; DES, 1985). This political convergence can be illuminated through how Baker and Blunkett, two former Conservative and Labour Secretaries of State, joined forces to endorse shared thinking and strategies (Baker and Blunkett, 2009). The difference is through delivery, while Joseph (1984, p 140) had talked about the need for an 'open discussion', New Labour was interventionist, initially through 'naming and shaming' the 'worst schools in the country' (Barber, 2007, p 31) as a form of what Barber (1997, p 188) called a 'missionary government'. This relentless delivery of national standards still dominated 10 years on with a National Challenge to improve 638 schools where less than 30% of pupils secured five A★–C grades at GCSE by being listed, offered support and threatened with closure (BBC, 2008). New Labour's reading of the situation was to argue that the Conservatives 'have relied too much on laissez-faire and have ignored the potential of active government' (Mandelson and Liddle, 1996, p 3), in other words intervention was crucial, as Blunkett (2001a, p 3) argued, 'you can't leave a school to sink'.

The New Labour government sought continuity with the Thatcher regime regarding economic growth in a globalising economy. In Marquand's (2009, p 16) terms, it was a form of 'demi-semi-Thatcherism' with a clear aim to tackle what it called a 'poverty of aspiration' (Brown, 2007) through drawing on neoliberal ideas and strategies. New Labour invested in public services but allowed private interests (both economic and moral) and 'hedonistic consumerism' to flourish, with Peter Mandelson once stating that New Labour was 'intensely relaxed about people getting filthy rich' (Marquand, 2009, p 19).[12] It seems that globalisation was understood as ensuring the right type of conditions for the movement of capital and ensuring that schools produced the right type of labour force to compete in this new brave world. Consequently, New Labour sought to modernise and transform public services through a combination of 'investment for results' (Blair, 2006) with accountability. The rhetoric of New Labour was that Thatcherism 'put the interests of the few before the many' (Mandelson and Liddle, 1996, p 3), and so New Labour made claims about equity where all can have a chance to succeed: 'New Labour advocates diversity and decentralisation, with bottom–up solutions and public goals sometimes achieved by market means' (Mandelson and Liddle, 1996, pp 17–18). This underpinned investment in workforce numbers and training, in pre-school opportunities through Sure Start,[13] in schools in areas of disadvantage through Education Action Zones (EAZ) and Excellence in Cities (EiC),[14] and in raising the status of those in need of investment and those employed to deliver it. However, in order to keep middle-class parents in the schooling system, the New Labour approach was that systemic reform had to have a strong accountability process in order to make sure that 'New' Labour did not revert to the 'Old' Labour attitude 'that the status quo is good and the private sector is bad' (Watt, 2009, p 6).

Conceptual architecture

This book is located in the tradition of critical policy studies where questions are asked about education policy 'as the authoritative allocation of values within education systems' (Lingard and Ozga, 2007, p 3). Consequently, I have underpinned the following analysis with the 'working principles' outlined by Byrne and Ozga (2008) regarding the need to link change in education with 'macro-social change' and 'to draw on resources from across the social sciences that enable understanding of that change', combined with the need for reflexivity 'that enables identification of the assumptions about the source, scope and pattern of education policy that are implicit in research on education' (pp 383–4). A number of projects have sought to develop this (eg Ball, 1990, 2007b, 2008a; Grace, 1995; Ozga, 2000a), to debate knowledge claims in School Effectiveness, School Improvement (SESI) studies (eg Thrupp and Willmott, 2003; Thrupp, 2005a) and within policy studies itself (eg Ozga, 1987; Dale, 1989; Ball, 1994b; Hatcher and Troyna, 1994; Raab, 1994). So, located within this tradition, this book aims to use Bourdieu's (2000) thinking tools to identify a logic of practice within New Labour's education policymaking with a specific focus on the leadership of schools. While the site of this theorising and investigation is England, the globalisation of school leadership as the solution to solving the problem of standards (eg Pont et al, 2008a, 2008b), combined with the globalisation of New Labour's school leadership products and delivery (eg Barber et al, 2011), means that the site of this research and analysis has resonance for policy watchers and leadership researchers in other countries. I intend to give recognition to the shared experiences of neoliberal projects (Anderson, 2009; Burch, 2009) and the movement of ideas and people around the world (Saint-Martin, 2001), and so create opportunities to, in Appadurai's (2006, p 169) terms, 'deparochialise' policy research.

This book contains eight chapters that could be read as independent essays but are linked through the conceptual architecture of Bourdieu's thinking tools, and my position and voice as author. The book begins with a mapping of the leadership of schools *game*, followed by an examination of the *game* players. I then examine institutionalised governance to open up the regularities in the *field*, followed by a theorising of the practice of knowledge production as regimes of practice. I then move on to focus on the impact of this on professionals and knowledge production, where alternative *games* are given recognition. I close the book by examining the legacy of New Labour with regard to education policymaking, and how the *game* is currently being played. So, following Rizvi and Lingard (2010, p 50), I would locate my position as undertaking an analysis 'of' rather than 'for' policy, and as such it is more about 'academic exploration' than the politics of 'political advocacy'. I bring to this task a realisation that authorship is an intellectual process that will draw on resources and produce a 'lacework of meanings' (Seddon, 1996, p 201), and I am also aware that in a post–Cold War world, the academy has been in difficulty where 'neoliberal doxa has filled the vacuum thus created and critique has retreated into the "small world" of academe, where it enchants itself with itself without ever being in a position to really threaten anyone about anything' (Bourdieu, 2003, p 21). So, like Bourdieu, I would agree that scholarship needs to be reconstructed, and, following Apple (2006a, p 681), I would argue that our job is to keep alive 'collective memories'; to not only make sense of and theorise about what has happened, but also to examine what this means and what the ongoing policy and practice trajectories are. This contributes not only to the record of events, but also to how other stories that are not officially endorsed can be heard. In building research and policy projects, there is a tendency for individuals and groups to understand their social reality and practices, like a 'fish in water' where 'it does not feel the weight of the water, and it takes the world about itself for granted' (Bourdieu and Wacquant, 1992, p 127). This book is a provocation for knowledge producers as *field* members in public institutions to challenge how they are being positioned and how they seek to position the self. Primarily by reading across epistemic boundaries, I provide as complete a map as possible of knowledge production and policymaking in relation to leadership, and through challenging the 'ritual embalming' (Bourdieu, 2000, p 48) of the orthodox canon, the book will be simultaneously applauded and loathed.

Notes

[1] National standards in education in England are measured according to: (a) Standard Attainment Tests (SATs); and (b) GCSEs at the end of Key Stage 4 or at 16 years of age.

[2] The UK government runs education in England, and the most senior minister is known as Secretary of State and heads the Department in London. When New Labour came to power in 1997, the national ministry in London was called the Department for Education and Employment (DfEE) after reorganisation had taken place in 1995 (prior to this the title was the Department for Education [DfE] and, before that, the Department of Education and Science [DES]). In 2001, the DfEE became the Department

for Education and Skills (DfES). In 2007, the DfES was split into two: the Department for Children, Schools and Families (DCSF) and the Department for Innovation, Universities and Skills (DIUS). DIUS no longer exists, as universities are now included in the Business, Innovation and Skills portfolio. Following a general election in May 2010, a coalition of Conservatives and Liberal Democrats was formed, and the DCSF became the Department for Education (DfE). Throughout the book, I will use the term 'Department', and the particular authorship of a policy text will enable the reader to identify the particular configuration of the Department at that time.

[3] I intend to use Bourdieu's thinking tools in this book to describe, explain and understand social practice, and in doing so I will explain these tools as I go along so that I interplay their meaning with conceptual argument and empirical research. This is consistent with Bourdieu's sociology, particularly his concern to problematise his relationship with 'canonical authors' (Bourdieu, 1990, p 30). Specifically, I will not abstract, define and apply a theory, but use Bourdieu's thinking tools to problematise the objective relations and social practices within policymaking. All will be fully referenced, but when I am using a particular tool I will use italics for particular words and phrases.

[4] The Secretaries of State with responsibilities for education were: David Blunkett (1997–2001), Estelle Morris (2001–02), Charles Clarke (2002–04), Ruth Kelly (2004–06), Alan Johnson (2006–07) and Ed Balls (2007–10). I also quote from two Schools Ministers, David Miliband (2002–04) and Jim Knight (2007–09).

[5] The National College for School Leadership (NCSL) was set up in Nottingham in 2000 and, following a change in remit, became the National College for Leadership of Schools and Children's Services (NCLSCS). Throughout the book, I will use the term National College.

[6] Fresh Start Schools were introduced to deal with failing schools – a school would be closed and then reopened with a new head and staff; there was no formal evaluation, but the policy was dropped due to the number of cases where schools did not improve (see Russell, 2000); Executive Heads were introduced to enable a successful head to run other schools in the locality (see Barker, I., 2009); and Federations were introduced to enable schools to collaborate or merge into one organisation (see Lindsay et al, 2007).

[7] The Academies Programme was launched in 2000 and was based on the aim of replacing failing inner city schools with flagship Academies outside of local authority control and sponsored by private interests (see Gunter, 2011).

[8] The National Literacy and Numeracy Strategies were introduced to improve classroom practice and standards (see Earl et al, 2003).

[9] The Office for Standards in Education (Ofsted) was established in 1992 by the Conservative government and its inspection regime was continued by New Labour (see McCrone et al, 2007). School Improvement Partners (SIPs) were established as part of the New Relationship with Schools policy. Under this programme, a school would be allocated a SIP to work with them for five days a year to examine progress and strategies for improvement (see DfE, 2011a).

[10] For example, the NHS Leadership Centre was set up in 2001 (NHS Modernisation Agency Leadership Centre, 2003) and the Centre for Leadership at the Fire Service College was launched in 2007 (see www.fireservicecollege. ac.uk/training/uk-fire--rescue-services/centre-for-leadership.aspx?rnd=178 [accessed 1 November 2010]). For a summary of leadership training and development initiatives across the public services, see PIU (2001, p 101).

[11] Saint-Martin's (2000) study shows that management consultancy grew under the Thatcherite governments from 1979 and there is the view within the Labour Party that 'consultants tend to be Tory supporters'. However, he argues that historically there is a need to recognise that 'it was not the Tories, but the Labour government who, in the 1960s, first legitimated the participation of business consultants in the process of bureaucratic reform and brought into government the notion of efficiency' (p 114).

[12] Shaw's (2007) analysis of New Labour from 1997 to 2007 is based on asking the question of whether Labour under Blair 'lost its soul'. He argues that on the basis of New Labour's commitment to social justice, the answer is 'no', as the focus on investment in public services has to be recognised, but the answer is 'yes' in regard to the acceptance of individual gains and how New Labour lost sight of the traditional importance of 'fraternity' or 'fellowship, co-operation and service' (pp 206–7).

[13] Sure Start provision was set up from 1999 in areas of disadvantage to enable early years education, health and welfare to be integrated (see NESSRT, 2008).

[14] Education Action Zones (1998) and Excellence in Cities (1999) were set up to invest in the improvement of schools in urban areas (see Ofsted, 2003a).

TWO

The leadership of schools

Introduction

Consider the following statements from New Labour education policy texts:

> The quality of the head often makes the difference between the success or failure of a school. (DfEE, 1997, p 46)

> The £19 billion is a substantial commitment on our part to do what we can ... investment for reform, for change and for pursuit of higher standards and excellence ... to bring this about there is no group of people more important than headteachers. (Blair, 1998)

> You can recognize a good school by the quality of its head and I believe good headteachers and good leadership are essential in the drive to raise standards in schools. (Blunkett, 1998)

> So this is a good time to be debating the future of school leadership. There is consensus on its importance. There is consensus on its key elements. There is ... consensus that school leadership in England is getting better, fast. (Miliband, 2003a)

> Excellent leaders create excellent schools. Secondary schools need strong leaders at all levels, enabling them to provide a rich and diverse curriculum taught by professionals committed to success for every learner. (Clarke, 2004, p 25)

> Good leadership is at the heart of every good school. A strong headteacher, backed by an able leadership team and governing body, is vital for success. (DfES, 2005, p 99)

> In excellent schools the teachers receive continuous training and professional development to update their skills and expertise, and there is always strong leadership from headteachers with the autonomy to lead their schools. (Brown, 2007, p 10)

> Strong leadership sets the tone for the whole community. It creates the ethos that makes clear exactly what a school stands for and what it's trying to achieve. (Kelly, 2005b)

> Strong and visionary world class leadership is essential if the UK is to sustain its competitive performance. The price of failure will be high. (Johnson, 2003)

This selection of gobbets is only a fraction of what is available to illustrate the knowledge claims that leadership matters: an enduring emphasis is on the single leader combined with increased recognition that all can and should do leading and leadership. *Codification* of leadership in this way has a ritual feel about it, with almost prayer-like blessings that are used to give grace to policy.

Policies that enabled the leadership of schools to be constructed and developed are therefore:

> statements which are typically expressed both in utterance and in textual form. They have a distinctive and formal purpose for organizations and governments: to codify and publicise the values which are to inform future practice and thus encapsulate prescriptions for reform. (Ranson, 1995, p 440)

A study of such texts combined with data from the KPEL project shows that New Labour governments from 1997 to 2010 made the leadership of schools, in Bourdieu's (1990) terms, the dominant *game* to play. A *game* that was and remains internationally endorsed and celebrated (Caldwell, 2006; Huber et al, 2007). This *game* is one where those outside of schools, and indeed outside of the UK, determined and controlled the leadership of schools. It was often a messy and inconsistent *game*, but significantly teachers were, in Ball's (1993, p 108) terms, an 'absent presence': teachers were present as objects to be reformed and as the audience in receipt of reforms, but absent because they were excluded from strategic reform processes. Indeed, as the decade moved along, more emphasis was put on 'generic' and 'effective' leadership from within and outside of public services. So a leadership *doxa* was codified (Bourdieu, 2000), and while some official scrutiny did take place by the House of Commons Select Committee (House of Commons, 1998), the design, questioning and evidence base of this enquiry was functional. To try to open up questions of knowledge production through debate and alternative evidence was a place to which such enquiries did not go, and New Labour regarded as unhelpful heresy. In this chapter, I intend to use New Labour policy texts to examine the leadership *game*, followed by an in-depth analysis of the National College[1] as an important site for *game* playing.

The leadership *game*

New Labour developed a leadership *of* schools *game* where they established a national framework of educational products and processes for schools in England, and required the delivery of this locally. This is revealed through empirical work, where, as one minister said: "we always knew we couldn't do what we wanted in education unless we turned round leadership" (Min2). The single person as leader was an example of 'structured structures' (Bourdieu, 1992, p 53) where ministers were disposed to leadership as normal, and this was further developed as 'structuring structures' (Bourdieu, 1992, p 53) through the way information and advice were sourced. The same minister said:

> "so you come to government with anecdotal evidence that heads make a difference, and … what we were being given from Ofsted and the rest of it seemed to show that leadership makes a difference … I don't think we make a decision that we'd concentrate on leadership, there was not a point when that decision was made, it was obvious."

The reconstruction of the headteacher identity as local leaders of reform took place in the following ways.

Modelling

This was constructed as follows: first, the role and identity of the headteacher was further separated from teachers, and reworked, fixed and labelled as delivery and performance leadership through the drawing up of National Standards (TTA, 1998; DfES, 2004b);[2] and, second, the preferred model of this leadership was imported as 'transformational' (eg Burns, 1978) and legitimised through named examples of particular charismatic headteachers who were regarded as exemplar good practice leaders (see Knight, 2006; Taylor, 2009) and the separation out of an elite group of heads 'as national leaders' (DfES, 2005, p 101).

In the Green Paper, *teachers: meeting the challenge of change* (DfEE, 1998a), the territory was mapped and claims staked for the headteacher as leader:

> All the evidence shows that heads are the key to a school's success. All schools need a leader who creates a sense of purpose and direction, sets high expectations of staff and pupils, focuses on improving teaching and learning, monitors performance and motivates the staff to give of their best. The best heads are as good at leadership as the best leaders in any other sector, including business. The challenge is to create the rewards, training and support to attract, retain and develop many more heads of this calibre. (DfEE, 1998a, p 22)

In developing this approach, primacy was given to private-sector leadership models to secure leader responsibility and accountability, provide the language, processes and legitimacy for delegating work, and command commitment through followership. Professionalism was redesigned as technical capability (eg data-handling competence) combined with personal attributes (eg charisma) and attitudes (eg responsibility), underpinned by an overt commitment to New Labour strategies and processes.

The removal of a headteacher became the *de facto* way of bringing about improvement and effectiveness (eg Stoll and Myers, 1998b; Barber, 2001). However, New Labour faced challenges, not least in that, despite their investment, there was a shortage of trained and accredited educational professionals. Additionally, New Labour remained concerned that 'heroic' headteachers could not be scaled up across the system because some 'Super-Heads' had not always been able to turn around failing schools. Particularly irksome was continued evidence that some headteachers had retained a professional identity in that they not only resisted or modified changes, but also continued to develop their own strategies under the radar. Some remodelling took place where the role of the effective local leader remained a consistent feature, but the person who might inhabit the role and what title they might adopt changed. So the emphasis was on leadership rather than professional knowledge and expertise:

> Over the next five years we will continue to give priority to developing effective leadership at every point in the system – from the small primary school to the DfES [Department for Education and Skills]. We shall support and encourage the development of the existing cadre of senior managers and the earlier identification and development of future leaders. We will encourage thinking about how organisations develop effective leadership teams. We shall ensure that successful leaders continue to be rewarded for their success and weak leadership is identified and tackled swiftly. (DfES, 2004d, ch 9, para 38)

Generic transferable leadership skills could come from any part of the public, private or voluntary sectors and this fitted with the *Every Child Matters* (DfES, 2004c) agenda[3] regarding the provision of children's services with a children's workforce through the collaborative provision of education, health, welfare and policing.[4]

Risk management

The modelling of the leader and leadership was communicated to headteachers through the use of policy opportunities with launch events, speeches and documents. Belief statements were used to inform headteachers that they made a difference to student outcomes, and this was symbolised by higher pay,[5] the award of honours (knighthoods and dames) and the nationalisation of training and accreditation where piloted programmes inherited from the Conservative government were transferred to a National College from 2000. New Labour operated through 24,000 heads rather than 400,000 teachers as their direct agents, with the training of heads and the labelling of their work as effective leadership, with particular investment through the Leadership Incentive Grant (LIG)[6] central to this. The use of targets managed the risk involved in local implementation, particularly through a tightening up of performance regimes with: thresholds regarding standards, with all schools being required to achieve 30% A★–C grades in five subjects at Key Stage 4; the production of data documents known as the PANDA (Performance and Assessment) and the Autumn package to enable between-school comparisons; and the production of authoritative guidance on how to structure and culture school processes (SEU and

DfEE, 1997; Ofsted, 2002), particularly regarding how to use data as a means of *Smoking Out Underachievement* (DfES, 2004a). Data analysis schemes such as Contextual Value Added (CVA) calculations with thresholds regarding what is and is not an acceptable standard enabled schools to be identified as successful or failing, leading to tighter surveillance or even closure. The complexity of this was handled through the launch of *A New Relationship with Schools* (DfES and Ofsted, 2004) with changes to the inspection system, the introduction of school self-evaluation (with the School Evaluation Form [SEF]), and the rationalisation of the demands on a school through 'a single conversation' with a SIP (Kelly, 2005b). Performance-related pay and inspection surveillance meant that spaces for professional judgement had been further reined in and this was increasingly supplemented by technical delivery checks and compliance mechanisms.

Reculturing

This took place through a combination of modelling and risk management: agenda setting and priorities were directly related to national policy, and challenges to this were only accepted if they came from headteachers who were recognised as leading the reforms in preferred directions or if headteachers in general raised concerns about the technical operation of change (eg in 2004, school budgets were given a three-year time horizon to allow for longer-term planning). Interestingly, Hyman (2005), as Blair's chief speech writer, went to work at Islington Green School, and while he recognised how hard delivery is at the level of working with children living real lives, he challenged the pace and not the substance of reform. A further feature is that the language and discourse of schools was strictly controlled through the use of 'improvement', 'effectiveness', 'targets' and 'standards', with, for example, Miliband (2003b) using business models when talking about 'meeting the productivity challenge'. The rebranding of schools as 'Academies' and 'colleges' with mergers known as 'Federations', led by 'principals' and 'chief executives', enabled the Thatcherite vision of the school as an independent small business to be further developed. Professional practice was either modelled as leadership or remodelled as work that others in the workforce could do. In Blunkett's (2001a) terms, teachers had a culture of overworking, and so professional dialogue was closed down through ministerial interventions. For example, Blunkett (2001a, p 12) stated that 'mixed ability teaching undermined comprehensive education' and so banding was presented as good practice; and the government made it clear that schools should have senior leadership teams (DfEE, 1998a). Significantly, pastoral and much 'teaching' work was removed from teachers to a wider workforce such as student services replacing teachers as Heads of Year, teaching assistants covering lessons for absent teachers, and curriculum resources being accessed as ready-made online delivery packages (see Butt and Gunter, 2007).

Behind the scenes, this has not run smoothly. While commissioned research emphasised that the top person need not have QTS as a chief executive (DfES and PwC, 2007), a leaked document from the Department called *Workforce Reform – Blue Skies* imagined the school of the future with one qualified teacher as the head, with learning supported by others brought in to deliver (Stewart, 2003, p 6). The debate clearly was taking place about the relationship between training and accreditation to teach, and whether it was necessary, and if it was, then teachers could be a highly qualified elite group who may design learning but who may not routinely teach children. While the rhetoric was about professionalism and freeing teachers to teach, in reality the process was one of deprofessionalisation with a lack of attention to a defendable model of pedagogic practice. It seems as if professionals have either exited (eg Yarker, 2005) or complied, what Ball (2003, p 216) describes as 'the terrors of performativity'. There was a 'struggle over the teacher's soul' (Ball, 2003, p 217) regarding the values and realities of professional practice in tension with the demands of 'policy technologies' (p 216), where 'teachers are represented and encouraged to think about themselves as individuals who calculate about themselves, "add value" to themselves, improve their productivity, strive for excellence and live an existence of calculation' (p 217). This was clearly evident in job redesign with a new emphasis on 'system leadership' where teachers have the work of the headteacher distributed to them under the label of empowered leadership, so that the headteacher can take on responsibility for more than one school (DfES, 2004d; Munby, 2006).

Restructuring

This has taken place through: first, partnership links with secondary schools securing private-sector investment, and then bidding to win specialist curriculum status such as a Sports or Business College[7] as a niched product in the marketplace; second, new schools being allowed to enter the marketplace through Academies where private interests (usually faith-based groups, private companies and individual philanthropists) could act as a sponsor (originally £2m), and so access public-sector investment and control the curriculum and workforce (Gunter, 2011); third, various formal and informal structural relations between schools by (a) Executive Headteachers (where the headteacher [and senior managers] from one or more schools support a school identified as not meeting national standards), all-through schools (where primary and secondary school[s] in a geographical area merge into one multi-site school) and Federations (where secondary schools in an area can cooperate or fully merge their leadership and governance structures); and, fourth, the closure (or threat of closure) of schools that are not performing to centralised standards. Initially, New Labour operated a policy called 'Fresh Start' with 'Super Heads' brought in to 'turn a school' around quickly, where a school would close in July and reopen in September with a new head and staff. With some high-profile resignations of Super Heads this strategy was buried, and gradually replaced with Academies, Federations and Executive Headteachers. So people had their jobs redesigned, but the retention of hierarchy meant that little was actually new. Restructuring arrangements and strategic decisions were controlled centrally by the Department, and through the use of modelling and risk management, together with reculturing processes, any assumed diversity was located as close to the customer as possible (on-site tactical delivery).

Exclusion

New Labour used all four methods identified by Hood and Jackson (1991) to 'suspend disbelief' regarding their knowledge claims: first, by 'attacking the doubters as *people* rather than dealing centrally with their arguments', particularly through 'character assassination'; second, 'the assertion of *time pressure*, building up a sense of crisis and urgency'; third, '*cargo-cultism*, as the linking of national economic performance with the quality of public management'; and, fourth, '*amnesia*' by presenting 'doctrines as new, in order to avoid disbelief on the grounds that the same doctrines have been tried before' (Hood and Jackson, 1991, pp 193–4, emphases in original). New Labour knowledge claims were communicated in belief statements and located in a form of data calculation that aimed to measure the impact of leadership on school outcomes. Consequently, other ways of knowing based on professional experience (ie what professional practice was like before New Labour imposed professional standards), independent research and policy scholarship were usually discounted as unmodern. Barber (1997, p 197) noted that the urgency of reform mattered more and that researchers were considered to be one of the problems:

It has been one of the frustrations of Tory ministers in the last decade that people within the education service often appeared to them not to share their proper impatience for change. Demands for consultation, longitudinal research projects, extensive piloting, waiting for more evidence – while each might separately seem legitimate – taken together and linked to the constant criticism of anything new, looked to ministers like self-interested defence of the status quo.

While major consultations did take place, particularly in regard to the workforce (see DfEE, 1998a; DfES, 2002b, 2002c), they tended to be highly controlled and were often designed to prevent debate.[8] Indeed, those who failed in the New Labour regime and/or sought to discuss the reforms and/or develop alternatives faced exclusion and even attack.[9] Hyman (2005, p 76) sums this up nicely: with supporters in a '"big tent" on the one hand, "enemies" on the other'. Those who tried to open up the debate were attacked by Miliband (2004a, p 9) as 'sceptics' and 'naysayers and doubters' who were automatically associated with a 'mindset of low expectations', and were identified by Barber (2007, p 35) as 'a few academics [who] continued to whinge on the sidelines'. As a result of visiting the Institute of Education in London for a meeting organised by *The Guardian*, Blunkett (2006, p 108) notes how he 'blew his top' and concluded, 'I wasn't prepared even to countenance listening to what they had to say. We would turn elsewhere for advice, information and insight, at least for the time being' (p 109). An examination of conference speakers, contracted consultants, authors of National College for School Leadership (NCSL) reports, as well as recommended readings for practitioners shows the reliance on preferred knowledge producers (Thrupp, 2005b; Gunter and Forrester, 2008), who Thrupp and Willmott (2003, p 7) identify as 'textual apologists'. Researchers who undertook commissioned research from the Department or the National College have reported micro-management and interference, and independent reports with unfavourable findings were routinely dismissed (Mortimore, 2009).[10] Harsh treatment was meted out to those who allowed the workings of the 'tent' to be exposed, and Beckett's (2007) coruscating analysis of the Academies Programme includes the story of Des Smith a former headteacher and member of the Specialist Schools and Academies Trust (SSAT). He 'was caught promising that honours could be lined up for supporters' (Beckett, 2007, p 28), and, following arrest and questioning, he found himself outside in the cold: 'the Government which had used him and disowned him did not bother to try to protect him from his lack of media experience' (p 31).

The leadership of schools and the National College

The leadership of schools as professional 'reformation' through the power of the state required a dedicated public institution with its own products and workforce to take over the *game*, and play it to win. The NCSL was launched in 2000, and rebranded as the National College for Leadership of Schools and Children's Services in 2008.

The problem of standards as measured by student outcomes was directly linked to the quality of the headteacher as leader, and in this section I will focus on the leadership of schools strategy with a particular emphasis on the contribution of the National College to how strong and visionary leadership was spoken and written into reality through a 'signature pedagogy' (Shulman, 2005). The pedagogy was to fuse selected ideas and evidence with professional values so that a New Labour delivery *disposition* was encouraged and developed; and the signature nature of it was based on the exclusivity of investment for results. Integral to this was a new building designed by Sir Michael Hopkins and Partners (NCSL, 2000) that cost a total of £25 million (Newton, 2003), with production values and hospitality to rival the best conference facilities. Photograph 2.1 shows the use of glass and steel, symbolising the investment and modernism of the New Labour leadership project, where the Director could be photographed with a backdrop that oozed status and glamour. Photograph 2.2 shows the driveway with colourful banners, with one greeting visitors with 'Welcome to the Future' and using key words such as 'Inspiring Learning' to communicate the truths of leadership to all who approached.

The webpage and publications enabled codification of the message to be controlled through in-house design and editing, with many of the texts: being unauthored (except by the National College by default)[11] so that texts can read as a disembodied voice speaking with authority; being undated so that the messages are all-pervading and timeless; and using categories such as 'school leaders' rather than role titles so that all who read them must regard that they are being spoken about and to. As Ball and Exley (2010, p 153) have said: 'overall, a shift in the types of knowledge deemed valuable in relation to policy can be observed, away from academic expertise and towards simple messages that can easily be understood by politicians, policy makers and the public'.

While the National College positions itself as different from a university, it legitimised itself through activity that is connected and

Photograph 2.1: The National College building

Photograph 2.2: The driveway to the National College building

shared, such as research, publication of research reports, keynote and paper presentations at national and international conferences, appointing visiting professors, and funding doctorates. Those who work in the National College are funded directly from the Treasury, there is no project bidding in open competition, no independent peer review and grading of research reports, no research quality audits such as the Research Assessment Exercise (RAE), no public access to data sets through the Economic and Social Data Service (ESDS), and no public statements on research integrity procedures.[12] A final point to make is that National College texts tend to be written in short statements and bullet points, where complex ideas and uncertainty are eliminated in favour of positive and clear messages. It seems that the urgency of reform has led to short turnaround times for design, fieldwork and reporting, and so under New Labour, the emphasis has been on the use of ready-made solutions with headline summaries that can be read and digested quickly.[13]

Knowledge production by the National College is governed by its remit from the government, where the role was outlined in the 2002–03 *Prospectus* as:

We aim to:

- Provide a single national focus for school leadership development, research and innovation
- Be a driving force for world-class leadership in our schools and the wider community
- Provide support to and be a major resource for school leaders
- Stimulate national and international debate on leadership issues. (NCSL, undated a, p 3)

The National College then outlined how it would do this:

Research seeking out, sharing and building best practice through research and learning networks

Virtual College providing online support through our web site and online communities

Programmes developing and delivering programmes that meet the needs of school leaders at every stage in their careers

Each area of our work supports the other – so that research informs the development of our programmes, and online learning ensures that leadership knowledge and resources are carried to the widest possible audience. (NCSL, undated a, p 3, boldface in original)

A study of knowledge production through an analysis of research, virtual college and programme activity is outlined in Table 2.1. First, research is focused on networking for educational professions and linking this to selected leadership theories and the work of preferred researchers. Second, the sharing of good practice and problem solving, and talking with decision-makers and leadership researchers, is through various online systems, particularly through *talk2learn*, which is described as 'the secure online community environment developed for school leaders by the National College for School Leadership … in partnership with Oracle and Ultralab' (NCSL, undated m, p 4).[14] Third, a Leadership Development Framework (NCSL, 2001) was devised to cover all aspects of workforce production and shift identities towards being a leader, doing leading and exercising leadership. Finally, as the National College developed, it took on a range of development and leadership

Table 2.1: A summary of National College activity

Official National College work	Examples
Research	Research Associates Programme: school leaders 'undertake study, engage in enquiry and impact on practice' (NCSL, undated b, p 5). Commissioned Research: funding of literature reviews and empirical projects (NCSL, undated b, p 5). International Research Associates: 'provides an opportunity for practitioners and academics from overseas to undertake a research sabbatical in England' (NCSL, undated b, p 5). Visiting Professors: for example, Michael Fullan and Brian Caldwell 'as critical friends' (NCSL, undated b, p 5). Networked Learning Communities: local projects designed to deliver on national priorities.
Virtual College	Information and practical tools, such as examples of school policies, news and events, and links to policy sites. Talking Heads: online community for heads. Virtual Heads: online community for aspiring heads. Online Hotseats/Leading Edge Seminars: online meetings with policymakers and 'leading thinkers' who 'discuss a specific issue and answer your questions online, giving community members unique access to the people who make decisions in government and education' (NCSL, undated a, p 8). Futuresight: using scenarios to undertake futures thinking. NCSL Leadership Network: group of 'headteachers who are capable of making a difference' in their own and other schools, and to examine achievement (NCSL, undated d, p 20).

Official National College work	Examples
Programmes	Emergent Leaders: Equal Access to Promotion; Leading from the Middle; Women in Leadership and Management. Established Leaders Programme. Entry to Headship: Early Headship Provision; National Professional Qualification for Headship; New Visions Programme for Early Headship; Headfirst. Advanced Leaders: International School Leader Placements; Leadership Programme for Serving Headteachers; Partners in Leadership. Consultant Leaders: Consultant Leader Development Programme. National Leaders of Education: from 2005, leaders from excellent schools can support failing schools and advise ministers, and gain accreditation. School Improvement Partners (SIPs): accreditation of SIPs role with schools from 2006. Future Leaders Programme: develop leadership in urban areas with people not currently working in schools (NCSL, undated a, p 13; undated d, pp 10–17; undated i, p 15; undated j, p 20).
Development and Strategic Initiatives	Community Leadership: developing 'leadership in school, community and multi-agency settings' (NCSL, undated d, p 14). Team Leadership: two programmes, 'Working Together for Success' and 'Developing Capacity for Sustained Improvement' for senior leadership teams (NCSL, undated d, p 14). Working with Schools of a Religious Character: contact made with faith groups and seminars held. Student Leadership: activities with school students. Strategic Leadership of ICT: training for heads devised with the British Educational Communications and Technology Agency (BECTA). Bursar Development Programme: training and accreditation for school bursars. The Primary Strategy Leadership Programme: training of consultant leaders to work with primary schools on improvement. The London Leadership Strategy: development of leadership capacity in London schools within the London Challenge initiative launched in 2003. The National Remodelling Team: located at the National College to work on school workforce remodelling. Leaders of Extended and Full Service Schools: from 2005 is seen as a part of the Community Leadership initiative (NCSL, undated g, p 25).

initiatives in order to respond to New Labour's workforce remodelling and school restructuring agenda (see NCSL, undated f).

An examination of National College outputs shows that both Mode 1 and Mode 2 knowledge claims (Gibbons et al, 2007) have been used. Mode 1 is through investment into disciplinary knowledge regarding change, effectiveness and improvement from within SESI epistemic groups and evidenced through projects, conferences and publication. Mode 2 knowledge is where experiential and contextual forms of knowing are based on belief systems and anecdotes that are shared in online communities and have been codified in advocacy statements about the direct relationship between identity, work and leadership.[15] So the National College works with preferred leadership gurus who undertake projects, give keynotes and write texts for publication and the website, but at the same time networks of practitioners share their working lives, their personal beliefs and problem solve. On the one hand, Heather de Quesnay, the first Director, outlined the reform agenda:

> Never has there been such an exciting and challenging time to be a school leader. Heads and other leaders now have new opportunities and responsibilities to be creative and innovative, to take risks and reap the rewards of change. The National College for School Leadership … is at the heart of this agenda for educational reform. Our role is to inspire, challenge and support leaders to be the best they can be. To stimulate debate, create new understandings, build worldwide networks and develop leaders who have the vision, skills, passion and energy to transform our schools and to change lives. (NCSL, undated a, p 1)

And, on the other hand, the emphasis is on how:

> we constantly involve school leaders themselves in the enquiry process. We start from the principle that what is known about school leadership in action is already out there, being lived out daily by school leaders throughout the country. Our research is strongly orientated towards innovation, action and applied research. Our aim is to find out what works well and why, building an evidence base and working within schools to apply that base to real life. (NCSL, undated a, p 6)

It seems that in adopting a 'focus … on closing the gap between research and practice' (NCSL, undated a, p 6), school leaders are told they have useful knowledge but that this has to fit with the reform agenda and the National College-espoused model of leadership. There is a homogenising process in play within the *game*: first, a myth of a 'chasm' between research and practice has been created,[16] and so researcher cleansing is necessary in order to remove those who do not think correctly; and, second, the National College research team are described as people with 'like minds' (Jackson, 2001, pp 2–3). So the rationales and narratives use selected Mode 1 evidence and Mode 2 beliefs to justify interventions at national/local/individual levels in order to enable commitment and alleviate any local tactical delivery problems.

A useful illustration of this can be seen by focusing on the link between policy imperatives and how the National College responded through research activity (see Table 2.2). An example is how the National College handled its requirement to produce new leaders, known as succession planning, and so new hybrids were considered and distributed leadership selected as the most appropriate way to lead educational provision.

Distributed leadership permeates National College discourse and the promotion of good practice through dedicated webpage provision with case study evidence. Hopkins (2001), in his Think Tank report to the Governing Body, made it number five in a list of Ten Propositions regarding how leadership can transform learning; and it remains a consistent feature of claims about effective school leadership (eg

Table 2.2: National College and the leadership of schools

Policy imperative	National College response
Enable headteacher (or principal) to deliver and be accountable for reforms	Scope the literatures (eg Ainscow et al, 2003; Bennett et al, 2003a, 2003b; Bush and Glover, 2003; Leithwood and Riehl, 2003; NCSL, 2007; Hartle, undated) Build compliance with National Standards (eg Alton, 2006; Cambell et al, 2006a, 2006b; Goulden and Robinson, 2006; Rodger, 2006; Scott et al, 2006) Build compliance with Reform Agenda (eg NRT, 2001; NCSL, 2006b, undated I; Steward, 2007; Macaulay, 2008; Hargreaves, 2010) Adopt model of effective transformational leadership (eg Harris and Chapman, 2002; Day and Harris, undated; Fullan, undated) Develop hybrids: Distributed Leadership (eg MacBeath et al, 2004; Kimber, undated) Emotional Leadership and Well-Being (eg Lee, 2006; Bristow et al, 2007) Instructional Leadership (eg Benson, undated; Stoll, undated) System Leadership (eg McGaw, undated) Teacher Leadership (eg Harris and Muijs, 2003) Examine leadership development (eg Abra et al, 2003; West et al, 2003; Bush and Glover, 2004; Coleman, 2005; Sharp et al, 2006) Undertake comparative studies (eg Wong, 2006; Caldwell, undated; Tucker and Codding, undated)
Remodel the school workforce	Succession planning (eg Hartle and Thomas, 2003; NCSL, 2006a, 2007) Personalising the curriculum (eg Cresswell et al, 2006) Job redesign (eg Court, 2003a; Glatter and Harvey, 2006)
Restructure the system	Scope opportunities from private sector (eg Hallinger and Snidvogns, 2005; Thompson et al, 2004) Examine types of schools (eg Ireson, 2007; Swidenbank, 2007; Chapman et al, 2008; Hill, 2010; National College, 2010a, 2010b)

NCSL, 2007), where annual reviews of research stress its centrality (NCSL, undated b, undated c). The necessary intellectual work to build distributed leadership as preferred good practice has been done through commissioned research (eg DfES and PwC, 2007; Day et al, 2009), and in particular by the National College with speeches (eg Munby, 2006), literature analysis (eg Bennett et al, 2003a), the funding of empirical team projects (eg MacBeath et al, 2004) and by individual professionals (eg Lloyd, 2005). However, it seems that distributed leadership is primarily a National College solution to the problem of leadership image, role and work overload, because ministerial speeches to heads show that while distributed leadership is mentioned occasionally (eg Miliband, 2003a), many texts do not mention it (eg Kelly, 2005b), and when they do it tends to be about issues of sharing (eg Morris, 2001) or to a non-school professional audience (Johnson, 2003; Knight, 2007). It seems that distributed leadership has enabled the National College to translate the New Labour mantra of the effective school leader, as illustrated at the top of this chapter, into a way of labelling and characterising professional practice as both efficient and effective, but also realistic and humane. However, it also enables neoliberal reforms to the workforce to be branded as both productive and an upgrade with new titles and job descriptions; where the headteacher (or chief executive) can lead other parts of the education system safe in the knowledge that accountability and responsibility for outcomes is clearly allocated.

Notes

[1] Approaches in other countries regarding leadership preparation are outlined in Lumby et al (2008) and Ng and Wong (2001); and for where there has been experimentation with leadership training through a College approach, see, for example, Davis (2001).

[2] In 1998, the then Teacher Training Agency (TTA) published National Standards for the profession. A pack of four booklets was produced that laid out National Standards for Qualified Teacher Status, Subject Leaders, Special Educational Needs Co-ordinators and Headteachers. The standards made clear the core purpose of the role and the key outcomes from effective practice, and so laid out the knowledge and understanding for, attributes and skills for, and the nature of the job (TTA, 1998). The National Standards for Headteachers were subsequently updated (DfES, 2004b).

[3] In 2003, New Labour published its vision for the restructuring of children's services known as *Every Child Matters* (ECM). This contained five outcomes that had been identified as important for well-being: Be Healthy; Stay Safe; Enjoy and Achieve; Make a Positive Contribution; and Achieve Economic Well-Being. The Children Act 2004 included provision for making changes: extending services offered by schools and improving working between schools and specialist services (DfES, 2004c) .

[4] A Freedom of Information request has confirmed the situation regarding Qualified Teacher Status (QTS) and headteachers. There is no legal requirement for headteachers to have QTS in England, and from 2003, headteachers were treated as a separate category from, rather than as a subset of, teachers. In the current School Teachers Pay and Conditions Document (DfE, 2010c), the definition of a headteacher is 'a person appointed to the teaching staff of a school as head teacher, and includes a person appointed as acting head teacher to carry out the functions of a head teacher pursuant to section 35(3) or 36(3) of [the Education Act 2002] but not a teacher who is assigned and carries out duties of a head teacher without being so appointed' (DfE, 2010c, p 19). So 'there is no assumption that a head will be a qualified teacher' (Mayers, 2010), and this is different from Wales, where the headteacher is defined as 'a qualified teacher appointed to the post of head teacher and deputy head teacher respectively in a school' (DfE, 2010c, p 19). In England, QTS is required for teaching, and so a teaching headteacher would be required to be qualified.

[5] The entrepreneurial drive of this type of leadership has led to some challenging cases. Beckett (2009) tells the story of a geography teacher and union activist, Hank Roberts, who 'blew the whistle' on the headteacher and senior management at Copland Community School in Brent, London. In return for generating £2m for new buildings, the headteacher, Sir Alan Davies, and the senior management team received illegal bonuses.

[6] The LIG was introduced in 2003 and was 'designed to secure and embed a transformation in the leadership and management of 1400 secondary schools in cities and in challenging circumstances elsewhere. It will do this by strengthening senior leadership teams through professional development and collaboration. Schools will receive £125,000 a year. Those in challenging circumstances outside Excellence in Cities and Education Action Zones will receive a further £50,000 a year' (Clarke, 2004, p 27).

[7] New Labour aimed to develop a diverse educational provision where secondary schools could bid to become 'specialist' regarding the curriculum, for example, languages, science, sports, technology (see DfE, 2011b).

---

[8] The process has a number of features: first, the framing of the problem was directly linked to teachers and their practice, for example, the Green Paper that outlined the reform of the profession is titled *teachers: meeting the challenge of change* (DfEE, 1998a, 1998b), with the direct message that teachers alone must face and accept the changes that will be delivered to them; second, the production of detailed glossy documents that presented the government's case together with easy-to-read summary leaflets (see DfEE, 1998a, 1998b, 1998c; DfES, 2002a, 2002b, 2003); third, the design of consultation 'response forms' that enabled policy to be endorsed (DfEE, 1998d; DfES, 2002c); and, fourth, the production of guidance materials to enable the policy to be delivered, which was included in the consultation pack (DfES, 2002d).

[9] This is also evident at the very core of government decision-making. Hattersley (2010, p 26) compares the Thatcher and Blair premierships and notes that 'both were blessed by generally supine cabinets', and he goes on to report that in the Blair government, 'a request for collective discussion was regarded as disloyalty'.

[10] The Transforming the School Workforce Pathfinder Project (Thomas et al, 2004) was commissioned by the Department to provide evidence about the pilot workforce remodelling project in 32 schools in England (see Butt and Gunter, 2007). Of interest is how policy moved ahead before the project evidence had been completed and how official reports told the story of remodelling without reference to the project or the findings (see Ofsted, 2004).

[11] Reference is sometimes made to 'we' and 'the research group' (eg NCSL, undated e, p 37), but these people are not formally introduced. Connected to this is a tendency for reports to mention approved researchers such as Brian Caldwell, Michael Fullan or Andy Hargreaves, but when there are research teams, the style used by private companies to author reports through the company brand rather than the actual authors (eg Hay Group) has been used for researchers in higher education. For example, in NCSL (undated c) 'Lancaster' and 'Manchester' are used rather than the names of the actual researchers who completed the work.

[12] A review of the webpages and research reports shows that some authors do make reference to ethical issues regarding data collection, but there is no formal process outlined that explains how research proposals are scrutinised, approved and insured.

[13] A good example of this is a booklet entitled, *Making the Difference: Successful Leadership in Challenging Circumstances* (NCSL, undated p). It presents eight strategies for improvement with each one given a page that presents the key messages, and each page folding out to reveal some more information. A set of questions is provided to help the reader link the messages with their school and work. It is like a child's picture book where the cover is an easy-to-clean, robust, rigid plastic, and with each turn of the page there is a stimulating message as a focus for required learning.

[14] In addition to online networking, the reach of the National College is through paper-based publications such as a magazine called *LDR* and advertising supplements in the weekly press. For example, an eight-page broadsheet supplement was published through the *EducationGuardian*, 4 November 2008 (NCSL, 2008). This includes updating information about training, advertisements and stories of leaders and changes to structures.

[15] Knowledge claims are mainly functionalist (see Chapter 1), and while there are a small number of publications that use the phrase 'social justice', this is a fraction of the overall output. For example, Harris et al (2006b) includes just one input regarding socially critical democratic development and democratic practices in schools. This is presented alongside functionalist distributed and facilitative leadership with frameworks for action based on what- and how- rather than why-type questions.

[16] My own work on the history of the field shows partnerships between educational professionals and researchers in higher education from the 1960s onwards regarding professional development and research (Gunter, 1999; Gunter and Thomson, 2010).

THREE

New Labour and intellectual work

Introduction

The leadership of schools *game* needed players who would generate and communicate beliefs, ideas and evidence. Specifically, New Labour needed to draw upon and construct intellectual work, and to do that it needed intellectual workers who would produce, package, transmit and legitimise knowledge and its mode of production. Such workers joined the *game* through invitations, by bidding for contracts, and remained in the *game* as trusted deliverers and contacts. So, in this chapter, I intend mapping New Labour's intellectual work and workers, particularly through the National College, with an emphasis on the control of knowledge production.

New Labour and research

Following Lawn and Lingard (2002, p 292), my argument is that intellectual work was produced by 'a policy elite that acts across borders, displays a similar habitus, have a feel for the same policy game' and so acts as 'bearers' of the New Labour leadership of schools *game*. In Bourdieu's (2000) terms, there was a *game in play* including officially located role-holders at national level, such as ministers and civil servants, and outsiders brought in to lead policy, such as Michael Barber in the SEU, and in NDPBs such as the National College, and knowledge producers and popularisers in the universities, think tanks, schools and private companies. For example, Collarbone (2005, p 77) describes the National Remodelling Team (NRT)[1] as 'an example of a public–private partnership' with the advantage of private-sector consultants who, 'not blocked by existing "assumptions", [are] able to introduce practices and tools often untried in the education sector, [are] experienced with working in large organizations and dealing with change ... and radiate a "can do" attitude, no matter how major the task'. This interplay between institutionally located powerful people and people who are powerful because of their preferred knowledge position and track record for delivery meant that hierarchy could operate to secure change. These people often knew each other (or of each other), worked in compatible ways and acted as gatekeepers to enable communication and workflow patterns to emerge. They shared a New Labour *disposition* for functionalist reforms and delivery methodologies. Let me begin with an illuminative example.

In *Excellence in Schools* (DfEE, 1997, p 46) the following statement is made:

> The vision for learning set out in this White Paper will demand the highest qualities of leadership and management from headteachers. The quality of the head often makes the difference between the success or failure of a school. Good heads can transform a school; poor heads can block progress and achievement. It is essential that we have measures in place to strengthen the skills of all new and serving heads.

There is no evidence or referencing provided, and so the policies seem to be based on beliefs transformed into assertions. This spoke to common-sense assumptions, but what gave New Labour both an entitlement and confidence to do this was that they drew from the epistemologies and research findings of school effectiveness and school improvement knowledge workers. Indeed, as Goldstein and Woodhouse (2000, p 353) have argued, school effectiveness spoke to the Conservatives from the 1980s as well as New Labour 'at least partly because it implied that changing schools could affect performance and hence that educational policy was relevant to educational "standards"'. So, prior to taking office, Barber (1996) argued in favour of research-based investment and endorsed the Sammons et al (1995) meta-analysis commissioned and funded by Ofsted. This identified the characteristics of effective schools through both textual description and references (see the summary in Table 3.1).

The authors present a number of caveats regarding reading and engaging with the findings: first, the authors separated out the 'characteristics of effective schools' from 'key determinants of effectiveness', particularly since the evidence base was based on 'small numbers of outlier schools (selected as either highly effective or highly ineffective)' (Sammons et al, 1995, p 1); second, they identified 'the dangers of interpreting correlations as evidence of causal mechanisms' (p 1); and, third, they stressed that 'the Review should not be seen as prescriptive and certainly cannot be viewed as a simplistic recipe for effectiveness' (Sammons et al, 1999, p 224). Nevertheless, the report shows an interesting difference in emphasis. For leadership, the opening statement is: 'almost every single study of school effectiveness has shown both primary and secondary leadership to be a key factor' (Sammons et al, 1995, p 8). But for teaching, the overarching judgement is: 'it is clear from the research literature that the quality of teaching is at the heart of effective schooling' (Sammons et al, 1995, p 15), and for students, they say:

> a common finding of effective schools research is that there can be quite substantial gains in effectiveness when the self-esteem of pupils is raised, when they have an active role in the life of the school, and when they are given a share of responsibility for their own learning. (p 21)

Table 3.1: Eleven factors for effective schools (Sammons et al, 1995, p 8)

1. Professional leadership	Firm and purposeful A participative approach The leading professional
2. Shared vision and goals	Unity of purpose Consistency of practice Collegiality and collaboration
3. A learning environment	An orderly atmosphere An attractive working environment
4. Concentration on teaching and learning	Maximisation of learning time Academic emphasis Focus on achievement
5. Purposeful teaching	Efficient organisation Clarity of purpose Structured lessons Adaptive practice
6. High expectations	High expectations all round Communicating expectations Providing intellectual challenge
7. Positive reinforcement	Clear and fair discipline Feedback
8. Monitoring progress	Monitoring pupil performance Evaluating school performance
9. Pupil rights and responsibilities	Raising pupil self-esteem Positions of responsibility Control of work
10. Home–school partnership	Parental involvement in their children's learning
11. A learning organisation	School-based staff development

The relationship between the characteristics of effectiveness and the nuanced use of language, such as 'key factor' and 'quite substantial gains', is something that the authors recognise, but they are concerned to provide 'an accessible format' (Sammons et al, 1995, p 2) to help policymakers and practitioners to engage with the findings.

The Sammons et al (1995) report has faced critique (eg Hamilton, 1999; Morley and Rassool, 1999), and, in reply, Sammons et al (1999, p 225) defend the listing with regard to accessibility as 'research should be made available to practitioners and policymakers', with Sammons (1999, p 184) stating that what this means is that reading the report and list 'did not require a detailed knowledge of the academic literature'. There is no evidence in the report that leadership is more important than teaching and learning or pupil rights and responsibilities, and the authors make it clear that 'ultimately, the quality of teaching and expectations have the most significant role to play in fostering pupils' learning and progress and, therefore, in influencing their educational outcomes' (Sammons et al, 1995, p 24). However, the rank ordering of the 11 factors translates a complex interweaving of organisational structures, cultures and practices into a clear and unambiguous hierarchy.[2] Barber (1996, pp 129–30) replicates (without the numbers) and endorses this list:

> The real power of research ... lies in the weight it gives to an argument, even where it simply confirms common sense. It provides overwhelming evidence on which to base suggestions to headteachers and teachers in schools, and policy proposals to politicians. For headteachers and teachers it is, for example, encouraging that research, in addition to suggesting the characteristics of effective schools also indicates that, if schools attempt to put those characteristics in place, they will improve. In other words, what the research suggests should be done in theory works in practice. For politicians, the research has provided convincing evidence on which to base some major policy and spending decisions. (p 131)

This example is illustrative of how education policy demands were based on a functional approach to knowledge production with the emphasis on the school as a unitary organisation, where people trained to show the right behaviours and skills can enable effectiveness, and how that training can be based on simple listings that translate complexity into easy-to-apply models of good practice. For example, it enabled individual teachers, departments and schools to be identified as effective or ineffective:

> the salvation of the education system depends on the subtle relationship between schools taking responsibility for their own improvement, and government (and other agencies) creating a climate and context within which they are encouraged to improve themselves. Neither on its own is sufficient. (Barber, 1996, p 132)

From school improvement work with a particular emphasis on change processes, such as Michael Fullan's,[3] New Labour identified that, as distinct from failing or stuck schools, successful schools: have a vision, set targets, produce and use data through self-evaluation processes, and develop staff (Barber, 1996). Consequently, functionalism is interconnected to everyday practices: questions asked, language used and the cultures in which people work:

> The assumption tends to be that ... [failing schools] are simply schools without the characteristics of effective schools. David Reynolds of Newcastle University suggests that this is too simplistic. Failing schools, he argues, have characteristics which actively militate against improvement.... Staff tend to blame pupils and the community for failure. They are fearful of outside intervention. There are feuds and cliques among staff. There is resistance to change. Good new ideas are met with cynicism. Effective staff in these circumstances often hide behind the norms of an ineffective group. Demoralisation is widespread, and teachers expect little from either the school as an organisation or from the pupils. (Barber, 1996, p 146)

Barber (1996) made the eradication of data-determined school failure non-negotiable and he endorsed bold strategies for improvement.

Intellectuals and intellectual work

Barber's (1996) engagement with SESI research shows a direct linkage between New Labour's beliefs (leadership by a single person at the top of a hierarchy is necessary and normal), ideas (the right type of leadership can bring about transformational change in public services) and evidence (leadership is the number one factor in school effectiveness). Standards, and more specifically failing schools, were how the problem of publicly funded education was conceptualised, with the leadership of schools as the solution. A *logic of practice* articulated through policy texts defined the problem and made rapid delivery, combined with enthusiastic *dispositions*, the only *game* imaginable. As Bourdieu states:

> Through the very peculiar logic of the *administrative commission* ... the bureaucratic field contributes decisively to the constitution, and to the consecration, of 'universal' social problems. The imposition of *problématique* that the sociologist – as every other social agent – suffers and of which he becomes a relay and support every time he takes up on his own account questions which are an expression of the sociopolitical mood of the times (for instance by including them in his survey questionnaire or worse, by designing his survey around them) is all the more likely when the problems that are *taken for granted* in a given social universe are those that have the greatest chances of being allocated *grants*, material or symbolic, of being, as we say in French, *bien vus*, in high favor with the managers of scientific bureaucracies and with bureaucratic authorities such as research foundations, private firms, or governmental agencies. (This explains why public opinion polls, the 'science without a scientist,' always beget the approval of those who have the means of commissioning them and who otherwise prove so critical of sociology whenever the latter breaks with their demands and commands.) (Bourdieu and Wacquant, 1992, pp 239–40, emphasis in original)

New Labour needed forms of knowledge that would allow them to govern and to make use of data central to performance calculations about the self and students (Ball, 2010). The leadership of schools *game* was based on a *doxa* that generated an '*illusio*' where 'being caught up in the game ... as a fundamental belief in the interest of the game and the value of the stakes which is inherent in that membership' (Bourdieu, 2000, p 11, emphasis added). The call to join in with modernising policy enabled players to stake their *capital*: this was *economic capital* through funding reforms (eg Academy sponsors); *cultural capital* through the embodiment, institutionalisation and objectification of leaders, leading and leadership as normal (eg ministerial and civil servant narratives about reforms) (Bourdieu and Wacquant, 1992, p 119); *social capital* through tapping into and generating 'a durable network of more or less institutionalized relationships of mutual acquaintance and recognition' (Bourdieu and Wacquant, 1992, p 119) (eg headteachers, local authority senior leaders and university professors taking on roles in government); and '*the symbolic effects of capital*' (Bourdieu, 2000, p 242, emphasis in original) is revealed within the *game* as the struggle for distinction and recognition, where a person enters a 'social fiction' through rituals (Bourdieu, 2000, p 243) (eg winning a commissioned research project contract, being awarded a title such as Sir or Dame, and taking on a prestigious delivery role in the National College).

A study of biographies through outputs and webpages does give a glimpse into the complex interconnections, and as this book is permeated with evidence, here I only give a couple of illuminative examples. First, in 1996, a review of the fields of SESI was authored by David Reynolds, Pam Sammons, Louise Stoll, Michael Barber[4] and Josh Hillman (Reynolds et al, 1996) and they acknowledge the interest by the Conservative governments at the time, but are explicit about the direct link with the New Labour opposition: 'the Labour Party will fight the next General Election on a policy platform explicitly based upon the insights of effectiveness knowledge' (p 134). Having won the 1997 election, Barber delivered on this aspiration, and a review of education policy and the leadership of schools *game* shows the significant contribution that SESI knowledge workers have made. Second, the National College Governing Council (NCSL, 2000) lists 13 members including: David Hopkins, at the time Dean of Education at Nottingham University, who headed up the think tank (2001) and who later took over from Barber at the SEU; Michael Gibbons, at the time a headteacher, who became the first Chief Executive of the Innovation Unit in 2006, and was asked by Jim Knight (Minister for Schools) to take over as Chief Executive of a Federation following an Ofsted inspection that put one of the Academies into special measures; Tony Mackay, Director for Strategic Thinking in Victoria, Australia, Chair of the Innovation Unit and President of the International Congress for School Effectiveness and Improvement (ICSEI); and Toby Salt, at the time a headteacher, who became an Executive Head of a Federation involving three schools, a Director at the Innovation Unit and is now the Deputy Chief Executive and Strategic Director at the National College.

It is interesting how interlinks between organisational and epistemic hubs enabled the production of intellectual work, mainly through information exchange located in an understanding of *field* position. Knowledge workers determined what is known about leadership, what needs to be known and who the trusted knowers are through books, articles, conversations, keynote lectures and hot-seat sessions (in meetings, phone calls, emails, online, conference papers and talks). Time was invested, outcomes delivered, products designed, narratives emplotted and schools imagined. They were both hands-off through thinking and strategising, and hands-on through providing answers for politicians to seemingly intractable problems and by working with practitioners on how to make the necessary changes. For example, the NET website has a paper by Sir Iain Hall (undated) who, in his capacity as a branded 'Leading Thinker', outlines the role that headteachers have gone through over 30 years. In this way individuals do thinking, provide descriptions and explanations, and so construct leadership knowledge.

A broad review of what was going on during New Labour's time in office shows that the staking of *capital* was through a range of practices and projects that can be identified as follows:

Branded

Claims were made about tried-and-tested products and often this is what the company/person is known for. For example, the Hay Group (undated) offers its '360 degree feedback process' for leaders;[5] the Improving the Quality of Education for All (IQEA) project enables a partnership between a school, local authority and the IQEA team to 'focus on the conditions within schools that can sustain the teaching–learning process' (Reynolds et al, 2000, p 220); and Headteachers into Industry (HTI) offers short-term secondments with a 'Stretch Programme' where leaders can 'stretch their own leadership skills in a new environment ... and ultimately understand what industry requires of young people who will become employees of tomorrow' (HTI, 2007).

Bespoke

Companies/people offer services (sometimes linked to a branded product) that can be customised to the needs of an individual and/or organisation. This could be a person of sufficient reputation and track record that they can provide dedicated services. This can be an individual, for example, Tony Mackay's website demonstrates his capital:

> Tony's work at state, national and international levels focuses on strategic thinking and facilitation for Government bodies, education agencies, think tanks, school boards and

leadership teams. It encompasses the areas of school and system leadership, improvement and innovation, teacher professionalism and curriculum and assessment policy and includes the design and implementation of Research and Development Programs and Leadership. (CSE, undated)

Or a company, for example:

Hay Group has been at the leading edge of educational change for decades. Many of our specialist consultants have experience working directly for education providers and so understand the unique culture and challenges that educational institutions and authorities face. (Hay Group, undated)

Bespoke work is also undertaken by companies, for example, Cocentra (undated) provide an 'Interim Management Service' for senior leadership to cover absences or to supplement a senior leadership through a period of change.

Bought in

Companies/people were contracted by a public institution on behalf of the state to deliver a particular project. The form and outcome of the project can be open to negotiation, but it tends to be tightly time-bound, with milestones and required outcomes. This seems to be the most active area of private involvement in leadership. For example, CfBT (undated a, undated b) were involved in writing materials for the NPQH; Hay McBer (2000) produced a model of teacher effectiveness and undertook a comparative analysis of headteachers and senior executives in private companies (Forde et al, 2000); and PricewaterhouseCoopers researched and scoped what school leadership is about and made policy recommendations (DfES and PwC, 2007). A team from the Universities of Nottingham, London and Toronto was contracted to research *The Impact of School Leadership on Pupil Outcomes* (Day et al, 2009), where they examined the relationship between headteacher activity and values, and improvements in test scores.

Brought in

Companies/people were contracted to deliver a service. For example, the Academies Programme was launched in 2000 with the goal of raising standards in failing schools in urban areas, where private interests (companies, individuals) either alone or in consortia could invest £2m in return for public investment in the building and running costs. Private interests can control governance, leadership, workforce conditions of service and the curriculum. So far, the official evaluation is that Academies have seen gains for students though the variation between Academies is developing rapidly. Sponsorship is generally seen to be beneficial to the modernisation of education, not least through funding, networking and how they 'have an unremitting focus on improvement and consistently challenge the Academy's leadership and staff in this area' (PwC, 2008, pp 11–12).

The staking of capital in modernisation projects enabled 'advocacy coalitions' (Ball and Exley, 2010, p 155) to develop, so private people and companies have invested in Academies (eg Innovative Schools, 2010). PricewaterhouseCoopers led the evaluation (PwC, 2008), and Conor Ryan, former educational adviser to Blair and Blunkett, together with Academy principals, provided evidence and intellectual arguments in favour (Astle and Ryan, 2008). 'Independent' people and organisations working in the same territory, even if in competition, are sutured together to produce a homogeneous marketplace where the consumer (Department, National College, headteacher) in search of support and development opportunities is linked either personally or online to particular people, ideas and products. As Ball (2010, p 131) argues, 'within this economy of policy knowledges, knowledge production that is fast, certain, unequivocal, "on message", and immediate and relevant is especially valued as a way of representing the world to government'.

The National College and intellectual work

Game playing with and within the National College is a power *game*:

> strategies are not abstract responses to an abstract situation … they are defined in relation to promptings, inscribed in the objective world, in the form of positive or negative indices which are not addressed to just anyone but which only 'speak' (as opposed to what 'says nothing to them') to agents characterised by possession of a certain capital and certain habitus. (Bourdieu, 2000, p 220)

So the promptings from New Labour were to endorse belief systems conducive to functional knowledge production and thereby render educational problems and solutions thinkable in particular ways: first, the normalisation of the single person as leader as the starting point for modernising professional practice and as the repository for leadership that should be distributed; second, the focus on the school as a rational organisational entity and the performance of personnel (particularly teachers); third, the development of the transformational model based on vision and mission, with ongoing rebranding and futuring through various hybrids such as distributed leadership; and, fourth, the refinement of methodology and methods designed to measure the impact of the single leader on school outcomes, and so be consistent with other parts of the government infrastructure (eg Ofsted, 2003b). The main message from Number 10 was that public services needed reform, but the leadership evidence and theoretical base lacked functionality and did not have clear messages for practice (PIU, 2001). However, even though evidence may be limited in quantity and quality, this should not stop the endorsement of the preferred models of good practice embedded in reform proposals.

Such promptings generated behind-the-scenes activity that only empirical work uncovers. As one consultant stated when talking about the National College:

> "There was a desire to ensure that at the point of the launch of the College, there was an evidence base around leadership that could be truly international. So that as the College began its work, it would be informed by a knowledge base that one felt was contemporary, that identified some of the best practice in both leadership development work and leadership generally and also the way in which a College would be able to function simultaneously within the policy environment, the environment of the practice of leadership of the field, cooperation with other key agencies, both professional associations, and other NDPBs and obviously supported by the best research base.... We went through a process of identifying and selecting, and most of that was throughout various networks, and then invited them to present short papers around a series of dimensions that we thought were appropriate." (PC4[6])

So the epistemic position of such consultants combined with their approval of what knowledge counts as significant. This may not be tangible or visible, particularly since the consultant talked about how their role was to facilitate, where:

> "my feeling is that there are a group of us who, you know, think about as being … connectors, networkers, facilitators, consultant advisers … I don't think it's a set of roles that has been explored perhaps as much as it might, but part of the reason is because it's not a set of activities that are always well understood, because by definition, success at it means that it's less visible, deliberately so." (PC4)

In addition to this, there are concrete illustrations of the products from this type of activity. The National College has been explicit about how it has commissioned, for example, McKinsey and Company (NCSL, 2006c, 2007) and Demos (NCSL, 2006c) to support the advice it gives to the government. In making claims about 'good leadership', the National College continues to draw on knowledge claims that reinforce rather than challenge functionality (National College, 2010c). An interesting focus is on SESI knowledge workers who have developed an impressive track record regarding the leadership of schools *game*, and did this through, first, projects that focused on framing the school leadership agenda (eg MacBeath, 1998; Day et al, 2000, 2007; Jackson, 2000; Southworth, 2002; Harris et al, 2003; Harris, 2005, 2008; Hopkins, 2007) and the types of knowledge that are relevant to practice (eg Fink and Hargreaves, 2006; Reynolds, undated); second, rethinking and developing the fields (eg Stoll and Fink, 1996; Stoll and Myers, 1998a; MacBeath and Mortimore, 2001; MacBeath and Moos, 2004); third, working directly on New Labour's reform plans (eg on personalisation, see Hargreaves, 2004, 2006; Miliband, 2004b; on school improvement, see Chapman, 2005; Harris et al, 2006a) and engaging with the New Labour innovation agenda (Hargreaves, 2003); and, fourth, developing and refining methodology and methods (eg Day et al, 2009). In relation to the National College, there is a lot of evidence of direct involvement in the shaping and development of the *game* through linking the leadership agenda to the National College agenda (Hopkins, 2001; NCSL, 2002), particularly since this approach to leadership is endorsed by close-to-practice professionals who popularised it through the National College (eg Munby, 2007, 2008, 2010; Salt, 2009; Collarbone, undated). Intellectual work also took place through participation in College structures, events and publishing database, and through taking up official roles within the College (eg Southworth, 2004; Coles and Southworth, 2005).

In order to illuminate this, I intend to draw on New Labour's aim not only to understand what was taking place in the leadership of schools (eg Earley et al, 2002; Stevens et al, 2005) and to set the agenda for the type of professional practice that was necessary to deliver reforms (eg DfES and PwC, 2007), but also to establish a clear evidence base for the direct link between headteacher leadership and student outcomes. In order to do this, the Department and the National College drew on the work of Leithwood who had contributed to the functionality of the 'high reliability organization' (Leithwood et al, 1999, p 211) and wrestled with matters of accountability (Leithwood, 2001) that fitted neatly with Barber's (2007) 'deliverology' approach. Furthermore, he pioneered measurement studies, and while he recognised that leadership is indirect in its impact on students, particularly through the work of Hallinger and Heck (1996), he was disposed to argue that 'nevertheless the demands on schools cannot await the outcome of such research' (Leithwood et al, 1999, p 32). Leithwood contributed to New Labour and National College thinking on school leadership (eg Leithwood and Riehl, 2003; Leithwood and Levin, 2004, 2005), and as already noted, in 2006, a team including Chris Day, Pam Sammons, David Hopkins, Alma Harris and Ken Leithwood was contracted to deliver a three-year project 'to explore the relationships between school leadership, in particular that of the head, and pupil learning outcomes' (Day et al, 2009, p 6). This was a major study that began with the functional assumption that the headteacher is the causal origin of all that is effective:

> the ability to continue to improve or to sustain effectiveness over longer periods is an indicator that improvement has become embedded in the school's work and culture and the result of heads' application of combinations of strategies within and across school development phases. (Day et al, 2009, p 1)

The key findings noted in studying such successful schools were: first, 'there are statistically significant empirical and qualitatively robust associations between heads' educational values, qualities and their strategic actions and improvement in school conditions leading to improvements in pupil outcomes' (Day et al, 2009, p 1); and, second, 'headteachers are perceived as the main source of leadership by staff, governors and parents. Their educational values, strategic intelligence, and leadership strategies shape the school and classroom processes and practices which result in improved pupil outcomes' (p 2). Consequently, the elitist nature of schools in England, and the deference to the single person as leader, is confirmed as culturally acceptable and making a difference.

Importantly, this team also produced a literature review (Leithwood et al, 2006a, 2006b), and then updated it in the final report (Day et al, 2009). The production of *Seven Strong Claims about Successful School Leadership* (Leithwood et al, 2006a) is crucial to moving forward in regard to Sammons et al's (1995) rank ordering of professional leadership as the first in the 11 factors of effective schools:

1. School leadership is second only to classroom teaching as an influence on pupil learning.
2. Almost all successful leaders draw on the same repertoire of basic leadership practices.
3. The ways in which leaders apply these basic leadership practices – not the practices themselves – demonstrate responsiveness to, rather than dictation by, the contexts in which they work.
4. School leaders improve teaching and learning indirectly and most powerfully through their influence on staff motivation, commitment and working conditions.
5. School leadership has a greater influence on schools and students when it is widely distributed.
6. Some patterns of distribution are more effective than others.
7. A small handful of personal traits explains a high proportion of the variation in leadership effectiveness. (Leithwood et al, 2006a, p 3)

Notably, these claims again recognise that the classroom and relationships between teachers and students is more important, but then the focus is on school leaders and leadership as necessarily requiring attention and investment. The authors have drawn again on functional literatures, mainly from non-UK sources, and have enabled the shift from role titles (eg headteacher, deputy headteacher, head of faculty, curriculum coordinator) towards generic leader, leading and leadership in ways that marginalise the requirement to have educational knowledge, and under workforce remodelling make organisational leadership open to anyone who can demonstrate leadership credentials. Indeed, the construction of the 'seven strong claims' is a very useful device for enabling the National College to justify its plans (see Munby, 2007, p 14).

The new improved leadership model of distributed leadership features strongly, and here I will raise just two problems. First, leadership is located in the leader as the repository of effectiveness, and is bestowed on others, where students in particular are positioned as beneficiaries, but, in reality they are the objects upon which elite adults impact and so generate data to prove that these adults are realising their targets. Second, leadership, and distributed leadership in particular, is a power process, and missing from this analysis is any overt theory of power or a recognition of how advantage and disadvantage are constructed and reconstructed through practice. Work by Hatcher (2005) and Hartley (2007, 2010) in critically examining the knowledge claims of distributed leadership theorists and developing alternative perspectives is missing (Gunter et al, forthcoming). Significantly, the world of the 'seven strong claims' seems to be one without social injustice, with no recognition that 'the notionally gender-neutral figure of the entrepreneur is, culturally speaking, a variety of masculinity' (Connell et al, 2009, p 332).

Notes

[1] The NRT grew out of the Transforming the School Workforce Pathfinder pilot project in 32 schools led by Pat Collarbone (see Thomas et al, 2004). From 2003, the NRT was located at the National College and was moved to the Training and Development Agency (TDA) from 2004 (see NRT, 2001).

[2] Such an approach to listing out factors of effectiveness or 'qualities of excellence' or 'common characteristics in high-performing schools' dominates and continues to put the emphasis on the importance of leadership (eg Taylor and Ryan, 2005, p 3).

[3] Each headteacher in a Transforming the School Workforce Pathfinder Project school was given a copy of Michael Fullan's (1999) book *Change Forces: The Sequel* to support the change leadership training process.

[4] Michael Barber was also on the steering group of the National Commission on Education funded by charity and private business, and wrote a chapter in the report *Success Against the Odds* (National Commission on Education, 1996). The chapters about effective schools in disadvantaged areas are co-written by various combinations of people from higher education, local government, voluntary-sector organisations and private-sector companies.

[5] There is an international dimension to this. For example, Brundrett et al (2006) show the antecedence of training programmes in England and New Zealand and report on the links with work by the Hay Group in Australia, England and New Zealand.

[6] See p viii for an explanation of the abbreviations identifying interviewees from the KPEL project.

FOUR

Institutionalised governance

Introduction

The explanation for the leadership of schools *game* begins in the conceptualisation of the state and its relationship with civil society as a form of institutionalised governance. The UK state has intervened in and adapted to the interplay between hierarchy, markets and networks in public and education policy in England. So, for the New Labour leadership of schools *game* to play and develop within policymaking, the state had to exercise forms of control through the operation of public institutions. This control was through the institution itself as the custodian and symbol of electoral legitimacy as the mandate to govern, and through forms of governance regarding how outsiders as experts were invited into policymaking and contracted to deliver on policy through advice, design, activity and promotion. In this chapter, I intend to describe institutionalised governance regarding the role of public institutions and how outsiders were brought into the design and delivery process, and I will use the origins and formation of the National College as an illustrative case.

Critical policy scholarship

Ranson (1995) argues that policy needs to be historically located through an analysis of the people and practices involved, together with theorising that interplays rather than separates out agency and structure. So understanding the emergence and development of the leadership of schools as a policy *game* needs to be linked to the relationship between the state, public institutions that produce public policy and civil society as manifest in forms of governance. A useful starting point is Newman's (2001, p 33) framework, outlined in Table 4.1, 'to suggest different models of governance, each with its characteristic form of power and authority, pattern of relationships and assumptions about change'.

Newman (2001) recognises that governments tend to operate in all four models, and this is the case with New Labour through 'a mix of approaches – delegation *and* central control, long-term capacity building *and* short-term targets – producing tensions in the process of institutional change' (p 37, original emphasis). The leadership of schools has: first, hierarchical elements, particularly through the state control of knowledge production, professional identity and practice; second, rational goal assumptions where managerial power to deal with problems (eg performance targets) was deemed necessary to deliver output data; third, open systems through which contractually controlled networks were used to deliver leadership products and training; and, fourth, elements of self-governance through socially responsible entrepreneurialism to enable improvements by elite interests operating independently but on behalf of the community.

Table 4.1: Models of governance (based on Newman, 2001, pp 33–7)

	Hierarchy	Rational goal	Open systems	Self-governance
Power	State control over policy and implementation through bureaucratic institutions	Dispersed and so institutions use management structures and processes to control	Dispersed and fluid within networks of actors. Institutions steer and influence as indirect control	Public institutions work in partnership with citizens to resolve problems and deliver services
Relationships	Vertical and bureaucratic power flows	Centralised targets locally managed in agencies	Dynamic and responsive	Integration of citizens and institutions of government in decision-making and delivery
Change	Slow and based on rule changes	Targets delivered through roles, contracts and incentives	Fluid and fast with self-directed and self-reflexive strategies	Partnerships based on communities as agents of change
Accountability	High on outputs and process	High on outputs	Low	Can be high through public institution–citizen partnerships

The tensions in New Labour governance identified by Newman (2001) are evident in education policymaking. The approach was to secure 'investment for results' (Blair, 2006, p 1), with Barber (2007, p 79) conceptualising his deliverology strategy as hierarchical, underpinned by 'the science (or pseudo science) of marshalling prime ministerial power to deliver significant measurable improvements in public services'. Centralised leadership of reforms through the leadership of schools (and penalties for those who strayed or resisted) operated through structures (eg the National College), cultures (eg private-sector models and practices), processes (eg targets, data-determined performance-related pay and contract renewal) and people (eg National College role incumbents and contractors who codified and transmitted reforms). So the leadership of schools developed and operated through a form of institutionalised governance: the central control of the public institution through hierarchy and managerialism interplayed with trusted people and organisations operating according to rational goals and within networked contractual systems. This is in contrast with the USA where a form of marketised governance operates through a school improvement industry located in 'an extremely pluralistic and heterogeneous environment in which new organizational forms, while easy to found, are also quick to fail' (Rowan, 2002, p 286).

The public institution

The New Labour decade shows that certain public institutions continued to matter. By public institutions I mean central and local government, NDPBs, and, in relation to education, schools. Such structures are meant to have a permanence that supersede the comings and goings of particular people, and so a permanent neutral civil service is meant to counteract the fashions and markets in outsider think tank 'intellectual arbitrage' (Mulgan, 2006, p 154). There is a system of interconnections regarding the law and finance as well as general day-to-day activity. In Hood's (2007, p 129) terms, there are four 'basic social resources' for how central government regulates civil society: first, 'nodality' or 'the capacity of government to operate as a node in information networks – a central point of contact'; second, 'authority' or 'legal power and other sources of legitimacy'; third, 'treasure' or 'assets or fungible resources'; and, fourth, 'organization' or 'capacity for direct action, for instance through armies, police or bureaucracy'. New Labour used such resources in the development and deployment of the leadership of schools by those outside of schools: the 'central point of contact' was Number 10;[1] the 'authority' was that of the Prime Minister to require and determine reform; the 'treasure' was through the investment made in the leadership of schools; and 'direct action' took place through the bureaucracy of reform packages (descriptions, guidelines, training packs, teaching

---

55

materials) with external policing by Ofsted and internal policing by performativity.

Béland (2005, p 3) argues that 'political institutions create constraints and opportunities for those involved in policymaking', and so histories impact on what might be done. Indeed, Barber (2007) is clear about how institutional logics were such that he had to work on the reform of Whitehall structures, processes and attitudes in order to enable New Labour's commitment to delivery to operate.[2] Essential to this was the role of central public institutions (the Prime Minister and Number 10 advisers, the Department, and the Treasury) in securing top-down control of education policy conceptualisation and delivery through the legality of the mandate.[3] Barber (1997, p 191) recounts a story that clearly impacted on him in regard to how reforms can be driven through:

> When I asked Kenneth Baker (former Secretary of State for Education and Science) why he had gone ahead with the National Curriculum in spite of the almost universal opposition among educators he said, very simply, 'we had a mandate'. He was right. The idea and the timetable had been set out before the 1987 election.[4]

The primacy of the national public institution remained, with delivery based on targets and the minister linking potential resignation to outcome measures (Barber, 2007). While the language may have been more inclusive with the use of 'we' rather than 'the government' (Mulderrig, 2003), and 'new' or 'modern' (Fairclough, 2000), research by Mulderrig (2003) shows the strong presence of the government in policy texts. She suggests that the shift away from an authoritarian tone does not necessarily mean that the asymmetrical relationship between the government and governed is removed, rather it could be a language of disguise. According to Newman (2001, p 85), 'the government tended to talk "over the heads" of the professions to win the support of the public and political stakeholders', and in doing so New Labour appealed to common sense in ways that were designed to chime with a population that also experienced managerialism in their workplace.

New Labour took office with a commitment to restructure and reculture through modernising Whitehall, where the emphasis was to be on ensuring 'that the policies we make, the services we deliver and the tasks we carry out deliver results, deliver the best results' (Blair, 1999a). Even Blair's departure did not interrupt the modernisation agenda, with Adonis (2010) showing how Brown approved of the reforms and wanted them to continue. The Department established Units, such as the SEU and the Innovation Unit, which had a delivery remit and operated according to 'new public management' methods, cultures and language, and were staffed with selected pro-reformers drawn from Higher Education Institutions (HEIs) and schools. The National College was established as an organisational delivery arm of the government with a requirement to secure high-performance leadership of schools as a means of enabling government priorities. And so, in Newman's (2001, p 169) terms, 'the dispersal of power ... did not mean the erosion of power', particularly since New Labour, following on from other governments, engaged in controlling professional practice from a distance.

This analysis goes some way to revising a shift from government to governance in political science, where it is argued that there are processes taking place which create a sense that 'we live in "the centreless society"' (Rhodes, 1996, p 657) and where government has been 'hollowed out' (Rhodes, 1994, p 138) through the increased role of networks. However, education policy in England remains firmly in the grip of the London government: unlike Scotland,[5] responsibility has not been devolved downwards to an English parliament or to existing local government, and it is a policy that has not been relocated upwards to Europe. And, while networks and networking have grown, they are 'still less significant than the hierarchical relations between institutions and actors' (Pierre and Peters, 2000, p 18). As Holliday (2000, p 175) has argued, the core remains strong even in a complex setting, and so 'the fact that agencies now sign contracts with the central state and non-state actors are increasingly prominent in the policy process does not change things much'.

While institutions do matter, certain institutions matter more than others. Examples of new alliances, or what Hatcher (2006, p 599) calls 're-agenting', can be used to illustrate regulated governance at a distance, and so, for example, Future Leaders is led by Heath Monk (who was previously Deputy Director in the Department) in partnership with Absolute Return for Kids (ARK), a philanthropic investment charity, and the SSAT, a charity that works with New Labour specialist and Academy schools. However, Future Leaders is an example of the New Labour delivery *disposition*, particularly through the promotion of specific cultural tastes regarding normalised good practice.[6] Hence, it is the Department, funding by the Treasury, the construction of NDPBs such as the National College and the promotion of contractual partnerships that seem to matter most. Local government institutions continued to be restructured and recultured as delivery and supervisory organisations through a combination of inspection, legislative requirements and outsourcing to private contractors.[7] Unions (with the exception of the National Union of Teachers) were incorporated into a social partnership with government, where they were directly involved in policy delivery. Hence, governance in the form of public dialogue and political debate was replaced by central government direction combined with contractual compliance and new partnership arrangements that fit with the New Labour delivery culture. The reliance on contractual relationships between NDPBs and consultancies, and the formation of charities such as Future Leaders, in the provision of educational services meant that the public relation to the institution is circumscribed, and so powerful private interests were able to act within a public institution in the name of the public. This is where governance in the form of networks fits in, and, in particular, how institutions of the state have worked with private interests to help frame and deliver public policy. As Béland (2005) argues, the focus on institutions alone cannot explain change, not least how certain ideas come to the fore and why others are prevented from reaching the agenda.

Governance

The challenge for government is that policies 'travel' to, enter and are interpreted and reworked in 'embedded' settings (Ozga, 2005, p 207), and confusion can be generated by 'ensembles of policies' that contradict or generate tensions between what is being required and what is preferred (Ball, 1994a, pp 25–6). Hence, there is a risk management imperative (Hood et al, 2004) where people had to be trained in the new ways, or at least enabled to publicly comply through displaying a New Labour *disposition*. Policy needed translation, monitoring and measuring to make sure that the government's intension was delivered locally in schools and classrooms and so produce outcome data (eg student achievement) to prove that the government had done what it promised to do and had made a difference. New Labour, like other governments, realised that it could not develop and deliver policy without help, and, as Saint-Martin (2000) has shown, knowledge about how to modernise had to come from outside because it is based on challenging bureaucracy. So by working through partnership and contractual relationships, particular interests could be brought directly into the policy process, building in a responsibility to cooperate and deliver. This proved to be 'an effective strategy for "shifting the blame"' (Power et al, 1997, p 13), and so, as Ozga (2009, p 158) has argued, 'the state does not "go away" ... rather it works in new forms and through new processes'.

So ministers read particular texts, called people in, gave people jobs and put contracts out to tender that enabled trusted researchers to frame policy ideas and strategies. The complexity and multi-levelled nature of this is neatly captured by Coburn (2005), who shows in another context how those in and out of the education system interlink in the generation and legitimation of ideas. In doing this, New Labour connected with people and networks already operating in the education marketplace, and constructed such roles and interconnections through this intervention.[8] Institutionalised governance is about 'trust networks' (Tilly, 2005) within and connected to people and institutions. There is no level playing *field* where all can join in, but a power process of involving particular individuals and organisations who present themselves and are acknowledged as market leaders in knowledge production and delivery. So there is a need to move beyond Actor Network Theory (Law and Hassard, 1999) regarding the moments of how translation into a network operates, and into analyses of why power works in the way it does. What is particularly helpful in doing this is Kingdon's (2003) analysis of 'policy entrepreneurs'. In education, these are ministers, civil servants and advisers appointed from schools and HEIs to Units in the Department or NDPBs such as the National College, and private consultants both as individuals and from large companies who are located in different institutions (private companies, universities, think tanks) and in different places (UK and internationally), but who reveal harmonised *dispositions* regarding neoliberal reforms. Following Kingdon (2003), these policy entrepreneurs associate and position themselves to take advantage of a policy opportunity window that opens, where ideas and ways of knowing can be 'recombined' as 'new' and so provide evidence, language and distinction to legitimise the types of change and the urgency of the reform imperative. Such networking is based on a 'willingness to invest their resources – time, energy, reputation, and sometimes money – in the hope of a future return' (Kingdon, 2003, p 122), and as 'policy groupies' they 'enjoy advocacy, they enjoy being at or near the seat of power, they enjoy being part of the action' (p 123). The 'return' on the investment is that their interests are enhanced through policy impact, status and business success, particularly since 'the provision of public sector services is now a large money-making enterprise' (Fitz and Hafid, 2007, p 293).

While Kingdon (2003) identifies the strategies and investment for gain within policy entrepreneurial activity, Moran (2007) provides more depth about how power flows actually work. There is a need to understand the workings and historical origins of the state, not least the endurance of 'club rule' (Moran, 2007, p 4) and its reformation in the current configuration of regulation within a marketised system. Elites in local government, Whitehall and the profession had made the system work during most of the 20th century through what Marquand (1981, p 36) identifies as 'government by a club, or rather by a nexus of clubs', where people may have not known each other but they knew that other clubs could be trusted to play the *game* fairly and appropriately. As Gewirtz and Ozga (1990, p 47) show, such partnerships are not based on pluralist bargaining over policy agendas, but are 'a closed policy community, operating an already agreed agenda, excluding alternatives and limiting outside access to policymaking'. Challenges to such power were particularly through influential ideas in texts such as Chubb and Moe (1990), Osborne and Gaebler (1993) and, recently, Bobbitt's (2002, p 213) thesis of the 'market state' where choice, personalisation and consumerism mean that public education, and hence the traditional elites who have controlled this, is identified as a thing of the past.

This rejection of what Bobbitt (2002, p 144) calls the 'nation state' based on security and welfare meant that the 'troika of providers' between the minister, schools/unions and local authorities (officers, advisers, inspectors) based on 'mutual regard, trust and commitment' (Williams, 1995, p 4) fractured. Club government only worked and survived many challenges during the 20th century because the rules of the *game* were followed (Bogdanor, 1979). Indeed, as Gewirtz (2002) has shown, such elites were seen to be the source of the problem, with the Department having to become more interventionist to ensure government reforms were delivered and the 'inefficient' and 'self-interested' in schools, unions and local authorities having to embrace reforms or be excluded. While new roles, new practices and new cultures and power relationships were introduced into public institutions under the banner of 'new public management', research has shown that such changes are slow to impact and can vary across the public sector (Boyne et al, 1999). So, while reform could go so far, and early retirements can remove change-blockers and those who are too tired of permanent revolution, it was the actual replacement of providers, either with new quangos (eg National College) or through private providers and partnerships, that enabled rapid shifts. Ironically, the overloaded state and public institutions of the 1970s that saw the government take on responsibility for solving such problems as the sugar shortage (King, 1976) faced reform, and groups such as trade unions and professionals were deprivileged, by Thatcherism, and the

Blair governments reaped the benefits of this. Club government was fractured, overlain and reworked through contracts and outsourced partnership arrangements, and so potential rival sources of power were neutralised as their power bases were dismantled or severely weakened. For example, while teachers paid from the public purse with a 'job for life' could go on strike, a contracted team from a private company would not, as their contract would be terminated and another company brought in. Local government is answerable for educational standards to the local electorate and as such there are debates between a range of complex interests, but contracting and promoting private sector/ interest groups to operate chains of Academy schools enables direct accountability to trusted entrepreneurs and not to the local community.

Clubness was relocated in private interest networks embedded within government (Ball, 2007a), and informally through people knowing and vouching for each other. Some members of 'club' elites positioned themselves in such a way as to remain actively involved in policymaking. Some served both Thatcherite and Blairite governments, for example, Michael Barber, Pat Collarbone, Steve Munby, Cyril Taylor and Chris Woodhead.[9] Some local government chief executives worked close to policy, for example, Tim Brighouse, Heather de Quesnay and Steve Munby;[10] some members of the profession (particularly headteachers) joined the Units or the National College, for example, David Jackson,[11] or remained in post but led on reforms, with honours following for many as a result, for example, Sir Kevin Satchwell, Thomas Telford School; and some professors from HEIs remained close to policy, led on innovations and changes, and/or joined one of the Units or the National College, for example, David Hopkins and Geoff Southworth.[12] In addition, elites from private-sector companies, as individual consultants or as team members, have also been brought into Whitehall (and other parts of the system, not least to take over from local authorities) to provide advice and models of good practice, help reforms to be communicated, and undertake research to support policy development, for example, Tony MacKay. Such policy elites overtly interact in ways to demonstrate their *disposition* to enable reform design and implementation as a means of sustaining their involvement through contractual relations. Their power base is dependent on institutional legitimacy, but is located in contractual renewal rather than in bureaucratic roles. Agenda setting is central to the *game*, with private interests handling uncongenial policy by using a shrewd combination of waiting and shaping the discourse.

It seems as if governance in regard to education is about the ongoing positioning and integration of elites rather than a complete opening up of policymaking to networks. Indeed, in studying government restructuring, Pollitt (2007, p 536) talks about a 'management reform community' made up of consultants and special advisers, and who form a 'cadre' with a 'vested interest in continuous change' through functional performance management and 'makeover' strategies that are quick to introduce. From a public administration perspective, the argument is about whether outside experts are 'demons' or 'saviours' of public services (see Lapsley and Oldfield, 2001), not least as to whether they eclipse the democratic logic through a denial of public accountability in how they operate.[13] However, evidence shows that the continued dominance of government institutions (Marinetto, 2003), particularly in education (Gunter and Forrester, 2009a), means that experts are invited into rather than take over policymaking. There are crossovers where consultants do the work of different governments, and underpinning this is 'how both sets of interests and identities feed off each other' (Fincham, 1999, p 349). Furthermore, research shows that consultants should not be essentialised into one formal grouping, as those in large corporations tend to position themselves differently from those who are sole traders (Lapsley and Oldfield, 2001, p 541). The evidence from the KPEL project shows that positioning is about constructing a distinctive readiness and capability to design and deliver reforms, where building the business does vary from those in large companies to those who are sole traders. While consultants do work in a range of ways, their aggregated impact can be recognised as acting as 'a lubricant for political and policy reforms' (Hodge and Bowman, 2006, p 121). Consequently, consultants are crucial to governments through the interplay between ideas and processes with the modernising image of private-sector delivery. And it is more than this because, as Sturdy et al (2009, p 173) have argued, when the realities of what goes on in everyday practice are opened up for scrutiny both 'complexity and dynamism' is revealed as well as the contextual nature of 'embeddedness in wider social relations'.

Institutionalised governance and the National College

The National College building, together with the nine regional outposts,[14] is the stadium in which the leadership of schools *game* is played out. It is the physical as well as symbolic location of the colonisation of the *field* and the nationalisation of leadership preparation. As Bush (2004, p 245) states: 'The government's decision that it should provide a single national focus for school leadership development and research is ambitious, probably not wise and manifestly untrue.' The

National College is an interesting site through which to examine the workings of institutionalised governance. I intend to do that here by examining the decision to set up the College, the design and remit of the College, and issues of governance and control.

Bottom-up local development and training partnerships between heads, local authorities and higher education had grown rapidly from the 1970s, with Masters degrees becoming *de facto* accreditation for promotion (Gunter, 1999; Gunter and Thomson, 2010). Bolam (2003) identifies the role of headteacher unions (the National Association of Headteachers [NAHT] and Secondary Heads Association [SHA]) as well as the British Educational Leadership Management and Administration Society (BELMAS), British Educational Research Association (BERA) and Universities' Council for the Education of Teachers (UCET) in *field* research and professional training. Furthermore, the selection of headteachers had been developed through the growth of Assessment Centres (Merrick, 1992; Lyons et al, 1993). Debates about a college for headteachers continued (eg Wood, 1983), with Bolam (2004) identifying various feasibility projects. Governments invested in the National Development Centre (NDC) (1983–88) (Bolam, 1986) and the School Management Task Force (SMTF) (1989–92) (SMTF, 1990). So, by 1997, the opportunity existed to build on this knowledge and experience, focus on developing professional practice and renew local government and build on networks of governance. However, New Labour proceeded as if the year 2000 was year zero with the emphasis firmly on the future, and with past professional achievements whitewashed out.[15]

An argument was constructed that leadership training was not taking place and if it did, then it was incidental rather than planned (Blair, 1999b). Specifically, the decision to have a College is located in discussions between ministers, civil servants, advisers and private consultants,[16] where there was a particular interest in the London Leadership Centre that was established at the Institute of Education, University of London.[17] The National College was created as an executive[18] NDPB (or quango).[19,20] Under the Freedom of Information Act (FOIA), I obtained the papers regarding the decision to set up the National College, and there are a number of key discussions which show that the legal status was key to central control: first, classification as an NDPB meant that there was control over the appointment of the Director and Governing Council,[21] pay, and compensation payments; second, a banker is named as a potential chair of a charitable body that would obtain donations to fund the College, and while this 'disappears' from the papers, subsequent events show that direct control was through

Treasury funding;[22] third, the banker asked about 'mutuality' or how an organisation is owned by its customers, and the view was that headteachers could only own and run the National College once they were alumni as they needed to be College products to do that;[23] and, fourth, the Department pursued the idea of Royal College status, but found out that this is not normally given to a new body. Interestingly, however, in a memo between civil servants (23 November 1999) it was made clear that ministers and Number 10 did not like the idea: 'we are looking to set the College up as a modern, forward looking organization rather than tying it to a more established image'.[24] So glimpses into the debates that took place regarding the legal and presentational aspects of the National College show direct control, where headteachers were kept at a distance.

Ongoing control of the National College is illustrated by the Remit letter from the Secretary of State that outlines the purposes, programme and finances,[25] and repeatedly demonstrates that it is a delivery arm of the Department. In the first Remit letter, Blunkett (2000, p 2) was very clear that:

> The main aims of the College are:
>
> - To provide a single national focus for school leadership development and research;
> - To be a driving force for world class leadership in our schools and the wider education service; and
> - To be a provider and promoter of excellence; a major resource for schools; a catalyst for innovation; and a focus for national and international debate on leadership issues.

Blunkett (2000, p 2) then went on to say two things that illustrate direct control. First, that the National College is a delivery arm of the government:

> I intend to involve the College fully in the development and delivery of Government policy on all relevant aspects of school improvement and will look to the College for expert advice on developing targeted leadership strategies in key national priority areas.

Second, that the National College needs to negotiate and obtain permission regarding its activity:

> I would like the College to work closely with my officials to
> reach agreement on an initial programme of pilot activities
> to take place over the next twelve months which can be
> announced by the College launch. (Blunkett, 2000, p 2)

Control of the National College was further secured in the appointment
of Heather de Quesnay (2000–04) and Steve Munby (2005–) as Chief
Executives who came from professional practice.

Centralisation was further illuminated when the College was
established and began its work. The National College was presented
as the '"champion" for school leadership' and with the aim to 'lead
the debate in the country, with teachers, senior managers, governors,
communities educational officers and politicians' by being 'an agency
sufficiently powerful to make the argument, to develop and implement
programmes in partnership and to link together policies and other
agencies' (Hopkins, 2001, p 15). The website demonstrates the
National College commitment to this and how a range of projects and
publications have contributed to the knowledge base, and, as Weindling
(2004) has shown, between 1998 and 2003, 36 out of the 59 leadership
projects identified in his survey were funded by the NCSL and six by
the Department. However, Blunkett (2001b) made it very clear that
the Department would undertake research as a means of evaluating the
impact of the College and to help in programme design, and while the
College did commission research, it was the Department who funded
and led strategically on projects and seminars that were integral to
government policy (eg Bell et al, 2002; Earley et al, 2002; Bell and
Bolam, 2004; Leithwood and Levin, 2004, 2005; Stevens et al, 2005;
DfES and PwC, 2007; Day et al, 2009).

Remit letters became increasingly detailed (Kelly's [2004] is 16 pages
long), often taking on a teaching role in telling the National College
about school leadership and research evidence (eg Johnson, 2007;
Balls, 2010). The main job of the Remit letters was to instruct on core
priorities and outline shifts that the government wanted to make to
the work of the College: identifying key features of government policy
that the College was expected to deliver on (Kelly, 2004; Balls, 2008);
changing its role from the provider of training to that of 'intelligent
commissioner' (Kelly, 2004, p 1); directing that the main way in which
the National College was to be evaluated was through the use of a
'balanced scorecard' (Kelly, 2005a), with Balls, by 2010, providing an
11-page list of specific key performance indictors and targets to measure
delivery against; and requiring the National College to work with other
delivery bodies such as the British Educational Communications and

Technology Agency (BECTA) (Johnson, 2007), Children's Workforce Development Council (CWDC) (Balls, 2008, 2010), SSAT (Kelly, 2004), TDA (Kelly, 2005a) and Workforce Agreement Monitoring Group (WAMG) (Johnson, 2007).

Notably, following the End-to-End Review, the College's development work was reined in and the Department micro-managed and required it to seek permission to do things outside the Remit (Kelly, 2005a), with the Secretary of State saying:

> I take to heart the messages in the End to End Review about the need for greater precision, discipline, outcome-focus and depth in the future work of the College. Activity must be both evidence-based and proportionate to College capacity. I recognize that we will need to exercise restraint and ensure you do not face unmanageably large burdens, spread across too wide a front. A sponsor unit in the DfES will accordingly play a gatekeeper role. Every aspect of improving school leadership is important, but not every priority can be addressed at once. (Kelly, 2004, p 2)

Within government, a close eye was kept on the National College. Blunkett (2006, p 619) was concerned that headteachers did not seem to be doing as they had been told, noting in his diaries the problem of '"reversion" to what we had inherited' because 'if you take your foot off the accelerator then the car slows to its normal pace'. Similarly, Barber (2007, p 187) reported how his delivery strategy was being thwarted by trainers on the Consultant Leaders' Programme who in training heads, had not given due attention to literacy and numeracy:

> a read of the materials suggested that this seminal programme, instigated by a minister to improve performance in the national tests, had been heavily influenced by the purveyors of management gobbledegook who are always lurking in the education backwoods, waiting for their moment. Indeed, we had evidence that some of the trainers on the course had even made explicit the view that focusing on literacy and numeracy was actually wrong. My faith in the NCSL, and in the department officials whose job it should have been to check every detail of the training programme before it began, was shaken.

Following a major speech communicating the government's requirements of schools, 'the NCSL was sent away to rewrite the contents of their training and put its house in order' (Barber, 2007, p 189).

The National College was repeatedly reminded (Kelly, 2004; Johnson, 2007) that 'the DfES is responsible for setting the strategic framework for the operation of the College' (Johnson, 2007, p 2) and that the upward flow is in the form of information, advice and support, which the Secretary of State can and did take a position on (eg Balls, 2007). Indeed, in 2008, the National College had an extension to its remit regarding developing leadership training for Directors of Children's Services, and the National College responded with a delivery strategy (NCSL, undated n). A review of National College documents showed that it played this rebranded leadership of schools *game* with gusto, with speeches that transmitted government policy (eg du Quesnay, 2004; Munby, 2006), advice to ministers (eg Munby, 2005, 2007, 2010; NCSL, undated n), compliance with remit (eg NCSL, undated h, undated k) and the repeated use of data (eg National College, 2010c) and scorecards (eg NCSL, undated i) claiming a causal link between programmes and student outcomes as a 'positive contribution' (NCSL, undated i, p 11).

Notes

[1] Beckett and Hencke (2004, p 202) shows how Tony Blair as Prime Minister operated as 'Education Chief', working with Andrew Adonis as adviser in the Downing Street Policy Unit. Gillard (2011a, p 2) reports on what has been called 'The Adonis Problem', where Secretaries of State 'felt that their role was not to make education policy but to promote the policies devised by Adonis and Blair'. In 2005, Adonis was given a Life Peerage and made a Junior Minister in Education, and in 2008, he moved to the Department of Transport.

[2] Barber (2001, p 38) was insistent that the reforms had to work because 'the last twenty years of education reform are littered with programmes which have been inadequately implemented or abandoned by governments without the courage or strategic sense to see them through to impact on student performance'. This proved to be challenging, and Barber (2007, p 33) notes in relation to education that 'the lack of ambition which characterised the education service as a whole inevitably affected the department too', and so he had to work on cultural change regarding delivery through targets and data.

[3] In 1997, New Labour won 418 seats on 43.2% of the popular vote. The first-past-the-post system can deliver results where a mandate to govern through

seats in the House of Commons can be challenged through obtaining less than 50% of the vote.

[4] Cummings' (2002) research into the origins of the NPQH shows that the Conservatives pre-1997 and New Labour post-1997 were very much in control. He quotes George Guyte from the TTA saying 'There was immense ministerial interest both from the Tories and the Labour ... everything had to be run past ministers. Drove me crackers!' (Cummings, 2002, p 38).

[5] Research by Alexiadou and Ozga (2002, p 690) shows that in Scotland, 'devolution appeared to offer opportunities for the reassertion of older models of public service and "policy community", with a new element of widespread consultation with the public'. This is in comparison with England where such older models are at the core of the critique of governance, and where 'new forms of management reflected an idealised version of the business world as knowledgeable, flexible and entrepreneurial. Effective management promoted a vision of enterprise, secured by monitoring and surveillance throughout the system' (Alexiadou and Ozga, 2002, pp 689–90).

[6] Scott's (2009) study of the role of venture philanthropy in the development of charter schools in the US shows the impact of the conceptualisation and deployment of terms such as 'choice', and she concludes that 'it distills the notion of where educational expertise rests, away from schools of education within universities and the teachers and leaders they prepare and toward alternative structures that draw on non-traditional educational reformers, many of who come from business, law or advocacy' (p 132).

[7] There is much research that charts the historical location of this trend. For example, research by Fitz and Halpin (1991) into the policy processes and establishment of Grant Maintained (GM) schools through the Education Reform Act 1988 shows that there was a deficit strategy regarding local authorities and the provision of education. They conclude that because of the introduction of the market through parental preference for school places and open enrolment combined with opting out of local authority control for GM status, the role of the Department in London strengthened. The direct relationship between the Department and individual schools was established through the setting up of a GM schools unit, and the Secretary of State had powers regarding decisions about proposals for opting out.

[8] It is out of the scope of this book to examine this in detail, but Denham and Garnett (2006) have described the relationships between think tanks and their clients as 'donors, government, political parties and the mass media', and

how the ideological positioning of these clients 'will continue to affect what British think tanks do, how they do it and why' (p 165). Nevertheless, studies of think tanks such as Bentham's (2006) examination of the Institute of Public Policy Research (IPPR) and Demos show that they have made connections with the Labour Party and a range of other people and groups, but also seek to pressure for social democratic renewal. In other words, there is a complex relationship between ideas and policy, some of which is shaped by government and some of which is located in the aims and strategies of the think tank.

[9] Sir Michael Barber was a member of the North East London Education Association that investigated Hackney Downs School by invitation from Gillian Shephard, the Conservative Secretary of State, and post-1997 he led the New Labour SEU and then the Prime Minister's Delivery Unit (see Barber, 2007). Dame Pat Collarbone was headteacher of Haggerston School in London, she established the London Leadership Centre and worked on the NPQH for the Conservative government, and post-1997 she led a number of projects for the Department and the National College (see Collarbone, 2005). Steve Munby CBE is former Local Authority Director of Education, and the Chief Executive of the National College for New Labour and, since May 2010, for the Conservative-led government. Sir Cyril Taylor was Chair of the SSAT and on his website (www.cyriltaylor.com) says that from 1987 to 2007 he was 'adviser to ten successive Secretaries of State for Education on the specialist schools and academies initiative'. Chris Woodhead was HM Chief Inspector of Schools (HMCI) 1994–2000 and so served both the Conservative and New Labour governments. Beckett (2000) shows that Chris Woodhead continuing as HMCI and head of Ofsted was Blair's decision, and that there were tensions and frustrations between him and Blunkett and Morris. He concludes: 'Woodhead doesn't need Morris or her colleagues – he has more powerful friends. The extent to which this public servant can publicly deride the most cherished ideas of his supposed political masters is extraordinary' (Beckett, 2000, p 12).

[10] Sir Tim Brighouse is former Director of Education in Oxfordshire and Birmingham, he set up the Centre for Successful Schools at Keele University, and headed up the London Challenge to improve London Schools. Heather de Quesnay is former Director of Education for Hertfordshire County Council from 1990 to 1996 and for the London Borough of Lambeth from 1996 to 2000. Steve Munby was Director of Education for Knowsley 2000–05.

[11] David Jackson was head of Sharnbrook Upper School. In 2000 he was appointed Director of Research and School Improvement at the National College and is now a Partner at the Innovation Unit.

[12] Professor David Hopkins was Dean of Education at the University of Nottingham and took over from Barber at the SEU. Professor Geoff Southworth is a former headteacher, was Professor at the University of Reading and was Deputy Chief Executive and Strategic Director of Research and Policy at the NCSL until August 2008.

[13] The boundary limits between the elected and unelected is not a new issue, with Hodgson (2006, p 252) quoting Harold MacMillan saying 'we've not spent centuries fighting the divine right of kings to succumb to the divine right of experts'.

[14] During 2003–04 the National College established nine affiliated regional (government region) centres (some housed in universities):

• Eastern (Eastern Leadership Centre);
• East Midlands (Northamptonshire County Council);
• London (London Centre for Leadership in Learning, Institute of Education, University of London);
• North East (North Leadership Centre, Newcastle University);
• North West (The Centre for Education Leadership, University of Manchester);
• South East (Education Management South East);
• South West (Plymouth LEA);
• West Midlands (HTI Leadership Centre); and
• Yorkshire and Humber (CCDU Training and Consultancy Ltd).

[15] New Labour inherited the NPQH from the previous Conservative government, and in doing so they decided to continue with the centralised control of this professional qualification. Cummings (2002) shows how there was a direct decision, supported by advisers and consultants, not to have a Masters. He confirms through Anthea Millet, Chief Executive of the TTA, 'that the Conservative government had considered the idea of a leadership college and that discussions with some university vice-chancellors had taken place before the NPQH became the preferred model' (Cummings, 2002, p 40). He quotes Millet as saying:

They decided (remember, it was a Tory administration) to use the market-based model – which was in fact an invitation to individuals from interested institutions to undertake that work – but they decided to keep control over what the qualification would look like within the central direction, and they devolved that direction to the TTA. So really it was a question of:

yes, we want a professional qualification, not an academic one. (Cummings, 2002, p 40)

[16] There was some discussion about having an 'equivalent' of an Ashridge Management School for Education, and also a 'Sandhurst' for heads. Discussion about a College that was virtual and based on the Open University model also took place.

[17] Cummings (2002, p 56) states that Rowie Shaw (from NAHT) and Pat Collarbone (headteacher of Haggerstone School) 'were directly involved in setting up the London Leadership Centre and facilitated the debate about leadership among policymakers, including Michael Bichard (Permanent Secretary at the DfEE) and Michael Barber (Head of the DfEE SEU)'. Collarbone's (1999) doctoral thesis focuses on the National College, and she uses her experience with the London Leadership Centre to make recommendations for how the National College can build effective professional training.

[18] Skelcher (1998) identifies three types of NDPB: one type is as an advisory body, where expenditure is not normally incurred, and a second type are tribunals, which have a quasi-judicial role with some expenditure involved. The National College was set up as an 'executive' type because 'they have direct responsibility for the execution of a particular function or activity, and consequently have their own budget and staff' (Skelcher, 1998, p 7).

[19] The NDPB status was confirmed in a letter from the Cabinet Office to the Department for Education and Employment (DfEE) (from Rob Wall, Cabinet Secretariat to Peter Swift at DfEE, 10 September 1999), and this was seen as appropriate because it could 'operate at arm's length from Ministers' and 'will operate, at a day-to-day level, independently of Ministers'. However, 'Ministers will be responsible for setting the College up; will appoint members to the Governing Council; and will ultimately be responsible for the performance of the College and for its continued existence'. As I show in the rest of the chapter, the interplay between 'arm's length' and ministerial 'responsibility' shows that on balance the latter won out.

[20] The National College as 'The School Leadership Charity' was incorporated as a private limited company on 19 June 2000 and registered as a Charity on 24 August 2000. It was deregistered as a charity and then as a company in 2002. The rationale for this is not clear from the papers.

[21] The papers show discussion regarding the appointment of Michael Barber, Michael Bichard, and Chris Woodhead as ex officio members of the Governing Council. The DfEE was advised by the Cabinet Office (10 September 1999) that Michael Barber as an adviser to ministers could not take on this appointment as it would question the 'arm's length' status of the College. The listing (NCSL, 2000) shows that Michael Bichard was appointed in an ex officio capacity. It is also said that the TTA and General Teaching Council for England (GTCE) should have an 'observer' role on the Council, and in the listing David Putnam, Chair of the GTCE, is listed as having an ex officio role. Finally, there was a suggestion from ministers to have a honorary patron or president as an 'elder statesman' to give advice and hold the Director accountable (memo from Peter Swift, civil servant in Schools Directorate, to Estelle Morris, Minister, 23 July 1990), but I cannot find any evidence of this.

[22] Ravitch (2010) shows how after Michael Bloomberg's election as Mayor of New York in 2001, a privately funded Leadership Academy was set up to undertake training and mentoring of in-post and aspiring principals: 'The mayor raised $75 million in private philanthropic funds for a three-year programme to train ninety people each year', and she goes on to say that 'in its initial three years, the academy produced about 150 principals. After the first three years, the DOE [New York City Department of Education] assumed responsibility for the academy' (Ravitch, 2010, p 72). It seems from the DfES papers that the raising of this type of investment was seen as key to the College, but between April 1999 when it was discussed and June 1999 when the Prospectus was launched, this disappeared from the papers. A senior civil servant confirms in a memo that the banker who was approached will not have a role (memo from Christina Bienkowska, School Leadership Programme Director, to Dominic Mahon, DfEE, 7 February 2000).

[23] An email between civil servants (Ffom Peter Swift, Schools Directorate, to Katie Farrington, role unknown, 7 May 1999) stated that:

> we are certainly a very long way from considering a full-blown mutuality model as a practical proposition for the College. We would need to be satisfied that it was safe and sensible to hand the College over to its alumni and that they would run [it] properly for the benefit of parents and pupils, who as the Secretary of State says are the principal stakeholders.

[24] Memo from Peter Swift, Schools Directorate, to Michael Richard, Permanent Secretary, 23 November 1999. Another option considered was a Royal Charter, but this was discounted because it would give the National College too much independence (it is free from *ultra vires*) and the process for amending a Charter

means that the original drafting would have to be very specific regarding what can and cannot be done.

[25] Working out the Departmental funding for the National College is challenging because of a combination of general grants and specific targeted funding. In addition to this, between 2002 and 2006 the Grant-in-Aid from the Department was specified in the annual accounts, but from 2007 this stops. I have therefore used the Annual Report and Accounts 2002–06 and the NDPB and Agency reports to show a total investment of just under £500m (2002–09). Funding rises sharply after opening and with the addition of the National Remodelling Team (NRT), with a total grant of £94.5m plus just under £19m for the NRT in 2005, and this falls to just over £78.5m a year later. This rises again with the additional responsibilities for leadership training for Children's Services. The National College Annual Reports are available from www.nationalcollege.org.uk/ and the NDPB and Agency Reports are available partly from www.civilservice.gov.uk/about/resources/ndpbs.aspx and from www.dcsf.gov.uk/ndpb/ [Please note that the DCSF documents have now been archived; go to www.nationalarchives.gov.uk.]

FIVE

Regimes of practice

Introduction

Institutionalised governance has provided an explanation for how public institutions have a *structured* and *structuring* policy relationship with elite private interests, and how they stimulate as well as seek to control those interests. I intend in this chapter to use regimes of practice as an explanatory tool for knowledge production within institutionalised governance. Drawing on regime theory (Harding, 2000) and Bourdieu's (2000) theory of practice, I intend to build regimes of practice as a means of explaining how people position themselves and are positioned in relation to policymaking. I will show how the policymaking landscape had two main regimes under New Labour: the NLPR, which is made up of ministers, civil servants, private-sector entrepreneurs, academics, think tanks and headteachers; and the PRR or research community, made up of academics and headteachers. Located in between is potential School Leadership Regime (SLR) activity, which includes education management knowledge workers (Gunter, 1999) and those such as teachers, children, headteachers and academics that are positioned as outsiders to the NLPR, rather than seeking to position themselves as a regime of practice.

Developing regimes of practice

As Ball (2008b, p 760) argues, studying the New Labour period in office shows that networks 'are a policy device, a way of trying things out, getting things done, changing things and avoiding established public sector lobbies and interests'. But what is not always clear is why particular people are brought in and others excluded, and how the process of inclusion and exclusion operates. A list of people could be drawn up that includes researchers and educational professionals in schools, universities and local authorities who are not invited in for talks, whose work is not listed on the National College website and whose practice has not been noticed or endorsed as 'good'. While conceptualisations of governance through networks enables some people to be recognised regarding their various roles in policy design and delivery, what is not clear as yet is which people matter and why (Christopoulos, 2006). Also, analysis has shown that 'invocation of the idea' of networks is automatically seen as a good thing (Frankham, 2006, p 674), and so if you look for consultants, advisers and their networks, you will find them, but beyond describing their existence, it is not clear how power works (Goodwin, 2009).

Important thinking is taking place regarding such matters. Goodwin (2009) argues that there is something about the capacities and capabilities of people to exercise power and access resources, and who they associate with also matters – as Christopoulos (2008, p 479) has argued: 'actors' effectiveness is determined by the structure of their networks'. There is a need to recognise that knowledge production is subject to a range of motives and possibilities, with some staying within their knowledge community while others travel over boundaries. Recent analysis of networks shows the latter to be an emerging feature with 'a promiscuity of ideas – relationships across traditional divides and a critique of traditional political forms and modes' (Ball and Exley, 2010, p 165). The tendency for an overproduction of ideas (not every idea is regarded as a good idea, and not every good idea is used at a particular moment in time) combined with portfolios with multiple contracts means that there is a sense of instability. There is something opaque about interactions and so causal links may not be traceable, particularly as much of what takes place is within the busyness of everyday life and also out of reach of inquiry – as Ball and Exley (2010, p 164) note: 'what occurs is perhaps a process of attrition and infiltration, with versions or traces of network ideas being written into state documents'.

Underpinning this are matters to do with mapping and investigating the way power is exercised within networks. While the people and work that is the focus of this book tend to be institutionally located in a business, a school or a university, they are operating in policy spaces that transcend these, with Lawn and Lingard (2002, p 292) in their examination of policy elites in Europe arguing that there is a culture of practice that 'exists in the interstices of formal operations'. Researchers are seeking to both capture and explain this, with Jessop (2002, p 52) identifying 'heterarchy of self-organization' as a means of understanding how networks operate and interrelate with government. Ball (2009) has undertaken a forensic analysis of networks in education policymaking, and has found this form of heterarchic governance to be helpful:

> different kinds of power relations may exist between the same elements at the same time. Various different kinds of

such relationships and asymmetries are currently in play in policy heterarchies – e.g. partnerships, contracts, inspection, competition, performance management and regulation, sponsorship, consortia, matched funding, consultation, etc. Actors and organisations in a heterarchy may play different roles, use different capabilities and exercise different forms of power, at the same time. Again this poses both considerable analytical and representational problems for researchers but at least begins to 'fill out' some of the conceptual thinness inherent in the notion of network. (p 690)

I intend to build on this through the deployment of regimes of practice, and as such take seriously the need for conceptual and empirical work to go hand in hand.

The incompleteness and strategising inherent in heterarchies enables activity to be opened up to scrutiny, and by putting an emphasis on the *power to do* – to put an issue onto the agenda, to change a word in a policy document, to influence thinking about how change takes place – means that regimes of powerful interests can form in ways that 'regularize ... relations of mutual support' (Harding, 2000, p 55). Regime theory enables a conceptualisation of the authority and legitimacy that interconnects and regulates people from different employment locations as a 'governing coalition' (Harding, 2000, p 55) who require entry into public institutions (as ministers, civil servants, contracted providers) in order to retain competitive advantage (win elections, get appointed to roles, renew contracts). A regime works on the basis that no one person or organisation can control all the necessary resources, and without a formal organisation holding the regime together, it is 'constructed through informal bargaining and the "tacit understandings" of its members' (Harding, 2000, p 55). Power is fragmented, with a range of bases where it is located (business, government, think tanks), and it flows in different ways, sometimes indeterminable and often contestable regarding origins and termini. So I intend to use the word 'regime' to describe people as government and non-government actors who associate over time, have an agenda and, through this, promote and defend their interests.[1]

By using Bourdieu's (1990, 1998a, 2000) thinking tools of *field, habitus, capital, codification, doxa, illusio* and *misrecognition*, I will develop understandings of how regimes work as a *practice*. I have so far argued that there is a leadership of schools *game* in play, one that New Labour formally entered in 1997, and one that they made their own, played strategically and with huge resources. This is a *game* that dominated policy actors, was defined by and entry controlled through the *doxa* located in values and discourses (Bourdieu, 2000, p 11), and had its truths promoted through New Labour policy texts based on a system of belief–informed evidence. So taking up a position within the New Labour *game* can be understood and explained through the *dispositions* of those playing and those who want to play:

> The habitus, as the system of *dispositions* to a certain practice, is an objective basis for regular modes of behaviour, and thus for the regularity of modes of practice, and if practices can be predicted (here, the punishment that follows a certain crime), this is because the effect of the habitus is that agents who are equipped with it will behave in a certain way in certain circumstances. (Bourdieu, 1990, p 77)

Within practice there are 'structured structures' where a person develops *dispositions*, and there are 'structuring structures' where *dispositions* are generative and, consequently, 'objectively "regulated" and "regular" without being in any way the product of obedience to rules, they can be collectively orchestrated without being the product of the organizing action of a conductor' (Bourdieu, 1992, p 53). *Habitus* does not exist as an abstract 'it' waiting to be discovered, but is revealed as practice, and so through empirical work the positioning of the person can be mapped through examining their *capital* investments.

Following Bourdieu (2005), invested *capital* was mapped as positioned in relation to proximity to and distance from the state, defined as power and economy (see the Appendix). This has produced regimes of practice as networked positions within a *field* (see Figure 5.1), and as such the staking of *capital* through entering and positioning provides a dynamic explanatory construct through which the location and practice of power can be understood.

The New Labour Policy Regime

This regime dominated the *game* in play because of its positioning regarding economic and political power.[2] Those who entered and sought distinction here were primarily in formal Whitehall roles (the Prime Minister and advisers at Number 10, ministers, civil servants) who had the legitimacy of the electoral mandate based on a strong belief in the central direction and regulation of educational reform. They were supported by those who provided services and who were often brought in or bought in as contractual deliverers of reform programmes.

This was in formal government-appointed roles in the Department, for example, in the Innovation Unit and the SEU, or at arm's length from the Department, for example, in the National College. Shorter-term positioning was through contracts to deliver on a project or lead on a particular reform initiative.

Figure 5.1: Regimes of practice and New Labour education policy (based on Gunter and Forrester, 2009b, p 9)

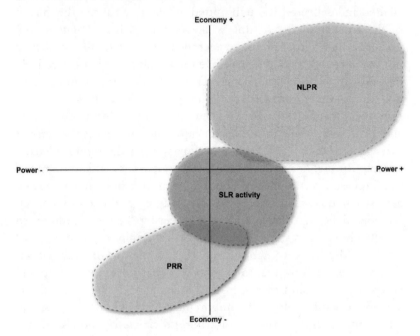

Those in government were very clear that the purposes of reform were to raise standards in schools and for the profession based on "a belief that disadvantage and deprivation are not a block on achievement, they're a hurdle to be overcome, they're an extra blockage in achieving it. But they're not going to be allowed to get in the way of bringing out talent, the ability, the self-fulfilment of students" (Min1[3]). By "being tough on standards" (Min2), New Labour sought to raise the quality of education for those on low incomes and the middle classes so that they would not abandon publicly funded education. Nothing short of a permanent revolution, which one minister called a "school improvement crusade" (Min2), was planned, with key interventions into the curriculum (the Numeracy and Literacy Strategies are regarded as the most significant) and into the profession as a means of delivery. The profession needed development and remodelling regarding roles and workload, and it needed to perform in relation to targets. A number of key New Labour people had experience of professional practice and brought that with them. This helped them understand schools as organisations, but this also created some tensions, particularly as one minister noted that knowing about culture and practice in schools was seen as 'weak' by some in Number 10, and was interpreted as not being "prepared to push the reform" (Min2).

The focus for achieving reforms was leadership: civil servants who advised and delivered also transmitted the *doxa*: "whatever the quality of the teacher in the school, whatever quality of staff in any organisation, whether or not you get the best out of them, whether or not you manage them and challenge their skills and talents effectively depends upon good leadership" (CS1). This required training: "we don't have enough of the twenty-four thousand [headteachers] who have their natural skills, so we need to nurture other people to be able to develop their innate leadership skills and to develop proper management skills" (Min1). Assumptions were made about leadership training through a National College: first, it was essential because of the limitations in leadership training "there had been no systematic approach to qualifications for leadership before" (Min1); and, second, it symbolised the importance attached to leadership, "it was commissioned to actually say, 'give us a generation of leadership for schools, at all levels'" (Min2). New Labour and the people around them *knew* this, recognised Tony Blair as a model of charismatic leadership and accepted his demand for world-class leadership in schools. Ministers and advisers talked about the importance of school effectiveness and school improvement data as confirming their views, and also that it was presented in such a way that in their busy lives they could read and absorb it. Nevertheless, they did note the changes they made to their thinking, particularly regarding how they learned that charismatic leaders were rare and difficult to scale up across the system. One minister said:

> "we had to, I think, learn that leaders are made not born, and that's quite important because once you accept that leaders are actually ordinary people who are helped to become good leaders, it becomes a different ball game. It's not about glossy headlines and holding figures up to be what everyone else should be. It's about … getting the basics right, teaching them leadership, bringing them on, learning from each other." (Min2)

In other words, the reality of leadership is that it is 'mundane' rather than 'sexy', but the rhetoric of policy both at the time of this Secretary of State and since put more emphasis on the latter than the former.

The *capital* staked was economic through public and private spending on the leadership of schools *game*, particularly through how private interests were enabled to invest in schools; was cultural through the normalisation of leadership; was social through bringing in those who helped codify and legitimise the *doxa*; and was *symbolic* through how the *logic of practice* in the *game* was made attractive to current and potential *game* players by communicating with the profession (particularly through headteacher conferences) and enabling those who were brought in as advisers to believe they had the potential to influence policy. Ministers and civil servants named people who took up roles in Whitehall and/or who were contracted to deliver on projects, were pro-school improvement and school effectiveness, and they trusted them as known people (often through professional links) who they liked, admired and talked about as inspirational. The Units were seen as crucial to ensuring that the right policies were politically possible, and appointments were important:

> "we knew then that there was somebody going to be giving us decent stuff on school effectiveness and what we also knew because we asked for it to happen and we made sure it was happening, that the people were recruited to the [Unit] were frontline deliverers." (Min2)

At the same time, ministers did not hold back on people appointed to key roles in delivery who were not responding to the remit that they had been given.

Those located in the NLPR revealed a New Labour *disposition* regarding policy and policymaking. All had an embodied sense of knowing what needed to be done and brought with them the culture and practice from knowing schools and business to influence and secure change. While there were disagreements with some policies, there were very few who resigned, most were able to focus and so bracket out issues that concerned them, and were able to wait for opportunities to suggest alternative ways of securing reform. In other words, a 'can do' delivery *disposition* ran alongside a 'wait to do' influencing *disposition*, and gains regarding the latter brought a sense of achievement. There is a sense of independence regarding how they were bought or brought in on their terms and they did operate outside of Whitehall and the National College, but there was also *misrecognition* of how this perceived autonomy was dependent on the status of being called in to help bring about radical reform. For example, consultants (in business and academia) claimed that they had a range of project funders, and that they were not dependent on the NLPR for contracts, but the winning of contracts outside of this could be based on being an insider.

Headteachers brought into Whitehall were able to list reform initiatives that they had 'invented' and that they believed made a difference. Their legitimacy as former heads meant they would be listened to by the profession and they knew the possibilities for 'wiggle room' in the implementation process (see Chapter 6). Academics rationalised their involvement as making a difference in the interests of children and teachers, with one professor who had sought "to locate myself at that intersection between policy, research and practice" (Ac8), and another who said:

> "what I've tried to do is to seek ways of working with, rather than against, government policy and trying to influence it. And I prefer to try and influence it from the inside, rather than snipe at it from the outside." (Ac9)

There is a strong link with professional practice in schools and local authorities in biographical accounts, and this is brought into the legitimising of positioning, though school effectiveness researchers tend to have been trained in higher education.

There is an ambivalence within positioning, with the university, formal networks such as the ICSEI[4] and involvement in policy being seen as essential to *field* development: the former provided scholarly legitimacy, the latter provided relevance, and networks enabled SESI to work out how to develop a secure position and rationale. Indeed, crossing borders between government and academia was a learning experience, as one professor stated:

> "it's very interesting being in government to see how irrelevant universities are, you know, as a seated policymaker in the government there was probably half a dozen at the most people in a university that you'd actually talk … to during that time." (Ac8)

Such positioning enabled the complexity of interests and values to be interrelated with the project and advisory demands of government, and for a number of respondents who had gained the prestige of being brought and bought in they could claim impact on policy, but also for some there was a 'price to pay' for doing this, with stories of how their work had been abused and how they had personally been bruised. However, the NLPR was dominated by trusted evidence deliverers on a range of research enquiries, who moved from project to project, within Whitehall and/or the National College. Business and academia are alike in this regard, with the former also being concerned to secure contract outcomes by doing speedy work "helping local authorities or agencies of government implement reforms within the modernising government agenda" (PC2). This role was presented as politically neutral; for example, one employee of a major international company stated:

> "but one thing we've got is that we're not part of the system, in the sense that we're not policymakers, we're not researchers, we're just there to deliver the outcomes that we're contracted to deliver, and to do a good job of doing that, which means that we don't have any axe to grind in policy terms." (PC7)

Interestingly, in establishing their place in the market, business consultants made it clear that they positioned themselves differently from universities. Such positioning enabled competitiveness within the NLPR, with a member of a multinational talking about the responsiveness and appropriateness of their company's research:

> "I think we bring our own style of research to government. So, say the [name of project] piece we did, if that had been an academic organisation, probably, based on my experience of being an academic, it would have taken about a year and a half or two years. And we turned it round in about nine months from start to finish ... so we tend to do things a wee bit quicker, and our reports ... tend to be reasonably well written and written in plain English and addressing the issues that policymakers are interested in." (PC2)

It seems that higher education was positioned as unmodern and disconnected, and this pre-dated New Labour with consultants carrying it forward in their work with different governments. Within this climate, some HEIs remained as players through setting up leadership centres (eg London, Manchester) and often shared a site and links with leadership developers (eg HTI and Warwick University). Important claims were made about the influence of the people involved, with one consultant talking about making leadership a dominant part of policy: "we wouldn't be where we are in this country in terms of leading the world on leadership and education if it hadn't been for people like [name] and me pushing, campaigning, lobbying, persuading, influencing for the last 10 years" (PC9).

The National College and its outposts stimulated and benefited from marketised knowledge production, with one consultant who moved out of academia into private work talking about new freedoms:

> "I've actually done more major research projects since leaving higher education than I ever did whilst I was in full-time employment, you know, I've had two quarter of a million [pounds] research projects in the last three years. And it's been fascinating and I love it and it suits me down to the ground and so now I am very much a portfolio worker, peripatetic, you know, I try to avoid the label consultant if I possibly can, teacher and writer, but basically doing my own thing in my own way." (PC6)

Individuals see their work as more relevant to practitioners than when they were in higher education: first, that university courses such as Masters programmes had developed for their own sake and did not connect sufficiently with practice; and, second, that university products were too expensive either as a programme or in the costing of research time and overheads, for example:

> "I can go to a local authority and negotiate a contract with them, and a big contract, and they know that all the money will be devoted to their contract. If I were working full time for a university, the university would slice it, and some universities are slicing 40, 50% … it's a major disincentive to be engaging with HEIs." (PC6)

Policy Research Regime

This regime is positioned at a distance from economic and political power.[5] Those who position themselves here are mainly located in HEIs, and seek distinction through the legitimacy of independent research and its relevance to both the academy and to professional practice, a contribution to knowledge, and the esteem of the *field* (with all its trappings, eg chair, journal editorships, ESRC funding). Notably, the regime is populated by those who locate their work epistemologically as critical policy studies with projects that examine, for example, globalisation, urban education and feminism. The regime's cultural *capital* comes not only from the independence of academia with accountability to and responsibility for the discipline and the integrity of research, but also from an orientation to understand and explain policy as well as the production of alternative conceptualisations and strategies based on the interests rather than policy implementation needs of practitioners. Some headteachers are located here, with evidence of direct associations with universities through research and postgraduate programmes; they tend to be headteachers who have had long careers and who critique New Labour from either the right (they benefited from Thatcherism) or from the left (they wanted to see more socially just policies from New Labour) (see Chapter 6). For this regime, economic and social *capital* is lower because many do not normally work for the government or its agencies; cultural *capital* comes from the status of particular HEIs; and symbolic *capital* comes from working outside of government policy and institutions, with resources from funding councils.

The *dispositions* of those who locate themselves in this regime are revealed through professional practice, which is about research. The majority of people interviewed who locate themselves here have a professional background in school teaching (only a few have come through the postdoctoral and research assistant route), with some who were headteachers or on a trajectory to take up this role. Consequently, they express a professional *disposition* and continue to work with practitioners through research, teaching and supervision, with the position taken being not to provide lists of 'can do' actions because, as one professor said: "I don't want to tell people what to do, but I want to help them to think about what they do" (Ac2). Respondents have given numerous stories about how they work with practitioners as intellectuals, who both want and enjoy the thinking space and tools to enable them to practise professionally:

> "almost all my students went on to be headteachers … and I have kept in contact with [name], on and off, ever since, and he was saying to me he still thinks about that course he did at [university] in the late 1970s and it still gives him tools that he says are still useful." (Ac2)

What seems to be distinctive about research and its links with professional practice is that this regime distinguishes between 'policy-driven research', which is funded and controlled by the government and considered of short-term value, and 'policy-relevant research', which "by focusing much more on processes, can still be of interest even when the particular policy has disappeared" (Ac27). As a result, research does not necessarily focus on leadership as demanded by New Labour project tenders, but on educational issues:

> "I wouldn't even associate myself with the term leadership, I suppose because I adopt a critical perspective, so the work I've done, what I'll call leadership just for your purposes, has been within the context of empirical work that I've done about the changing culture and values of schooling." (Ac6)

Identity is focused around what interests them rather than what deals might be done with the National College: "I don't do the L-word, I don't teach leadership, I don't teach management, I'm interested in schools and what heads do and I'm interested in kids and the curriculum and parents and all sorts of things" (Ac47). A number of respondents have developed this position regarding the links between research and practice through their experiences not only in schools as teachers and leaders, but also through taking on roles in higher education as Head of School or Dean. The experience of managerialism (targets, redundancy procedures, budget cuts) has enabled them to recognise and empathise with the idea that neoliberal reworkings of the school as a business are damaging to the profession, children and communities.

So this regime recognises the importance of leadership in the organisation of teaching and learning, with one professor describing how he worked with headteachers as follows:

> "And I think the leaders are important, but I think if we construct them as individuals, and also construct them as new managers and outside of all the social changes going on, and outside of things educational, it's a real danger. So what I was trying to do was work across those sort of two discourses and pull the educational bit back in. And they seemed to really, really like it and argue that that's the way that they see leadership in schools, it is educational leadership and it is about trying to get the best sort of practices for the best sort of student learning outcomes." (Ac41)

This approach means that this regime tends to work with the profession in revealing and developing alternative strategies to those recommended as official good practice. This can be on a number of levels: first, the need to return to issues of teaching and learning, curriculum and assessment, so that leadership is less about organisational outcomes and more about educational matters – classrooms; and, second, by adopting a normative agenda with a need to connect public-sector reform to wider issues of democratic development and how the role of students, parents and the community can be involved in ways that are more socially just.

The relationship between professional practice and knowledge is through social science disciplines, particularly sociology, but also references to history, economics and philosophy:

> "what I try to do in my work is to move in a creative but productive way between research and theory, between data and theory, to inform data with the interpretive frameworks offered by theoretical possibilities, but also to address, challenge theory with data." (Ac2)

This regime works against *misrecognition* by using reflexive approaches to knowledge production, and through discourse about the relationship between power, the economy and professional practice. There is a strong link between this position and 'the real world', with one professor arguing that academics have to "get their hands dirty" and work with professionals because:

> "it's easy to stand back and critique and say, oh this is all wrong you should be doing it differently, it's much harder to ... take seriously the perspectives of the people you're studying and to think what could they do differently, and it shouldn't just be up to them to sort that out because that's the hardest thing to do, academics should be working on this as well." (Ac6)

Another professor explained their approach:

> "I really reject the notion of research being imposed on headteachers [and] schools ... and even the idea of them as translators ... I always think it's leaders and teachers working with research and me doing research with schools rather than research in or on schools." (Ac41)

There is a strong emphasis on describing and understanding the social world, particularly how power operates at different levels either within the organisation or by examining the reach of globalisation into everyday practices. A shared social justice agenda means that these regime members are concerned with bearing witness to injustice as well as doing political activism. There is a strong feminist strand among the biographies of the women respondents, a clear concern with educational disadvantage in urban settings and the number of Australians in UK universities means that post-colonialism and working with indigenous peoples is a feature. Radicalism features through research, teaching, writings and membership of political organisations such as unions and pressure groups. This position recognises contradictions and what it means to pursue a critical agenda at a time of neoliberal modernisation. Those who position themselves here cannot stand outside of the globalised economy and there is a recognition that their work is inevitably shaped and funded by it.

This regime plays the academic *game* required of the university and the educational *game* required by the profession, but does not support the leadership of schools *game*. This is manifest in a number of ways: first, by opening up reforms to critique where the 'transformational' claims are challenged: "they might introduce *Every Child Matters* and all sorts of other things, but actually at root it's about reproducing a particular kind of society" (Ac39); and, second, by critiquing the heroic model of transformational leadership as just plain wrong, and while distributed leadership is seen as more helpful to the realities of professional practice, it is also recognised as being about retaining rather than challenging hierarchy. It is argued that the problem with the leadership of schools is not only the centralised control of professional practice, particularly through the National College as an arm of government regulation, but also through the unreflexive adoption of business rather than educational approaches. Indeed, the National College does not feature on the radar of these researchers. Although a few have undertaken projects, in the main the funding of research is seen as linking ideas with the social sciences through the ESRC. Any comments about the National College are within analysis of the leadership of schools *game*, with its role being understood as integral to bringing about reform through the control of knowledge production and practitioner access to ideas:

> "one of the influences of the National College has been that the secret lies in the leadership style, it doesn't actually ... [and they are told] you don't need to read more widely ... there's all these other books in some other section of the library that you can just ignore." (Ac14)

Interconnected with this are arguments that the evidence about school leadership is somewhat tenuous and unconvincing, but that policy has become so deeply intertwined with it that it is difficult to reposition for government and their intellectuals:

> "where else can you go if you've harnessed yourself to a ... model that's predicated on mistrust of the profession, then the only place left for you when you reach this kind of plateau is to invoke some kind of charismatic individual who can make a difference, who can turn a school round, who can lead. And so I assume that that's where they ended up, with a concept that seems to me to be fairly empty and also flies in the face of quite a lot of the good research evidence about the significance of the teacher in the classroom as the key factor in making a difference to school performance." (Ac58)

There are concerns both about the underlying knowledge claims of the SESI *fields* that lead to technical and decontextualised solutions to educational issues, and the political pragmatism of the SESI *fields* in serving an agenda, with names being given of people who are regarded as having either compromised their scholarship or, indeed, 'sold out'. Located within this is a preference for research networks in Europe, Australia and South America, where regime members identify more with the scholarship and social science traditions there than with what is regarded as the parochial and positivist nature of much school research in the US. Furthermore, some members articulate how they would welcome scholarly debate but have experienced behind-the-scenes attacks from SESI members.

Potential School Leadership Regime activity

In between the NLPR and PRR is activity that is focused on the school as an organisation by people who have a strong identification with leadership as the prime focus of their activity. The majority have been teachers and so have professional experiences that shape their orientation to their practice:

> "teaching history and some geography and some social studies, I was heading a humanities faculty. And then from there moved into higher education, initially because of my interest in what was going on in the classroom. So it was,

if you like, leadership and management of the classroom and how that was taking effect that was intriguing." (Ac26)

There are a lot of natural scientists in this territory, with a few economists, sociologists and historians.

The emphasis has traditionally been on working and networking with practitioners through postgraduate programmes such as Masters and doctorates (particularly the EdD) and continuing professional development both at home and internationally. There is a strong tradition of networking through BELMAS and internationally with linked organisations such as the Commonwealth Council for Educational Administration and Management (CCEAM) and University Council for Educational Administration (UCEA)[6] Intellectual work has been through these networks, with a strong emphasis on reading and developing perspectives rather than funded projects. A shared professional *habitus* enables those in higher education to support practitioners at times of rapid and potentially damaging reforms:

> "one of the things we can do with our little bit of agency as academics is to provide as powerful an argument as we can for a different approach and to try to get people to listen … we would never go so far as to prescribe it because we think that the contexts of practices are unique in the detail, they're not unique in the broad sense, but actually handling a particular incident in a school is deeply contextualised … if anything we are encouraging practitioners to be a touch subversive, as we believe many of them are." (Ac63)

Indeed, respondents showed concern when practitioners displayed technical compliance with markets, with one professor talking about how they had read in the newspaper about heads who had admitted to unethical practice in school admissions: "now these are the new brand of heads that have all been through educational leadership. They've got the words, they've got 'transformative', they've got 'distributive', they've got 'democratic', but they don't practise what they preach" (Ac56). This respondent identified that part of the problem is with researchers: "and yet we have been fairly passive in the area of educational leadership in drawing that to others' attention" (Ac56).

While this is a general overview of this territory, positioning tends to be more in relation to the NLPR and PRR regimes. There are a few who present themselves as independent, and who undertake descriptive and ethnographic-style work in schools, but they are very much a product of the *field* of educational management that grew out of the 1970s. What was a very busy territory that grew through postgraduate taught programmes and publications regarding educational reforms has declined over the past decade due to the NLPR colonising their territory, and through retirements and untimely deaths of *field* leaders who located here (see Gunter, 1999).

There are those who work on school and leadership issues who identify with school improvement and effectiveness, and so are on the fringes of the NLPR. Their predisposition to practitioner interests means that they are less interested in ESRC bidding than in undertaking commissioned work from local authorities, schools and the National College. There is an ambivalence towards the National College as it is seen as controlling the profession and set up without due consideration to the Continuing Professional Development taking place in local areas pre-2000. However, the National College is also seen as a realisation of the government's commitment to professional development and as an important source of income for projects and training delivery, particularly since the national training programmes have caused the postgraduate market to collapse, and so they are likely to participate in the University Partnership Group (UPG)[7] to ensure some stake in the *game*. This is a territory that includes SESI people who may not be directly involved for a time in policy work, some are new entrants with great expectations, others are those who have been inside and find themselves outside. This is a busy place because, as Chapter 6 will show, headteachers are officially located in the NLPR as reform deliverers, but many find themselves variously distanced from it.

There are those who are working on schools and leadership and are located on the fringes of the PRR. They are interested in research but do not have the type of social science underpinning or ESRC funding that those firmly located in this regime have. They tend to come to this position through an interest in organisations and leadership as places for the exercise of power, and so micro-politics and change is a strong feature of their discourse. One professor talks about work on "the relative unmanageability of change" which is:

> "largely ignored by the people who are dominant in the field of school leadership ... we would like to inform practitioners and policymakers but we are absolutely sure that nobody is going to listen, certainly not the policymakers, because the messages that come out of our work are very uncomfortable." (Ac63)

Women researchers in particular have raised the issue of social justice in regard to the experiences of women and black and minority ethnic (BME) practitioners in schools and colleges, and how the standards agenda is doing damage to young people. This speaks more to the PRR than to others on this terrain, but for a more formal move into this regime, these knowledge workers would need to present themselves less as leadership researchers and more as social science researchers.

Notes

[1] While much work has taken place regarding Urban Regimes (Harding, 2000; Mossberger and Stoker, 2001) and International Regimes (Hasenclever et al, 1997), with critiques outlining limitations (Domhoff, 2006), it is beyond the scope of this book to engage in a full analysis. The use of regimes within institutionalised governance goes some way towards dealing with Harding's (2000) point that regimes are different in the UK compared with the US. Hence, in the UK, the role of government and public institutions is stronger in policymaking both at national and local levels, and so hierarchy does impact on regime formation and contribution.

[2] I have written this text about the NLPR in the past tense as it reflects the regime as it was at the time of the New Labour government. The dynamics of regimes with issues of dissolution and permanence will be discussed in Chapter 7, and examined in relation to post-May 2010 in Chapter 8.

[3] See p viii for an explanation of the abbreviations identifying interviewees from the KPEL project.

[4] ICSEI had its first meeting in 1998, and is described as follows by the current president, Tony MacKay (2011):

school effectiveness and improvement is the common cause that brings us together. Whatever our country affiliation we share a desire to make our schools more effective. It was effectiveness studies that gave birth to our movement just over two decades ago, a period in which we have amassed an impressive corpus of knowledge on effective schools, effective leadership, effective teaching and how those inter-play with one another to enhance student learning. School improvement emerged as the natural offspring of that movement, seeking to apply the lessons learned while urging caution on policy makers overly keen to apply simplistic remedies.

[5] I have written about this regime in the present tense because even though the research took place during the New Labour government, the PRR remains (see Chapters 7 and 8).

[6] BELMAS has its origins in a meeting in 1971 and was formally set up in 1972. BELMAS is described as 'an educational charity that aims to provide a distinctive, independent and critical voice in the pursuit of quality education through effective leadership and management. We are concerned with ideas and practice and the interrelationship between the two' (BELMAS, 2011). There are formal networked links with CCEAM and the USA (UCEA), and field members have links with networks in Australia (Australian Council for Educational Leaders [ACEL]), Canada (Canadian Association for Studies in Educational Administration [CASEA]), New Zealand (New Zealand Educational Administration and Leadership Society [NZEALS]) and other parts of the world.

[7] The UPG includes representatives from certain HEIs. The UPG is informed of National College developments and has worked on linking the NPQH into postgraduate degrees.

SIX

Professional practice

Introduction

That those identified as ultimately responsible for school outcomes, variously called 'headteachers', 'principals' and 'chief executives', are and should be better leaders continues to travel around the world as a legitimate *game* to play (about Australia, see Addison, 2009; Eacott, 2011). It is an example of what Rizvi and Lingard (2010, p 17) identify as 'global flows' of abstracted generic effective behaviours and improvement strategies that 'are "vernacularized" in the context of specific nations as they meet local cultures and politics'. There is some emerging independent evidence of the realities of working lives in England and internationally, and in this chapter I open up the dilemmas and tensions in how heads position themselves in regard to regime practices.[1] Following Thomson (2008), there is a need to move away from binaries of 'resistance or compliance', towards 'the idea of the discursive positioning of headteachers, and/or interrogate their habitus and their "stakes" in the field, in order to show what actions are possible in specific circumstances' (p 87). Headteachers were meant to be consumers in the educational leadership industry and some have become manufacturers and retailers, but it is also the case that some have retained and continue to use rival products.

Policy, policy, policy

I intend drawing on thinking by the critical education policy community in order to frame the positioning of and position-taking by headteachers during the New Labour period in office. I take from Ball (1994a) and Gewirtz and Ozga (1990) that there is a need to examine what educational professionals actually do and how they position themselves at a time when policy is clearly positioning them within neoliberal projects, using managerialism to maintain the boundaries and denying the possibilities of other positions. Whereas policy science seeks to examine whether what was intended has actually been delivered, policy scholarship is concerned with the antecedence, experience and trajectories of policies and how they interrelate and are experienced by professionals (Grace, 1995). As Ozga and Jones (2006) have argued, policy ideas may travel, but the embedded reading of those policies matters, with reading taking place with and against what is proposed: 'faced with homogenizing traveling policy; particular groups or societies can be encouraged to revisit and reconstruct the value basis of their organizations; and generate new energy in its production within social and cultural institutions' (p 14). Furthermore, the reality of policy is that it is not just the preserve of an elite, and there is recognition that professionals make policies, and through this 'parts of texts will be rejected, selected out, ignored, deliberately misunderstood, responses may be frivolous, etc.' (Bowe et al, 1992, p 22). So, as Ball (1994a) has argued, policy does not enter empty lives, people have histories, are located within power relations and are committed to values and practices that they believe in, and so 'policies pose problems to their subjects, problems that must be solved in context' (p 18). Consequently, policy opens up and closes down spaces and possibilities for thinking and action, particularly for developing alternatives, and it controls who can speak and who is listened to (Ball, 1990, 1994a). So when a new policy is spoken or written and sent/received, the oral and written text usually presents clarity and normality: the *logic* is transparent and it seems that there is nothing more to say on the matter. However, as Bowe et al (1992, p 21) argue:

> the ensembles and the individual texts are not necessarily internally coherent or clear. The expression of policy is fraught with the possibility of misunderstanding, texts are generalized, written in relation to idealizations of the 'real world', and can never be exhaustive, they cannot cover all eventualities.

So examining policy interventions into professional practice is a form of 'policy archaeology' (Morley and Rassool, 1999, p 131) where not only are the layers uncovered, but how current practice is informed by experiences is examined. As Ball (1994a, p 21, author's emphasis) argues, the emphasis is not on 'constraint *or* agency' but 'the changing relationships between constraint *and* agency and their inter-penetration'.

Headteachers and professional practice

It is a truism that much is written about headteachers but there is little actual research, and while headteachers are expert talkers, they may not always go on the record in a formal publication. Nevertheless, there is sufficient to be able to say something substantial about work and identity issues, and how the complexity of positioning has been grappled with.

Arrowsmith (2001) was commissioned by Gleeson and Husbands (2001) to write about headship and performance, and he opens his chapter with an account of his year:

> I came to my performance management training in the last four weeks of a year in which we had: had an Ofsted [Office for Standards in Education] inspection; introduced asset management; planned for the new sixth-form curriculum; debated whether and then how to implement the new key skills qualifications; gone through the threshold process and received 52 applications; run the longest Dialogue 2000 project in the country; begun preparing the specialist college bid; prepared for the revised national curriculum; sketched in the issues for citizenship; run our first summer literacy school and follow-up programme; and coped with a very high level of staff absence and illness in an extremely difficult budget year. Already on the horizon for next year are the coming of 'connexions', and the new code of practice for special needs. (p 33)

From the literatures regarding headship, pre-1997 accounts of this intensification of reforms with the responsibility for delivery are reported in research about headship and the development of comprehensivisation from the 1960s and the quasi-market from 1988 (Grace, 1995). Indeed, pre-1988, Hall et al (1986) conclude their study of *Headteachers at Work* by arguing that government policy aimed at 'more systemic curricula and staff effectiveness policies' would require a planning imperative at school level, but that 'the time demands to carry out these could be incompatible with some interpretations of headship which we observed' (p 218). Just over a decade later, Whitty et al (1998) reported on how markets had led to overload vulnerability through personal responsibility for outcomes, with headteachers being 'increasingly forced into a position in which they have to demonstrate performance along centrally prescribed criteria in a context over which they often have diminishing control' (p 63). While Hall et al (1986) had concluded that role clarity was needed to help heads handle the new managerial demands, it seems that Whitty et al (1998) had identified how direct intervention by the state into the requirements of professional practice meant that headteacher identity was undergoing change through

external definitions of headship as business management (Ball, 1990).
Writers such as Ball (1994a) and Southworth (1999) show that the
demands of local management challenged educational leadership by
headteachers, and Ball (1994a, p 86) goes on to argue that while the
optimism of 1988 had given a glimpse of more autonomy through
the shift from bureaucratic control to market responsiveness, his data
suggest 'that flexibility is more apparent than real, or trivial rather than
substantial'. Massive structural and cultural changes had impacted on the
type and volume of headteacher work and their identities: the quantity
and quality of change had led to saturation levels with concerns for
health and the system (Weindling, 1992); the separation of heads from
their professional colleagues led to concerns about isolation (Mercer,
1996); the centrality of the headteacher role meant that they were
involved in everything from the incidental to the strategic, and that
keeping the balance between keeping the system moving, fire-fighting
and innovating challenged values, begged questions such as 'What am
I here for?' and strained the intention to collaborate with the demand
to get things done (Hayes, 1995; McEwen and Salters, 1997).

Reforms intensified under New Labour,[2] with Arrowsmith (2001,
p 33) reflecting further:

> Major planning issues now come along on average at the
> rate of one per month for teachers; each with an emphasis
> on the processes of planning, implementation, monitoring,
> review and evaluation. They all go into the melting pot and
> we teachers do our best.

The headteacher as moderniser and transformational leader was central
to the New Labour intervention into professional practice (see Chapter
2) and this was enabled through the production of a new type of
headteacher. Prepared and trained in the post–1988 period, the change
in the headteacher from Ms English to Mr Jones at the Beatrice Webb
school (Gewirtz and Ball, 2000) not only shows the shift from welfarism
to managerialism in ways that problematise the rationality of reform,
but also how change is layered in ways that do not eradicate previous
practices. Indeed, the literatures show an endemic tension between
reform implementation and protecting educational values (Hall and
Southworth, 1997; Bottery, 2007a; Maloney, 2009), particularly how
working with children is a key feature (Weindling, 1992). The KPEL
project illustrates this:

"I love working with people. I am a people-orientated person. Right so I love my kids. I came to teaching to teach kids, I still teach, right ... but most importantly what I believe is, my fundamental principle is, that together in this school we are changing lives of young people for the better." (Hd27[3])

It seems that protecting educational leadership matters, but there is a widespread frustration with the reform agenda and the detailed interventions that miss the point of schools: "I think we are assessment crazy, and that concerns me. We seem to want to be assessing children and not concentrating on teaching and learning, as much as I would like" (Hd15). The point was made that no matter how hard heads and teachers work they never catch up because of turbocharged reforms where whatever is achieved is never good enough:

"If you take 2004, then every secondary school head would have had their kids doing modern languages, 14–16. If you take 2002, every secondary school would have had every single child doing modern languages up to 16. You take 2006, well it's up to you whether kids take it or not. You take 2008, and we're encouraged that 60% should do it. How can all that be right, you got me? And then you have things like the three-part lesson, so you take the clock back three or four years and there is this massive encouragement for three-part lessons as the way to go forward. And then probably people like you research to show that the three-part lesson is shown to be inadequate.... But we all do it, we don't question it.... And it isn't right. So what I worry about headship is that we are part of a system in which the notion of being a profession ... I don't mean independently, I mean working with our peers, our communities, but in which we ourselves will debate what it is that is most worthwhile for our young people or community does not occur and we somehow too easily give up. We haven't given up here ..." (Hd4)

One head talked about how they had to implement reforms they did not agree with and motivate teachers and then "the government policy would change again and I felt quite, not stupid, as if I'd been a pawn in the game really" (Hd17). This resonates with reports from heads about the impact of being labelled a National Challenge School with targets for speedy improvement or face closure, particularly when value-added data and Ofsted inspections generated different labels (Tobin, 2009). As Leggett (1997) has shown in regard to reforms in Western Australia, the realities of school and administrators are different, and 'different values dominate, and underpin routine decision making. They are needed to ensure that the diverse needs of individual students are met on a daily basis' (p 286). So externally determined effective professional practice may not speak directly to people who face difficult situations every day, largely because such models do not help handle the consequences of poverty, but that has not stopped such people being labelled as inefficient or even outright resistors. So headship became, in Thomson's (2009, p 1) terms, 'a risky business', where those at the end of their careers claim that if they were starting out they would not be applying (Biott and Spindler, 2005). It seems that in spite of massive investment in headteachers as leaders, it is a job that fewer and fewer trained teachers want to do, with a major supply problem (Thomson, 2009), and where social injustice regarding gender and race remains problematic (McNamara et al, 2009, 2010), and through business remodelling, there are reports on the increasing role of non-Qualified Teacher Status (QTS) school leaders in senior or even principal roles (Morrison, 2009). The vulnerability of the job is illuminated by media reports of the sacking of secondary heads and deputies (Marley, 2009), and research by Goss (2008) for NAHT shows that the inspection system is inconsistent and unsafe, leading headteachers to fear losing their jobs with the knock-on effect on headteacher applications.

Regimes and headteachers

Positioning by headteachers needs more attention, not least the complex way how over a career and a number of appointments heads might talk about work in ways that show that the discourse of modernisation is not necessary totalising (Bottery, 2007b; Coupland et al, 2008; Gewirtz and Ball, 2000). Indeed, the heads in the KPEL project had developed narratives about how their approach had often developed through phases, and how they had come to understand their role over time. By using regimes of practice analysis, I intend to show how positioning and position-taking operated during the New Labour period in office.

New Labour Policy Regime

All headteachers were positioned here by virtue of New Labour's intervention into their professional identity and practice. This has antecedence in the post–1988 period where Grace (1995) identified a group of 'headteacher-managers' who embraced school leadership as a form of organisational control: 'they saw the role of the headteacher as becoming primarily managerial but believed that greater management effectiveness would generate an improved professional performance from the school and its teachers' (p 73). Headteachers have normalised reforms as what the profession should enthusiastically comply with and have popularised managerial knowledge and language (eg Barry and Tye, 1972; Craig, 1989; see also Tomlinson et al, 1999; Robinson, 2011). This embracing of reforms as generating headteacher autonomy is also evident in professional practice post-1997, with those who took up the New Labour invitation to be active modernisers illustrating a number of key features. First, there are those who accepted roles within public institutions to help frame policy and implement change, for example, David Jackson, former headteacher of Sharnbrook Upper School and Community College, took up the post of Director of Research and School Improvement in the National College, later moving to the Innovation Unit; Dame Pat Collarbone, former headteacher of Haggerston School, led the National Remodelling Team in the National College; and Sir Iain Hall, former headteacher of Parrs Wood High School and National College Governor. Second, there are those who have remained in schools and have: taken up offers to act as Executive Heads (eg Sir Dexter Hutt, who is Chief Executive of Ninestiles Plus, a school improvement company, and is an Executive Head at the Federation of Hastings schools); become Academy principals (see Astle and Ryan, 2008; Leo et al, 2010; Daniels, 2011); rescued 'failing' schools (eg Peter Clark CBE [1998] at the Ridings School; Lady Marie Stubbs [2003] at St Georges; and Sir William Atkinson at Phoenix High School; see Wilby, 2009); and built schools as educational businesses (eg Sir Kevin Satchwell at Telford; see Ball, 2007a). Third, there are those who have remained in schools and quietly played the *game*, may have implemented reforms they did not agree with and possibly been alienated, but overall rarely write or are written about (see Gillborn, 1994; Yarker, 2005).

The KPEL data show that about a quarter of the sample positioned themselves here and they recognised the gains that have been made: "is [name of school] a better school … since Blair came in power than it was before he came in power? The truth of the answer is 'yes'. In lots of ways, even down to the money we've got" (Hd1). Another head states: "I think it's a great interest in the job that we have these challenges to implement so many and various policies, and as I say I still love it today, which is fabulous" (Hd20), and there is a sense that even if a head is unhappy they will still do as required: "now we will do it … we will implement change in our schools so we have all sorts of initiatives, directives and ultimately we are public servants and we will make it happen because we have bosses at every level" (Hd11).

   Some heads talk about being called in to give advice and to work on particular National College programmes:

> "I have been invited twice to Downing Street to discuss government policy and changes in educational practice. So I think they do listen…. And I have been able to have telephone conversations with them to say, 'look I approve of this, but do you realise the implications of the other?' [Name of Government Adviser] has been to this school. I think they have made themselves available and they have not hidden in ivory towers, and I think that is very laudable." (Hd27)

There is concern about reforms and the manner in which they are imposed, and there is a sense in which they are pragmatic by trying to influence the agenda. However, the dominance of functionalism is accepted and these heads try to ensure the right type of interventions are made in schools so that centralism does not cause new dysfunctions and accelerate workforce demotivation.

Policy Research Regime

Research shows that headteachers can and do locate themselves differently than the official positioning, with, for example, headteachers such as Bernard Barker (1999, p 73) recounting the challenges of his '40-year campaign for comprehensive education'. This position is illustrative of what Grace (1995, p 74) identifies as a small group of 'headteacher-resistors' who were annoyed at the imposition of change with some raising questions about the quasi-market and opting out of local authority control. But Grace (1995, p 74) goes on to show the dilemmas in this positioning: 'that the policies to which they objected to on philosophical and professional grounds were policies which, if adopted, could bring to their schools and their pupils considerable material and resource benefits'. The philosophical and educational values base of headteacher positioning around the 1988 Education Reform Act (ERA) is evident in the interviews undertaken by Peter Ribbins (Pascal and Ribbins, 1998; Ribbins, 1997; Rayner and Ribbins, 1999). Winkley (1998) in talking about the training of heads argues against the technicist 'how to do' mode that can be picked up on the job, and in favour of the more demanding reflexivity involved in thinking about how to create and sustain 'a learning environment' (p 236).

Research shows the ability of headteachers to design and deliver educational change that is bottom up and exceeds that demanded by reform (Winkley, 2002; Hollins et al, 2006), and that there are strong beliefs in the socially critical project that shapes thinking and practice (Taysum and Gunter, 2008; Thomson, 2008; also this is shown internationally, see eg Thomson, 2001; Ryan, 2010). In the KPEL project data, about a quarter of the headteachers located here, and there is a strong sense of being political where local practice can impact and change the national scene: "those heads who fit the agenda the government talks to and listens to, those heads who don't they either tolerate or find ways around them" (Hd4). Heads of successful schools continue to work on protecting their position:

> "I'm the sort of head that believes my place is in the school. I think if I'm not on the corridors and I'm not in the classes, I'm not talking to kids and I'm not talking to teachers and support staff and parents, they cannot afford to have that person visible in a leadership role ... I have deliberately not wanted to be part of the NCSL or NPQH ... I'm very selective about where I go to look for good practice." (Hd13)

There is a sense that the profession has been damaged by over-inspection and testing: "it's a cold data-led profession and I don't like that particularly", and this head goes on to say:

> "I don't think they [the government] have a full understanding at times of what's entailed in the role. So I suppose the most successful schools ie in terms of data ... I would think they are probably valued and held up as a model. But there must be lots and lots of schools that work so hard and maybe don't achieve the standards that we all strive for one reason or another. And I don't think that's particularly valued." (Hd26)

Heads associate with the social justice aim of New Labour, but are concerned about the managerialism embedded in strategic thinking and delivery: "eventually they would want one head over several schools or one head over a very large school. And I do think it's a business model that they aspire to but it is a people-orientated profession" (Hd26).

Heads have examples of how the profession is being damaged, with one head talking about how they had admired a colleague who had worked to turn around failing schools, but who had decided to retire claiming that they would "not set foot in another school" (Hd26). Heads remain active in their work for a caring profession, not least through their practice. As one headteacher puts it:

> "it's still that thing about: (1) making sure that every child actually can thrive in terms of our social democracy, (2) making sure that you create a sense in which you open up what it counts to be successful in terms of a learner rather than just five A to Cs, and (3) that you have an absolute remit to work in a sense of social justice and community and to build up fairness and a model of community so that you model something in a sense which you yourself can approve, appreciate and enjoy." (Hd4)

These are heads who do Masters degrees and doctorates, who do research and write, and have links with people in universities.

Potential School Leadership Regime activity

The bulk of data and analysis about headteacher positioning identifies what is called a mediation role between policy requirements and what actually happens in schools. Sometimes principles are drawn on to support this, and at other times it is pragmatism that dominates. For example, Bottery (2007a, p 104) reports on two heads:

> Julian said that he would measure the importance of a new initiative, or consider the worth of a macro-level issue by continually asking himself one question: 'what relevance has this got for the children at this school in terms of raising their attainment and achievement?' The local framing of macro-issues within this value prioritization was also true for Harry, for Ofsted was not viewed as some governmental mechanism for either steering schools towards governmental determined aims, nor as a quality measure for raising attainment and achievement, but as a hurdle to be jumped through before he could deal with what he regarded as the real problems of the school.

Bottery (2007a, p 98) sums up his analysis by identifying different accounts of agency with different views of feeling powerful/powerless, and 'all the headteachers saw their role as working within the legislative architecture surrounding them; none saw a full-blown revolt as sensible or possible'. As Ball (1994a, p 95) argues, it is not that all heads 'succumb to the temptations of cooptation, but rather that the pressures and conditions of their work ... make certain leadership roles less easily obtainable and more risky than others'. This is consistent with Grace's (1995, p 74) identification of 'headteacher-professionals' who, in response to the 1988 ERA, were concerned about the potential damage of business management to collegiality and their own opportunity to teach, but 'some headteachers believed that it might be possible to evolve a workable compromise between the two cultures over time ie, to "make the best of things" in the interests of the children' (p 74). The endurance of this type of positioning has led Moore et al (2002, p 186) to demonstrate that what is happening is a form of 'strategic pragmatism' which:

> involves a conscious practice of creative – sometimes subversive – response to reform and to the effects of reform, with each issue being carefully measured and judged in terms of what is and is not acceptable when set against the institution's or institutional manager's preferred philosophy and practice. Such a response, rather than being configured in terms of submission to dominant but unpalatable ideologies, might be alternatively understood as offering the best hope of professional and institutional health and survival in times of rapid and extensive mandated policy change.

The media give illustrations of this type of positioning (eg O'Hara, 2010), and the KPEL data show that at least half of the heads would identify with this position: there is ambivalence but at the same time a recognition that reform has to be implemented and much of it is welcomed:

> "there is no headteacher I believe would argue with the *Every Child Matters* agenda nor the policies for development education that have come out in this government since it's been in power, I don't think I have seen so much money in education. But having said that there are elements of its strategies that are putting a completely new perspective

on headship and I'm not sure I'm happy with that little
bit." (Hd14)

So there are opportunities to read into policy and look for spaces, and
the experienced head can take a position: "we get a lot of initiatives,
and yes you could easily get overloaded, but I think I have learned
in 15 years that if it's not right for your school, don't do it" (Hd15).
However, the accountability regime weighs heavy on heads, and a
particular criticism is that while many reforms make sense, there is
the case that some initiatives have not been thought through and so
implementation is going to be very difficult.

There is a drive in some of these heads to take risks to protect the
local situation, which is usually about filtering national demands in
relation to school priorities, but can be more dramatic, particularly for
schools where national standards and Ofsted inspections could threaten
survival. For example, one headteacher talks about setting up a local
nursery without local authority permission, and this combined with
other changes to service provision has meant that there have been no
redundancies. Crow and Weindling (2010) show that political leadership
both within and outside of the school is both evident and essential for
headteachers. Indeed, Arrowsmith (2001) witnessed and participated
in 'headteachers behaving badly' in regard to the new performance
management requirements, but while it was problematic, in the end
they made it work:

> The question arose during the training day as to whether
> heads were cynics, idealists or frustrated romantics. This was
> because the nature and tone of the training puts us in an
> odd position. One is made to feel strangely unpatriotic by
> questioning the motives or procedures of major initiatives.
> The government clearly wishes to improve educational
> performance even if it does not yet have a broader
> educational vision, and it is quite challenging for a head
> of eleven years' experience to know why it does not feel
> better to be in such an improved and beneficial climate. It
> may be that this government shares with its predecessor
> the view that the only way to improve schools is the way
> it has decided and although no-one can doubt the extent
> of the consultation process on this issue, it has not been
> about whether, it has been about 'how'. It is no secret how
> badly some regional meetings went. Did the government
> ever seriously consider dropping the initiative as a result?

Was a significant alternative ever considered which might have achieved the same or even better outcomes? What was the real agenda? Listening to the earnestness of ministers like David Blunkett and Estelle Morris, it seems such a pity that many heads still feel that they are in opposition and have to develop those skills which enable them to 'render unto Caesar that which is Caesar's and render unto God that which is God's'.... We are by no means all on the same side yet. (pp 34–5)

Conceptualising heads having to make unpalatable reforms work is an enduring feature in the literature (eg Southworth, 1999), and there is realism that while heads retire or are removed, not all can or should do this. There is a sense of trying to protect children and staff from the worst excesses of reforms that could do serious damage. While some researchers try to put a gloss on this, with Gold et al (2003, p 136) arguing that their case studies show examples of 'values-driven leadership' where heads 'have a strong commitment to their "mission", determined to do the best for their schools, particularly for the pupils and students within them', others have raised serious questions. Wright (2001, p 275) has argued that reforms have created 'bastard leadership' using a metaphor from medieval history to make the case that it 'represents a capture of the leadership discourse by the "managerialist" project' (Wright, 2003, p 139). In reply to Gold et al (2003), Wright (2003) argues that what are raised as important values such as teamworking and participatory decision-making are 'second order values' (p 140), which can make implementation seductively attractive and justifiable. Indeed, Arrowsmith (2001) recounts how government training for performance management recommended to heads to use the 'trick ... to make staff see that performance management is an opportunity and an entitlement' (p 39); and New Labour speech writer, turned reform deliverer, Peter Hyman (2005) realised the complexity involved in the local delivery of big system reform where there are no 'quick wins' for Jimmy the pupil he was working with, and so the pace of reform needed differentiating rather than the reforms needing to be rethought. However, the purposes of schools and education and the control over those purposes, which Arrowsmith is reflecting on in the longer quotation earlier, are first-order values that remain externally defined through policy.

Consequently, the positioning of headteachers through the NLPR can continue to operate, though other assumed positions by headteachers of holding on to social justice values (PRR) and/or taking a pragmatic approach (SLR) remain difficult and incredibly tiring. This analysis goes some way to recognising the various positions that heads take at the same time, and, as can be seen from their biographies, this complexity can shift over time. So, as Thomson (2001, pp 5–6) has argued in her study of Australian principals, 'there is a need for pictures of principals as embodied moral subjects dealing with complex and shifting situations' and so she proposes that 'in current neoliberal times principals would be well served by the production of multiple readings of their work, and deliberate efforts to construct more disruptive representations of "principalling" are required'. Critical policy analysis can help to reveal this situation, show that heads and teachers are not the main cause of the problems they are required to solve and, through research, show that policy 'is struggled over, not delivered, in tablets of stone, to a grateful or quiescent population' (Ozga, 2000a, p 1).

The National College and professional preparation

Bates (1999, p 87) tells the story of visiting the locality to meet with people and introduce herself as the new headteacher of Lilian Baylis School in Lambeth:

> On my first excursion into the local community shortly after taking up my post I met a number of local traders in Lambeth Walk. I introduced myself cheerfully as the new headteacher at Lilian Baylis. Several looked horrified, others looked doubtful, one looked sad, took my hand and said pityingly, 'You poor cow'.

The leadership of schools *game* was meant to change all of this with the need to tackle school failure and hopelessness head on, and to make headship a higher-status profession. As I have shown, the main way this was to be achieved was through the direct control of knowledge production within the *field*, particularly by the National College.

Research into the national training programmes has been officially endorsed by the Organisation for Economic Co-operation and Development (OECD) as positive (Huber et al, 2007). Earley and Evans' (2004) survey reports show an increase in positive views about National College training, though the 'reality shock' of taking up a post compared with their preparation is also recognised (p 330). They go on to report that about a third of heads and just under a fifth of deputies had an involvement with the College, and it was expected that this would increase as the College developed its profile. Expectations were high, with the 2003 survey showing that:

> just over three quarters of headteachers thought that the college would play a significant role in developing the school improvement agenda and over four-fifths saw it as significant in promoting leadership development in schools. Only a very tiny minority (around 2 to 3 per cent) thought the NCSL would be of no significance in these endeavours. (Earley and Evans, 2004, p 332)

While the data show a higher rating from secondary compared with primary heads, overall the National College was seen in official evaluations to be positive with the potential to make a difference. The ongoing claims of the College in its scorecard and other materials have continued to be positive by showing its contribution to the standards agenda (National College, 2010c). However, the challenge of such evaluations is that it is difficult to make a direct link between such professional development and practice, particularly since there are other professional experiences and training that can have an impact, and the data on drop-outs and the linking of training with a headship application and appointment is hard to track.

There are positive views from within the KPEL data, and of the 25 respondents, only four had not undertaken any National College training. Prior professional development experience does not predict the amount or type of engagement: there are those who only have National College credentials, but their opinions vary, and those who have both Masters and doctorates as well as the Leadership Programme for Serving Headteachers (LPSH) or NPQH are also varied in their views. One head, based on his experience of working closely with heads through the National College, said:

> "What I find when I talk to colleagues, I find it varies hugely. Some have got a lot of time for it, some read stuff and are involved in the College and have been on courses and some people don't even know it's in Nottingham, it doesn't register on their radar at all really." (Hd9)

This is evident in the KPEL data, and on the positive side there are stories of how heads are involved through training programmes (NPQH, LPSH, HIP), they act as Consultant Heads, have been Research Fellows, undertaken coaching and been called in to give their views on things, and as one head said, they had been invited to a 'Dine and Discuss' (Hd27) event. The enthusiasm is summed up by one head:

> "and at the moment my role as headteacher has also diversified into that of a Primary Strategy Consultant Leader, so I am able to go out and support other schools with the work and the vision of their school, and so I have been very lucky, I feel, in the job to date." (Hd20)

Heads talk about the impact of the LPSH on how they thought about and practised leadership; serving heads who had completed the NPQH talked about productive experiences, and how it convinced them that they could do the job:

> "it was very time-consuming but it allowed me perhaps to be talking with people who already were heads and people in senior positions reflecting on how they saw the role and I think that was a very useful experience." (Hd2)

In general, the National College is seen as an important resource for the profession:

> "I know it's going to play a crucial role in addressing the issue or the concern that they've got about the lack of future leaders. Clearly a big professional development support for leaders at all levels. An information source, a professional development source, an ideas source." (Hd19)

Materials online or through the post are helpful, and they are seen as affirming what they know and do, and that being a part of the College helps with the isolation of being a head:

> "I think the NCSL ... do listen to us and what it is that we are saying we need, the kind of stuff that they put on is the kind of stuff that I think, 'oh I would quite like to go on that'." (Hd21)

Some heads know the National College personnel either personally and/or professionally, and so have an affiliation with like-minded people, and have direct contact by phone or email.

There are few detailed critiques of the National College, and this book is the first independent serious examination of the College in relation to the policy context. Evidence does show that positive professional development experiences did take place before the National College with a rapid growth in postgraduate education as well as short-term training opportunities (Gunter and Thomson, 2010). While the NPQH was subject to critical evaluation (Gunter, 2001b), official reviews of the NPQH trials shows that engagement with the training programme prior to the National College demonstrated 'improvement in their professional knowledge and understanding and how they improved in relation to the leadership skills and attributes in the national standards' (TTA, 1997, p 2). In Scotland, the Scottish Qualification for Headship (SQH), launched in 1998, has had both a positive impact and critique, but the model used was through 'a consortia of higher education institutions [HEIs] working with a number of education authorities' (Menter et al, 2005, p 8). It seems that effective professional development is taking place within Scotland based on a collaborative model that used to operate in England. So a National College was not necessarily the solution, and even if upgrading and coordination was needed, the Scottish model shows that a different approach could have been taken. However, the Scottish approach was located in a devolved policy context where performance leadership and audit was rejected in favour of a 'more developmental approach' (Menter et al, 2005, p 8), and where partnerships between universities and local authorities were central to the scheme. In England, there is clear evidence that the type of conceptual work valued in Scotland had already been rejected (TTA, 1997; Cummings, 2002).

There is some critical work on the National College regarding the technical challenges involved in setting it up (eg Crow, 2004; Mulford, 2004; Walker and Dimmock, 2004; Riley and Mulford, 2007[4]), and some of the heads give recognition to improvements that could be made. Heads note that the NPQH provides certification, but has had little impact on them in their approach to the job, and in reality, training for the actual job is impossible. One head compared working with heads through the National College and in North America, where s/he likes the reading and research culture in Canada amongst principals, and argues that the National College also has a coherence problem that could easily be sorted:

> "lots of good ideas, very hard-working people, people working their butts off. But you think sometimes, 'Well if you just sat down for a little while and thought about this, you could strip a lot of this out and get down to the

real nitty gritty', but it's again the same problem, too many vested interests." (Hd1)

Other heads are concerned with expectations of engagement that they don't have time to respond to: "Talk2Learn and all that, goodness no ... for the life of me, I just think there is so much to be done in the job" (Hd2). Other costs also impact as a number of heads have never visited the Nottingham site, and courses are not always accessed at the regional centres because of budget constraints.

Concerns have been raised about technical evaluations because of 'a mutual tendency to view the NCSL as a largely beneficial development' caused by close connections with NCSL activity (Thrupp, 2005b, p 13). However, the College has been subjected to socially critical analysis and arguments (eg Grace, 2000; Thrupp, 2005b; Thomson, 2007; Gunter and Fitzgerald, 2008): first, that the knowledge production underpinning training and research is highly functional, producing what Gronn (2003, p 7) has identified as 'designer leadership' produced by a cadre of policy entrepreneurs (Gunter and Fitzgerald, 2008). As Grace (2000, p 242) has shown, the intellectual heritage is in policy science with its emphasis on 'what headteachers "need" in order to meet effectively the many challenges which they face'. While Grace (2000, p 233) shows that the job is more complex than the NPQH assumes because it has 'outcomes [that] are technical, logistical and relatively predictable', and Thomson and Blackmore (2006, p 176) report on ways in which the job can be redesigned to 'support and build up principal agency, rather than reiterating research findings and one-best formulae'.

The KPEL data show that some heads give recognition to these arguments: one head describes how s/he left a training session early because of the quality combined with a lot of school work that demanded attention, and while s/he has been directly involved with the National College, looking around the room s/he realised the way inclusion and exclusion was operating:

> "I know it's NPQH and Leading from the Middle and I have actually lectured on, I have been a Consultant Head with a New Visions programme as well ... but I felt that it's, 'jobs for the boys' springs to mind, that I think that they appoint and nurture their own people ... I think it's hard to impact on what they're doing, I don't think that dialogue is as open as they would like to think. And they are certainly not impacting on heads that I know round here." (Hd15)

Second, researchers show that control of headteacher professional identity by the government is somewhat predatory as there is no escape from the National College (Gunter and Fitzgerald, 2008), and it acts as 'a conduit or relayer of New Labour policy into schools' and so is 'promoting an approach to school leadership which is very much dominated by New Labour's educational policy agenda and it's drawing on academic work which is, by and large, unlikely to challenge that agenda' (Thrupp, 2005b, p 18). The KPEL data show some recognition of this: one head said that "my impression of what I've seen from it has been that in actual fact, it's rather become the servant of government and DfES and the strategies and that side of it" (Hd24). Another notes that the professional appointment process has had to deal with cloning of the perfect professional:

> "What you're finding when you interview people actually for senior posts now, is that you are getting NPQH speak. And I think the way you interview is changing because you want to get beyond the NPQH speak. It's becoming a straitjacket for leadership." (Hd13)

Another very experienced headteacher who has a PhD noted: "when I heard people from it speak I've been slightly nonplussed, I didn't know what they were talking about to be quite honest. There were so many acronyms, phrases that were new to me" (Hd25).

Third, all writers raise issues of educational processes regarding the primacy of teaching and learning, and philosophical complexities around ethics and decision-making, and how official knowledge production at best skims this or at worst ignores the reality of leadership dilemmas and tensions. Thomson (2007) has analysed National College texts in relation to leadership in urban contexts, and she concludes that while there were opportunities to undertake robust conceptualisations of the urban, what she found was research and commentary that 'is part of a large policy discourse which demonizes inner urban children, families and neighbourhoods while individualizing their behaviors and needs and ignoring their strengths and assets' (p 1070). In other words, while the language is one of transformation, in reality the framing of policy problems and the generation of solutions preserves the status quo, and the historical link between education and democratic development is fractured (Grace, 2000).

The KPEL data illuminate some issues regarding the impoverished nature of learning and the *disposition* of heads to want something different than technical training:

> "I actually think they are not about learning, and they are about learning how to fill your forms in better. Whereas if it was a course about influencing this or learning about that then of course I would do it. So that is why I chose to do a PhD rather than all that stuff. It's a deliberate choice, but is not because I think they are crap, it's actually because where I am … it ain't me." (Hd4)

Another head talked about how unconvincing emotional intelligence is as a way to proceed as a headteacher, and there are heads who are frustrated that they want to read differently but cannot spare the time. Thomson (2007) tops and tails her chapter with the story of a headteacher who eventually gives up his EdD studies due to the pressures and demands of the job.

Overall, while the heads in the KPEL project showed positioning within regimes of practice, attitudes to the National College are not always directly related to this positioning. There are extremes of support from those in the NLPR and opposition from those in the PRR, but the bulk of heads from both regimes note some gains, although also problems: some focus on the need for technical improvements, while others argue that the National College does not speak to their interests, and more often than not these are experienced people who find 'needs analysis' old hat and not very challenging. In addition, the bulk of heads have had at least some involvement, but over time have either disengaged or are pragmatic as the day job dominates or they do not see National College activities as relevant to their concerns or affordable. So the leadership of schools *game* is played by the heads (even opponents realise they have to engage in relation to their own colleagues' accreditation), with some who do misrecognise how they have been drawn in to legitimise policy, particularly newer heads, but the majority use or do not use the National College to support their goals, and try to maintain a sense of autonomy about how they want to play in school and locally.

In summary, Currie and Lockett's (2007, p 365) study of leadership in public services confirms that it 'appears to be less about transforming circumstances … and [is] more about embedding change that others, policy-makers, have initiated'. They go on to show that the individualised approach to leadership is very applicable to education, due to the longer-term experience with markets, the tradition of the headteacher role and 'because teachers enjoy less power than other professions, such as doctors in hospitals' (Currie and Lockett, 2007, p 366). New Labour used this tradition and sought to rework headship through increasing status for the local delivery of reform, and through this gave recognition to headteachers who have not only delivered, but also sought to develop delivery with creative ways of thinking about the role and the system. In speaking to new headteachers, Blair (1999c) said:

> you are the critical agents for change and higher standards school by school. And there is literally no more important job in Britain today than yours. As I never tire of saying whenever I visit a school, as soon as I meet the head you get a pretty good idea of whether it's a school that's going places or not.

Listening to headteachers speak about what the *game* meant for professional practice compares with studies of other public-sector workers where 'self-presentation can also be a matter of bricolage, creatively fusing multiple and sometimes contradictory positions in their turns and their utterances' (Iedema et al, 2003, p 29). What does come through is the positive response to autonomy and the demand 'to be left alone', and, as Thomson (2010a, p 16) argues, this is integral to the *game*, where school self-management:

> creates a drive in agents that makes them operate accordingly to the rules of the game as they stand. It works to make agents not only manage the field, but also compete over what is at stake – not to change the rules of the game or the knowledges, *dispositions* and strategies that constitute the winning formulae and its contribution to the wider mission of the state and the field of power. In other words, headteachers must not simply massify/democratise, but also hierarchise.

Thomson (2010a, p 17) goes on to argue that whether heads play in the interests of the students and school 'is always framed by a decision about whether they are prepared to play to their own positional detriment'. This goes to the core of the narratives from the KPEL project, and how the NLPR sought to control both individual and collective interests through the National College, but how it could not be totally hegemonic because the leadership of schools *game* needed doubting and even non-players in order to make claims for recognition and distinction.

Notes

[1] I am focusing on headteachers as this was central to the KPEL project. The wider profession has been examined in Butt and Gunter (2007), and I am currently a member of a team led by Dave Hall and including Joanna Bragg at Manchester on how leadership is discursively constructed by educational professionals through their practice, for the ESRC-funded *Distributed Leadership and the Social Practices of School Organisation in England* project (RES-000-22-3610).

[2] Blackler (2006) shows that National Health Service (NHS) chief executives also faced rapid reforms and centralised control, and this is different from the normative images of effective transformational leadership. They had 'to function in an increasingly rigid hierarchy in which there was a lot of fear' (Blackler, 2006, p 15), and he concludes that his data show:

> the popular image of empowered, proactive leaders has little relevance to the work of the NHS chief executive in the UK at the time of the study ... New Labour's policy for the NHS appears to have been driven by a sense of crisis, a populist agenda, an urgent desire to demonstrate early performance improvements and the belief that managers could not be trusted. (p 19)

[3] See p viii for an explanation of the abbreviations identifying interviewees from the KPEL project.

[4] If readers do access this paper please note there is an error. The Office for Standards in Education (OSE) is identified as having undertaken a review of the National College, when the accurate name is the Office for Standards in Education (Ofsted).

SEVEN

Regime practices

Introduction

The deployment of regimes of practice has so far enabled the presentation and analysis of positioning by knowledge producers and their relationship with each other and with education policy. Knowledge production as a social practice can be for and/or about the *game* in play: political and economic elites determined the purposes of schools and the professional practice of the workforce through a codified *doxa* and attracted players through the *illusio* of how the *game* spoke to them. The mapping of the NLPR and PRR has revealed the need to understand how power works within and between regimes, and specifically that a regime of practice has a *logic of practice* in the staking and *symbolic exchange of capital* where boundaries are drawn. In this chapter, I intend examining regime practices through a review of social relations and exchange process before I then go on to focus on the impact of this on knowledge production about educational leadership.

Regime practices

All of those interviewed for the KPEL project espoused a commitment to students and their learning and educational organisations such as schools, and there is a strong professional experience background amongst policy entrepreneurs. However, it is clear that there are groups of people who have been and are institutionally located in universities, and in public and private organisations, who are variously networked nationally and internationally through distinctive hubs and special interest groups. What has been identified in the regime knowledge production processes is the importance of professional 'genealogies' (Bourdieu, 1992, p 15), with relationships based on a form of contractual kinship where people who know and who are in the know reveal particular *dispositions* and are central to its generative potential through how they engage in practice (Bourdieu, 1990, p 13). What distinguishes location and positioning is the *structure* and *structuring* of relations within epistemic groups, and so *capital* and hence identity is conceptualised and shaped in distinctive ways. However, kinship is not unconditional.

This is because there is 'the good player, who is so to speak the game incarnate, does at every moment what the game requires' (Bourdieu, 1990, p 63), but, as already acknowledged, 'anything goes' is not allowed and indeed is punished. So this makes boundary activity and relocation very difficult because in order to move, a person and/or group needs to question the underlying epistemology and professional practices, and as Bourdieu (1998a, p 5) states:

> It is well known that no groups love an 'informer', especially perhaps when the transgressor or traitor can claim to share in their own highest values. The same people who would not hesitate to acclaim the work of objectification as 'courageous' or 'lucid' if it is applied to alien, hostile groups will be likely to question the credentials of the special lucidity claimed by anyone who seeks to analyse his own group. The sorcerer's apprentice who takes the risk of looking into native sorcery and its fetishes, instead of departing to seek in tropical climes the comforting charms of exotic magic, must expect to see turned against him the violence he has unleashed.

Examples have been given in Chapter 2 of this taking place under New Labour, where those who generated different data and alternative policy proposals tended to be either ignored or 'portrayed as out of tune with the times/self interested mouthpieces of vested interests/impractical dreamers or academic theorists, without "hands on" experience of their subject' (Hood and Jackson, 1991, p 193).

In the NLPR, government players entered into *symbolic capital exchange* with elite private interests who had their own *game* in play in regard to expansion into the public arena. All shared a 'doxic acceptance of the world' regarding organisational leadership as an 'objective structure' where the conceptualisation of the local chief executive was the product of structured and structuring practices revealed through what is normal and necessary to secure domination (Bourdieu and Wacquant, 1992, p 168). There was an exchange of *symbolic capital* based on shared *dispositions* to deliver in the interests of children and parents as consumers, with the government giving private capital access to new markets through educational provision and private capital giving the government access to a modernised status through policy advice, solutions to seemingly stubborn problems and language, cultural tastes and change strategies that were familiar and normal to parents who work in the private sector. Central to this was an acceptance that the traditional public-sector worker with expertise and credentials need not do delivery, as others from the private and voluntary sectors can be deployed in ways that are efficient and effective. The *logic of practice* that produced such policy strategies was based on unspoken rules of the *game* where there was 'knowledge and recognition' (Bourdieu, 2000, p 198) of both domination and dominated. *Misrecognition* can be detected in the failure to speak about the interplay between the 'subjective truths' of the leadership of schools as the only thing to do, with the 'objective realities' of how this has been constructed through the *game* in play (Bourdieu, 2000, p 142).

Illusio was generated by the *symbolic* effects of this *capital exchange*, where the opportunity to be directly involved in government and to work within market relationships was based on the experience of playing it before or seeing it played, and having a 'habitus predisposed to anticipate it' (Bourdieu, 2000, p 12). Headteachers from schools, professors from universities, trade union representatives (ie social partnership arrangements) and senior leaders from local authorities were provoked and were predisposed to the *game* of making the New Labour difference for children, and this spoke to them as 'agents characterized by possession of a certain capital and a certain habitus' (Bourdieu, 2000, p 220). The leadership of schools *game* could only work if those who were at a distance from classrooms had the status of knowing more and better than those in classrooms, and this was generated through the *misrecognition* of those enabled to take up a position in Whitehall and/or Non-Departmental Public Bodies (NDPBs). The 'esteem, recognition, belief credit, confidence of others' in headteachers and professors as advisers and project deliverers was 'perpetuated ... [because] it succeeds in obtaining belief in its existence' (Bourdieu, 2000, p 166). While there was dynamism within the *field* with universities facing claims of irrelevance from within their own community and from the private sector, this was not usually publicly spoken or written about, and it seems as if the emphasis was more on doing deals with government than with publicly attacking competitors. While there was evidence of attempts to create power bases within the regime (eg both the National College and the SSAT developed leadership training), with 'new' leadership products and internal conflicts, any actual practice that threatened the regime was dealt with through contract termination. This acted as a disciplinary process and those who were on the fringes of the NLPR sustained this existence by their loyalty to the *doxa* in their teaching, research and writing, and so were ever ready to take up invitations to position more centrally in the *game*.

Those who were the objects of the leadership of schools *game* were: first, those presented as beneficiaries, such as teachers, parents, students and communities, and who were dominated through the 'representations of power', such as the titles, roles, pay and expertise of those who dominate (Bourdieu, 2000, p 171). Nevertheless, they showed the capacity to dominate: for teachers, it can be through the interpretation and enactment of reforms; for parents and communities, it can be at election time and through the exercise of interests in regard to educational provision such as Academies; and for students, it can be through absenteeism. The second group who were the objects of the leadership of schools *game* were those presented as irrelevant to the *game* and not invited to play, and those who do not find the *illusio* of the NLPR *game* to be congenial. These were located in the PRR where another educational policy *game* is in play: to open up the NLPR *game* to scrutiny and reflexive theorising, particularly through 'historical critique' (Bourdieu, 2000, p 182); and to develop an *illusio* located in issues of power processes where the interplay between agency and structure can reveal the rationalities of practice. The *doxa* is one of research, theorising and the co-production of knowledge in an unjust world. Those in the PRR who are close to practitioners have a *game* in play of enabling them to develop alternative models and narratives about practice, with the inclusion of teachers, students and communities as valid knowers and as legitimate participants in dialogue about changes to their lives and work. Within the PRR are those who hold major grants from funding councils and esteemed chairs, and stake *symbolic capital* in research that speaks differently to the New Labour project, and as such there is a *capital exchange* with others in higher education, local authorities, unions, schools, parents and communities. While the New Labour leadership of schools *game* may not directly speak to these interests, the PRR may speak to matters of social justice and radical change, and hence they provide *symbolic* effects of countering the charges of irrelevance from the NLPR.

What is currently 'not in play' is a third regime based on school leadership activity, the SLR, with a *doxa* focused on researchers, headteachers, teachers and children in a pedagogic relationship. It could resolve the concern raised by Whitty (2002, p 8) that too much attention to quick fixes means that 'there are some forms of knowledge production which are in danger of not taking place anywhere'. Currently, the people who do talk about this or who might create the necessary rationale and narratives to invite investment are too few in number, and have positioned themselves as actual players within or on the fringes of the NLPR or PRR. This is mainly due to the lack of *symbolic capital* around teachers and students as active subjects in educational change, and how investment, exchange and positioning operate in ways to render their *capital* worthless. For this potential SLR activity to emerge strongly, there would need to be a *symbolic capital exchange* between members of HEIs and schools through research and postgraduate study combined with forms of activism (see Apple, 2006a). While the data show that this exists, it tends to be in the PRR or under the radar and/or it is not a widespread feature, not least because HEIs have been positioned by the NLPR as irrelevant to the needs of professionals.

Taking stock

New Labour began playing the leadership of schools *game* before they took office and played it robustly for over a decade. So the relationship between the state, public policy and knowledge was one whereby the state colonised and took control of the production, interpretation, *codification* and communication of ideas and evidence in order to structure education policy and practice. Specifically, the commitment to the single person as the leader and their preferred practice as transformational leader has remained a constant feature, with rebranding taking place, the most virulent being distributed leadership. This approach to leadership has been discredited by research: first, such approaches to knowledge production, particularly its 'bunkered' (Thomson, 2001) nature, had been thoroughly challenged in the decades before 1997 (eg Foster, 1986; Smyth, 1989) and has continued since in the UK (eg Gunter, 2001a; Bottery, 2004; Hoyle and Wallace, 2005; Gronn, 2010) and internationally (eg Lingard et al, 2003; Bogotch et al, 2008; Anderson, 2009); second, models adopted as preferred professional practice by the National College have been critiqued because they are directly linked to policy delivery rather than educational processes, and fail to deliver in the ways intended (eg Barker, 2005, 2007; Currie et al, 2005; Currie and Lockett, 2007); third, the relationship between the neoliberalism and reform strategies that have created schools as businesses has been scrutinised in ways that problematise the leadership of schools strategy (eg Smyth, 1993); and, fourth, the role of leadership models as power relays has been shown to be integral to the replication of social injustice and the denial of equal opportunities (eg Blackmore, 1999). In summary, it is clear that the leadership of schools *game* was played by the NLPR even though the evidence was limited, certainly mediocre and possibly a perversion.

More specifically, the SESI knowledge base on which the *game* is based has faced a relentless thumping (eg Hatcher, 1998; Slee et al, 1998; Morley and Rassool, 1999; Thrupp, 1999, 2005a; Fielding, 2000; Ozga, 2000b; Thrupp and Willmott, 2003; Wrigley, 2008; Coe, 2009; Gorard, 2010). Important ideas have been communicated and debates have opened up issues and drawn on a range of intellectual resources, but perhaps the opening of Fielding's (2000) paper, which uses philosophy to think out loud, is helpful in understanding the position that is taken when articulating the mess that education is now in:

> We are facing a multiple crisis within this country, a crisis of intellectual and imaginative nerve that currently afflicts policy makers, teachers in schools and the research community alike. We remain prisoners of an outmoded intellectual framework and a properly zealous political will; taken together they present a well intentioned, if mistaken, symbiosis and as a consequence our demise is likely to deepen rather than disperse. Just as school effectiveness and school improvement articulate the moribund categories of the frightened, unimaginative society so the aspirant hegemony of the technologies of teaching provide a classroom equivalent which will do more damage more quickly and more widely than its institutional predecessor. (p 397)

While there have been some commentaries that reply to particular criticisms (eg Sammons, 1999; Townsend, 2001), these knowledge workers are struggling to reposition in the post–NLPR world (see Chapter 8).

An illustrative example can be found in the SESI response to Barker (2010a), who wrote a short piece for the *Times Educational Supplement* about his new book (Barker, 2010b). Barker (2010a) challenges 'five assumptions that have dominated thinking for more than 20 years': first, that trained leaders can boost examination results; second, that disadvantage can be overcome by attendance at an effective school; third, that quality can be improved by the market; fourth, that improvement can be secured through regulation; and, fifth, that performance can be improved by the transfer of 'best practice'. He argues in the article for reforms 'based on children's personal growth, rather than test performance' (Barker, 2010a). In response to the article and not the book, Sammons et al (2010) regard the presentation of different knowledge claims and evidence as 'dangerous because they promote the view that policymakers and practitioners are powerless to effect positive change, whereas considerable bodies of research provide valuable evidence on strategies that promote improvement and can enhance life chances for the disadvantaged'. The two positions are clearly evident here: the SESI acceptance that the system can and should be functionally improved (see Sammons, 2008), and the socially critical argument for systemic change to eradicate disadvantage by focusing on children and learning (Barker, 2010b). Further research will be needed to examine how SESI reposition in relation to the social relations within the Conservative-led government policymaking process and with employers in higher education. There is no reason to expect that SESI members' espoused commitment to policy and practice will not be popular with the new or successive governments (see Chapter 8), but potential exists for independent research and professional development work that is crucial for this part of the *field*. There is a vacuum here due to the decimation of the SLR that had vibrancy as 'educational management' in the 1970s and into the early 1990s (Gunter, 1999). The decline of this regime was due to repositioning around policy science through SESI and business models, combined with retirements and deaths. So there is an opportunity to revitalise working with educational professionals in ways other than delivering data about reform implementation.

Knocking leadership off its pedestal

The New Labour leadership of schools *game* may have been dominant in terms of *capital* investment, and may have been dominated through the breaching of the educational *field* by powerful economic and political elite interests, but there is a need to examine if this *game* is hegemonic. Evidence from the KPEL project reported in Chapters 5 and 6 shows that it is not and that *game* playing requires non-players – exclusion makes the *game* more distinctive. Interestingly, the advocacy of more socially critical approaches to the *field* in England can be clearly seen in Southworth's (1995) conclusion to his study of a primary headteacher, Ron Lacey. Southworth (1995, p 196) argues that teachers dominate children, and take this into their role as headteachers: 'the asymmetrical distribution of power in schools results in the head's domination of the staff group and is antipathetic to democracy'. Foster (1989, p 49) argues that leadership 'is not just the property of enlightened individuals', and Southworth (1995) uses Foster's (1986, 1989) arguments that leadership is a power process, and hence is sympathetic to how authentic transformational leadership is not about charismatic visioning and delivering organisational efficiencies and outcomes with empowered followers, but is about changing the world. However, Southworth (1995, p 202) is troubled by the lack of prescription: 'Foster does not say how leaders are to undertake their journeys, nor does he appreciate that the journey involves a transition from one identity to another.' In other words, hierarchy is deeply embedded in the English consciousness, and professional identity is firmly located in organisational and pay structures that constitute knowing your place and responsibilities.

What Southworth (1995) in his concerns about headteacher and occupational identity did not follow through is that the approach of critical knowledge workers such as Foster is not to give answers, but to work with educational professionals through social practice as intellectual work. As Anderson and Herr (1999) have shown, there are teachers who do not want 'one hundred steps to reading success' and they state what is also applicable to the *field* in England: 'unless both university academics and school practitioners are willing to take intellectual risks and push their comfort zones, we will end up with nonrigorous programs that short change us all' (p 20). Certainly in the time prior to 1997, and indeed pre-1988, the type of professional learning conditions that Southworth (1995) was calling for were developing, particularly through the contribution of the social sciences to headteachers' intellectual work (Gunter and Thomson, 2010), with warnings that management training[1] without such a foundation 'is all too likely to be either useless, or illiberal in its consequences or both' (Taylor, 1976, p 48).

Smyth (1985, p 179) opens his paper by stating that 'leadership is an alluring, seductive, even magnetic word', and so he asks what would 'leadership look like if we were to … depart from a view that construes leadership only in terms of influencing others towards setting goals and checking on their achievement?' (p 179). My contribution to answering this question is to suggest that if, as the SESI have found, teachers working with children are more important than headteachers as leaders in improving learning outcomes, then why do we not take this as a starting point and, in paraphrasing Ozga (2000a), knock leadership by elite leaders off its pedestal? In this way, I would agree with Smyth (1985, p 186) that leadership should be located within pedagogic processes, where change is 'as a consequence of dialoguing, intellectualising and theorising about their work'. There are a number of resources that can enable researchers to do that.

Focus on children

There is research that examines the nature of childhood and the damage being done through 'institutionalized suspicion and state-authorized scaremongering' (Guldberg, 2009, p 178); concerns about how too much genuflecting to parental belief systems means that children are indoctrinated rather than educated (Law, 2006); and detailed accounts of how and why children drop out (Smyth and Hattam, 2004; Smyth, 2005) and how this needs to be seen within the bigger picture of how people living together in communities is conceptualised (see Squires, 2008). This is just the tip of a large iceberg of debates about the consequences of transformational modernisation and the *games* that adults play regarding the damaging impact on raising children as critical citizens (Gunter, 2009). However, what is important is that there is a whole range of research with and for children about how they might be positioned differently than the compliant recipients of effective headteacher practices. Fielding's (2006) and Rudduck's (Rudduck and Flutter, 2003) work in England has been crucial in pioneering research with children and pushing at the boundaries of involvement in school policymaking. Specifically, there are challenges to the assumed immaturity of children 'that gets in the way of our seeing students as responsible and capable young people' (Rudduck and Fielding, 2006, p 225). Authentic democratic development needs to be based on the idea and practice of schools as places where young people learn to both contribute ideas and take responsible action as co-researchers in ways that do not cause the professional or indeed national policy façade to crumble (see Thomson and Gunter, 2006; Cammarota and Fine, 2008).

Focus on teachers

There is little independent research in England that focuses on teachers and their work, but what does exist shows that there are cases where educational professionals are seeking to understand how they have been positioned and how they might hold onto their educational values (eg Helsby, 1999). Research in Australia is particularly helpful: first, work by Smyth (2006a) shows how ethnography in classrooms can enable teachers and students to work on pedagogic changes, and so begin with what is already known and may have been overlooked in the drive to install the new reforms and auditing; and, second, the 'productive pedagogies' project reported on by Lingard et al (2003) conceptualises leadership as pedagogy, and by using Bourdieu's thinking tools, the team reach into research traditions by recognising forms of agency:

'teacher–leaders flourish in environments where they are regarded as intellectuals and provided with opportunities to engage in critical reflection about their practice' (p 42). Interestingly, Lingard et al (2003) walk on terrain that SESI would find familiar regarding cultures and structures, but what is different is the direct engagement with a theory of power to distinguish between 'productive leadership ... that allows for generalization, and the influence of place and time specific lived relationships that constitute leadership' (p 149). Leadership is in its proper place as a dynamic process that enables productive pedagogies and assessment, and is underpinned by a commitment to social justice.

Focus on schools

Examining schools from a perspective other than producing correlations about output data from outstanding and failing schools yields some different perspectives. There are studies of schools that are ordinary in the sense that they do not hit the headlines as 'the worst school in England' or 'the most improved school in England', instead they do a great job for the children and community. Indeed, Maguire et al (2009) show that schools find it difficult to be ordinary because to do so would make it vulnerable to the marketplace and additional external audit. Researchers working within schools and studying how professional practice operates through the process of commodification enable *field* members to access how the education boundary is being breached. In addition to this, there are studies of schools that do go against the grain, for example: Apple and Beane's (1999) study of democratic schools in New York; Apple's (2010) collection of cases from Israel/Palestine, Japan, Mexico and the US, which provides evidence of how travelling global education reforms can be interrupted through local action; and Smyth et al's work in Australia on how pedagogy and values can survive the relentless attack on public service values (Smyth and McInerney, 2007; Smyth et al, 2008).

Fielding and Moss's (2011) exploration of the 'common school' as a school for all children provides huge potential for critical intellectual work. The 'comprehensive' label for the secondary school has been discredited by Thatcher and New Labour, but at the same time primary schools have always been comprehensive in the sense that they have open access to all children up to the age of 11. Socially critical researchers are seeking to rehabilitate schools as integral to democratic learning and the starting point is defined by Fielding and Moss (2011, p 89): 'we mean a school that is open to and attended by all citizens living in its local catchment area, children, young people and adults, without admission criteria, except residence, and without specialisms that enforce selective attendance'. They propose a radical education as a productive alternative to the niche-marketed, specialist, faith-based, sponsor-controlled school.

This provides an important space for agenda setting, dialogue and development, and democratic renewal. There are two things in particular to say here: first, it enables the *field*, in Bourdieu's (2003) words, to handle and 'fire back' on the undemocratic nature by which schools are being converted to Academies (Gunter, 2011) and how Academies can and should be returned to local control (Hatcher, 2008); and, second, it enables the ongoing restructuring of schools into Academies, trusts, Federations and all-through schools to be challenged in relation to leadership as hierarchy and roles such as chief executive. Notably, there is recognition that the distribution of power and working for democratic opportunities is more important than forms of distributed leadership that maintain the status quo (Hatcher, 2005). Finally, debates about structure can and should challenge the leader-centric nature of English thinking with research that not only speaks the heresy of 'leaderless schools' (Davies, 1997), but also presents case studies of how schools can be organised differently (Court, 2003b; Grubb and Flessa, 2006). It also raises questions about whether this should happen in some schools to pragmatically handle the crises in recruitment to the top job, or whether debates and restructuring can be located in democratic development and so be related to the repositioning of children and the whole workforce.

Focus on justice and communities

Hatcher (1998) has argued that there is an egalitarian tradition in England that has a long history and is in evidence daily through the professional commitment of what is now called the children's workforce, but it has been largely unspoken for many decades due to how it challenges neoliberal projects. However, there remain important examples of how *field* members can work for social justice and, as Bates (2006) has shown, this has a long history in the *field*. So I take Fraser's (2007, pp 32–3) arguments seriously about the need to combine 'a politics of recognition with a politics of redistribution' in ways that are 'bifocal' rather than seen as a binary. What this requires is not only an ethical approach to the design and delivery of teaching and learning, but also a political approach to opportunities to bear witness to inequality, to work to include people in ways that previously they have not been and, as Shields (2004, p 128) has shown, 'we must ensure that educators do not celebrate some legitimate differences and pathologize others'.

Thomson (2010b, p 132) is very helpful to the *field* on this matter by showing how 'virtual school bags', 'funds of knowledge' and 'place-based education' enable all of those in education to 'do social justice'. By 'virtual school bags', Thomson (2010b, p 132) means 'the knowledges, experiences, and *dispositions* which all children bring to school', and she argues that schools often only draw on some of this, and therefore children 'in the know' do better. In other words, there have to be challenges to what is regarded as the knowledge that should be known. This links to the 'funds of knowledge' that are 'embedded in the labour, domestic, family and community practices', and which can be ignored in education, and so Thomson (2010b, p 132) argues that 'the affirmation of home and community practices also builds positive social identities for students and sensitises their teachers to the myriad ways in which the mandated curriculum excludes some and privileges others'. This requires a 'place-based curriculum' that enables education to be directly involved in regeneration, where children are educated to want to build the community rather than leave it. Teachers connect learning with local issues and events, but interconnect this with bigger-picture globalisation issues, and so it is not about narrow parochialism: 'place-based projects provide opportunities for situated identity work, as students engage with difference(s) and are assisted to produce texts in which they describe/inscribe themselves, those with whom they are in dialogue, and their mutual place in the world' (Thomson, 2010b, p 131).[2] What is important about taking this position is that it counters charges of utopianism and irrelevance to everyday issues, particularly by learning from children about who they are, their sense of self and how they want to create their lives (Shields, 1999). As Apple (2006b, p 41) has argued, there is a need to speak to people's everyday common-sense understandings of the world, and 'we can also use these progressively inclined elements to show that it is not only the right that has answers to what are real and important issues of educational practice'.

Just this short exploration of socially critical thinking, research and professional practice shows the rich potential for developing and playing more inclusive educational *games*. Social theory has a place to enable intellectual work to support ideas and practice, and a range of methodologies and methods, particularly researchers working with young people and professionals in schools, communities and in universities, to open up education to a range of enquiries. What does this mean for leadership? Leadership is important as a social practice, but it is dying in England because of the obsession with hierarchy, and supplying governments with evidence about how a particular type of leader, leading and leadership can work better. Rethinking the *field* requires researchers and educational professionals to: first, study the realities of educational organisations and the complexity of what it means to practise leadership (Smith, 2002; Collinson and Collinson, 2005; Johnson et al, 2009); second, develop forms of leadership that are educational and educative (Gunter, 2005); third, be upfront that leadership is a benign word for manipulation and influence, and so power issues need to be central and Hoyle's (1982) questions about how leaders are prepared for the job in relation to the moral issues embedded in practice needs engagement; fourth, relate teaching and learning to democratic development, and so leadership as a relational and communal process (that includes children) needs to be linked to the imagination as well as to participation and inclusion (Glickman, 1998; Corson, 2000); fifth, rebuild research and professional development partnerships between schools, local services and higher education (Smyth, 1998), and higher education has to value such partnerships as places where valid knowledge production takes place (Anderson and Herr, 1999); sixth, frame research around what it means to do projects in a socially unjust world (Griffiths, 1998), and, as Alvesson and Sveningsson (2003, p 379) argue, there are too many measurement studies 'carried out by researchers ideologically and commonsensically committed to the idea' and so there is a need for more 'openness, suspicion, and reflexivity'; and, seventh, challenge thinking about leadership for a more socially just world and what it means to be activist through practice and research (Ryan, 1998; Rusch and Marshall, 2006; Bogotch et al, 2008; Normore, 2008; Anderson, 2009; Shields, 2010).

These are not easy issues, and working both 'within' and 'against' takes courage (Lather, 1991). It is possible, and from the world of policy Ravitch (2010) has exposed her 'road to Damascus' revelation about how she learned that the 'policy of coercion' in the US educational reform programmes had not created great schools for all, and 'if a get-tough policy saps educators of their initiative, their craft, and their enthusiasm, then it is hard to believe that the results are worth having' (pp 66–7). However, while repositioning can take place, researcher reflexivity about the interplay between the state, public policy and knowledge can generate important perspectives:

> Policy research is always in some degree both reactive and parasitic. Careers and reputations are made as our research flourishes upon the rotting remains of the Keynsian Welfare State. Both those inside the policy discourse and those whose

professional identities are established through antagonism towards the discourse benefit from the uncertainties and tragedies of reform. Critical researchers, apparently safely ensconced on the moral high ground, nonetheless make a livelihood trading in the artefacts of misery and broken dreams of practitioners. None of us remains untainted by the incentives and disciplines of the new moral economy. (Ball, 1997, p 258)

Therefore, socially critical research is not an answer, because it does not seek to present the answer. The emphasis on teaching and learning as intellectual work means that problem posing and working for a more socially just world requires challenges to knowledge production, particularly as democratic development can be dominated by elite interests, as Western (2008) has shown. So, in order to bring children into decision-making, it will take 'courageous leadership' to challenge those interests (in research networks as well) (Smyth, 2006c, p 287). Bourdieu (1999, p 629) is helpful here in showing that research which helps people realise they are not responsible for the situation they are in is not depressing:

what the social world has done, it can, armed with this knowledge, undo. In any event what is certain is that nothing is less innocent than noninterference. If it is true that it is not easy to eliminate or even modify most of the economic and social factors behind the worst suffering, particularly the mechanisms regulating the labor and educational markets, it is also true that any political program that fails to take full advantage of the possibilities for action (minimal though they may be) that science can help uncover, can be considered guilty of nonassistance to a person in danger. (p 629)

Notes

[1] See Gunter (2004) for an account of the historical relabelling of the same professional practice as successively administration, management and, more recently, leadership.

[2] A really interesting example of collaborative learning between experts and communities is illustrated by the 2010 BBC TV series, *Story of England*. The history of the village of Kibworth in Leicestershire is told by Michael Wood

reporting on research with local and young people who were enabled and challenged to generate data, develop narratives and report on their findings by and through the expertise of archaeologists and historians.

EIGHT

New games?

Introduction

The New Labour period in office continues to be the focus of scholarly analysis and debate (Walford, 2005; Chapman and Gunter, 2009), and what the specific focus on the politics of knowledge production has achieved is to interrelate policy texts and research evidence with the power relations that produced and used it. So the original questions that I began the book with can now be answered: first, what type of knowledge was used and why? A *doxa* of beliefs about schools and the profession, together with effectiveness and improvement data to support the delivery of radical reforms, was used to enter and play the leadership of schools *game*. Second, what forms of knowing were deemed legitimate and why? Common-sense belief statements combined with correlations and/or normative claims regarding the correctness of particular leadership structures, cultures and practices were used to stake claims for distinction within the leadership of schools *game*. Third, who were regarded as knowers and why? Trusted knowers with shared *dispositions* to play the *game* within and for central government and its arm's length bodies, and who revealed the *habitus* to stake their *capital* within the leadership of schools *game*. Such regime practices enabled the normality of politics – debate, disagreement, negotiation and resolution – to be regulated or, indeed, rendered unnecessary.

The mapping and critical analysis of knowledge production has shown how regime dynamics are located within institutionalised governance, and how policymaking can best be understood through the formation, development, stability and dissolution of regimes of practice by knowledge workers who variously located their research and professional projects, and staked claims for recognition and distinction. While the leadership of schools *game* has a legacy and may continue, the end of the New Labour mandate to govern in May 2010 means that the NLPR has lost its institutional base, and a new government has taken office. This has implications for social relations within regimes and how positioning and repositioning may be happening. Therefore, while this final chapter brings the book to a close, it cannot be the actual end because ongoing work is necessary in the charting and analysing of education policy as a place where dominant economic and political interests have sought to take control. So in this chapter, I return to the standards issue and the place that leaders, leading and leadership have had within it, and examine what is happening post-May 2010. A change of government begs the question: when is a regime a regime and when might activity be activity? I go on to examine the contribution made by a focus on knowledge production in regard to educational policymaking, and how this work might be developed further.

The cult of standards and standardisation

Smyth (2006b, p 279) reports that:

> if we want evidence that muscular policies of testing, scripted and prescribed teaching, an ethos of competition, along with dehumanized and irrelevant curricula are not working for large numbers of students, then we need look no further than the 30–40% of students in most western countries who are not completing high school.

The impact of neoliberal projects based on the standard of public provision is not a new issue.

Callahan's (1962) book, *Education and the Cult of Efficiency*, describes and analyses what he calls 'an American tragedy in education' through the introduction of business processes, where between 1900 and 1930:

- 'Educational questions were subordinated to business considerations';
- 'Administrators were produced who were not, in any true sense, educators';
- 'A scientific label was put on some very unscientific and dubious methods and practices'; and
- 'An anti-intellectual climate, already prevalent, was strengthened' (p 246).

Current research shows that this business of education continues, with Molnar (2006, p 621) arguing that recent 'commercialisation pushes schools away from being centers of learning serving the public good and toward becoming profit centers for private interests'. Indeed, Burch's (2009) in-depth analysis of 'hidden markets' argues that, while education needed radical change in the US, markets are not a neutral or benign deliverer of equitable change, and may even do irrevocable damage.

Ravitch (2010), as a former enthusiastic policy insider, has come to realise this. The emphasis on counting through testing and accountability with the No Child Left Behind (NCLB) Act in the US from 2001 is highly problematic:

> NCLB was a punitive law based on erroneous assumptions about how to improve schools. It assumed that reporting test scores to the public would be an effective lever for school reform. It assumed that changes in governance would lead to school improvement. It assumed that shaming schools that were unable to lift test scores every year – and the people who work in them – would lead to higher scores. It assumed that low scores were caused by lazy teachers and lazy principals, who need to be threatened with the loss of their jobs. Perhaps most naively, it assumed that higher test scores on standardized tests of basic skills are synonymous with good education. Its assumptions were wrong. Testing is not a substitute for curriculum and instruction. Good education cannot be achieved by a strategy of testing children, shaming education, and closing schools. (Ravitch, 2010, pp 110–11)

Charter schools mean that there is a move from reforming schools to be business-like, to business and philanthropy providing schools:

> the charter school receives considerable autonomy from traditional public school regulations. Charter schools can recruit and enroll students without the confinement of an encatchment zone, thus providing parent choice; they can hire and fire their personnel independent from the school district where they are located, and they can innovate and develop their own instructional focus and curriculum. (Goldring and Mavrogordato, 2011, p 186)

The evidence about impact on standards is inconclusive, and, according to Ravitch (2010, pp 146–7), there are key questions that need to be answered:

> Whether charter schools are a sustainable reform, whether they can proliferate and at the same time produce good results, is a question yet to be resolved. Whether there is the will to close low-performing charters remains to be seen.

Whether there is an adequate supply of teachers who are willing to work fifty-hour weeks is unknown. The biggest unknown is how the multiplication of charter schools will affect public education.

This is just one example. A global discourse about standards in publicly funded education continues to travel, and while the charter programme, along with philanthropic and for-profit investment in the US, has not been directly copied by UK governments in England, learning about systemic reforms did confirm and provided inspiration for similar policy developments from the 1980s onwards (Whitty et al, 1993). Ideas along with their promoters get on and off planes, particular texts are read and used to encourage and justify changes, and knowledge exchange takes place. Caldwell (1999) under the headline 'The world is watching, Tony' showed how Australia was receptive to New Labour policies:

> In Australia, the conservative Liberal National government in Victoria has made structural changes along the lines of the 1988 Education Reform Act and now looks to the new British arrangements for ideas for the next stage of reform. Michael Barber, head of the Government's standards and effectiveness unit, spoke at an Australian schools conference in April. The visits to Melbourne in May by education minister Estelle Morris and Anthea Millett, the Teacher Training Agency's chief executive, are testimony to a developing exchange of ideas and information. Both countries have an interest in an expanded role for the private sector, new approaches to teacher development, high-level training for heads, and state-of-the-art applications of new technology.

England, as a laboratory of educational experimentation, has been watched and studied, with former colonial links in particular having shown a predisposition to look and learn (on South Africa, see Berkhout, 2007; on New Zealand, see Fitzgerald, 2007; and on Australia, see Vidovitch, 2007).

A similar tragedy to that in the US and other countries has been unfolding in English education over the past 30 years through, paraphrasing Callahan (1962), a cult of standards and standardisation:

- an overemphasis on outcomes through testing, audit and inspection;
- the categorisation and labelling of people (including children) and organisations as either successful or failing;
- the dominance of private interests and gains at the expense of collective needs and opportunities; and
- the deprofessionalisation of teacher skills, knowledge and practices as the means through which the workforce can be trained to be efficiently deployed.

Data can be and has been used to justify and question the standards agenda. Mansell (2009) has shown how GCSE scores have risen, but the Programme for International Student Assessment (PISA) results[1] have declined:

> In 2001, 50 per cent of young people (mainly 16-year-olds) in England achieved five or more A⋆–C grades at GCSE. By 2010, that figure had been transformed, rising by a half to a new high of 75 per cent. Now compare the test results of those same two cohorts of pupils in the PISA tests. In 2000, a more-or-less representative sample across the UK of that same 2001 GCSE cohort scored, in PISA, 523 points in reading, 529 in maths and 532 in science, where 500 points represented average performance across all OECD countries. Now, in 2009, a sample of UK pupils who go on and take GCSEs in 2010 scored 494 for reading, 492 for maths and 514 for science.

For Mansell (2009), teaching to particular tests may bring gains regarding home data, but the transferability of skills to other tests, particularly where PISA 'stress the need for pupils to apply their understanding', has not been as successful:

> the PISA figures cast doubt on Labour's literacy and numeracy strategies ... if these strategies had truly raised pupil's long-term understanding, progress ought to be seen in all international testing studies, for both primary and secondary pupils, not just in some of them.

Other research has enriched understandings about what has been taking place: with Crace (2006) reporting Shayer's conclusions that '11 and 12 year old children in year 7 are "now on average between two and three years behind where they were 15 years ago" in terms of cognitive and conceptual development' (see Shayer et al, 2007); research showing that incentives to change the curriculum (some of them rather perverse) have taken place, with children being entered for easier exams (Wrigley, 2011) and with reports of increases in cheating (Galton, 2007) and truancy (Harrison, 2010); Gillard (2011a, p 33) showing that, while 'a third of heads' were planning to retire by 2011, the evidence shows 'only 4 per cent of teachers wanting to become heads in the next five years'; and reports that attitudes to learning by adults and children have increasingly focused on doing the right thing, with Maloney (2009, p 267) arguing that the National College 'gives headteachers the security they are on the right lines both in terms of their own practice and in supporting the key discourses', and, complementary to this, Galton (2007, p 170) showing that children are working hard but testing has 'reduced and limited their horizons to merely doing what they need to do in order to succeed in gaining the required levels'. Significantly, the *Cambridge Primary Review* (Alexander, 2009; Alexander and Flutter, 2009) reports on the politicisation of the curriculum through the standards agenda, where 'the curriculum is subject to excessive prescription and micro-management from the DCSF, the national strategies and the QCA [Qualifications and Curriculum Authority], and many believe that the extent and manner of control from the centre has been, on balance, counter-productive' (Alexander, 2009, p 8). While New Labour had made claims that such interventions were necessary to improve the quality of education and the life chances of children, research shows the complexity of how schools and their leaders have responded (Barker, B., 2009), and that class continues to be the best predictor of achievement (Wilkinson and Pickett, 2009; Kerr and West, 2010).

The thread running through education policy has been to promote and copy independent schools as the model to aspire to, particularly to prevent middle-class flight from state education, especially in urban and multi-ethnic areas (Tomlinson, 2003). Thatcher did it through the Assisted Places Scheme, and both Thatcher and Blair worked on enabling schools to operate outside of local democratic processes through, for example, GMS schools, CTCs and the Academies Programme. New Labour sought to invest in public provision as a means of enabling the business of education to be attractive to the middle classes, and to create middle-class cloning aspirations for those in socially and economically disadvantaged settings (Gewirtz, 2001). Integral to doing this was the leadership of schools *game*, with a single charismatic leader doing leading and exercising leadership: from 1988, the headteacher was to be an entrepreneur in the quasi-marketplace where other roles operationalised strategic planning, marketing and bidding; and from 1997, this was overlain with the headteacher (or potentially a non-educational chief executive) as reform deliverer in their own and potentially other schools, where other leadership roles assumed distributed tasks to ensure compliance with reforms, generate and analyse data, and performance manage the workforce regarding the delivery agenda.

New games, old games?

In May 2010, a Conservative-led government was formed based on the support of the Liberal Democrats, and Whitehall-watching suggests that, without a mandate, the NLPR has dispersed, and what seems to be emerging on the same territory is a Conservative Market Regime (CMR). It is clear that the new government wants to present itself as different: symbolically the *Every Child Matters* rainbow logo has gone, and there is a disclaimer on the Department's website that even though some NLPR policies and advice remain, 'the content on this site may not reflect current government policy'. While New Labour invested in public services, the Conservative-led government is mainly disinvesting, but with some targeted investments, with Gillard (2011b, p 8) reporting that 'by the beginning of July the government was talking about cuts of up to £3.5bn in the schools budget as part of the most drastic public spending squeeze since the second world war'. However, the standards agenda remains in place, and while 'a quarter of all primary schools had boycotted the summer's tests ... schools minister Nick Gibb defended the tests and confirmed they would stay' (Gillard, 2011b, p 8).

Continuities with New Labour are evident with the extension of the Academies Programme,[2] and the emphasis on private interests as providers has generated further opportunities through 'Free' Schools[3] outside of local democratic processes: 'We will give parents, teachers, charities and local communities the chance to set up new schools, as part of our plans to allow new providers to enter the state school system in response to parental demand' (HM Government, 2010, pp 28–9).

Current Secretary of State for Education, Michael Gove's use of quotes from previous Labour politicians (see Gove, 2009, 2010a), combined with similar claims about having a moral purpose 'to make opportunity more equal' (Gove, 2010a), suggests affiliation with the civic position. However, the acceleration of competitive marketisation, with headlines like 'Gove has no "ideological objection" to firms making profits by running academy schools' (Barkham and Curtis, 2010, p 6), rather than the renewal of public institutions as the solution to the problem of standards, suggests that the Conservative approach is about gaining an advantage (DfE, 2010a). Gove's (2010a) argument is that structural reform will enable more social mobility, and the pupil premium[4] means that reallocated funds follow disadvantaged children into school, acting as a subsidy and incentive. The globalised economy is being used to reinforce the Thatcherite conceptualisation of a school as a local small business:

> And far from difficult economic times being a reason to scale down our ambitions, the economic challenges we face are only reason to accelerate our reform programme. Because the days are long gone – if they ever existed – when we could afford to educate a minority of our children well while hoping the rest were being schooled adequately. Already China and India are turning out more engineers, more computer scientists and more university graduates than the whole of Europe and America combined. And the success of other nations in harnessing their intellectual capital is a function of their determination to develop world-beating education systems. Across the globe other nations are outpacing us – pulling ahead in international comparisons, driving innovation, changing their systems to give professionals more freedom to grow, adapt, improve and learn from each other. (Gove, 2010a)

Like New Labour the delivery of a globally ready workforce is the job of schools, and the leadership of schools *game* currently remains in play, with policy texts that have echoes of 1997:

> Great schools are the product of great leadership. There are many superb heads in our state system doing a wonderful job. But there are also many schools which are still not giving children the start in life they deserve. We still have one of the most unequal education systems in the world and half of young people leave school without the basic qualifications you need to succeed. That's why we will invest in recruiting more great heads to turn around our weaker schools and extend the academy model so more strong schools can help weaker schools. The Coalition Government is relentlessly focused on making our school system one of the best in the world and making opportunity more equal. (Gove, 2010b)

The local leader of reform remains within the rhetoric, with approved-of headteachers celebrated in speeches as role models for the kind of leadership that brings about the type of changes required (see Gove, 2010a).[5] Consequently, existing headteachers are automatically located in this policy regime, and are meant to be excited about Academy conversion, about 'Free' Schools opening in their area and competing for students, and about how standards are to be measured through the English Baccalaureate.[6] The New Labour emphasis on school failure, and importantly the fear of failure, remains central to the *game*, and the New Labour endorsement of system leadership has been carried forward through increased investment in heads who support other heads from '£4.2million in 2010–11 to £7.2 million by 2013–14':

> NLEs [National Leaders of Education] are serving headteachers who have achieved excellent results in their schools, in inspections, national tests and examinations … NLEs use their knowledge and experience to provide additional leadership capacity to schools in challenging circumstances. Local Leaders of Education [LLEs] are successful headteachers who provide coaching and mentoring support to headteachers of other schools. (Gove, 2010b)

Institutionalised governance continues to be helpful as the means by which to describe the interaction between public institutions and networks of private interests. There is an emphasis on delivery:

> Because for any reforming politician the most important thing in preparing for Government is not passion, ardour or zeal but the ability to prioritise. Nothing is so fatal to hopes of change than the unfocussed energy of a well-intentioned Government which dissipates its majority, its mandate and its good will by chasing every desirable end rather than pursuing a proper, structured, programme of reform. (Gove, 2009)

The government remains firmly in charge regarding permission to become an Academy and set up a 'Free' School. In addition, new legal powers mean the Secretary of State has 'the right to order a local authority to close a school that is in special measures, requires significant improvement or has failed to comply with a warning notice' (Vasagar and Shepherd, 2011). Despite opposition,[7] conviction politics is in play and policy is running ahead, even with reports of financial inducements being used to generate buy-in to the reforms (Millar, 2011) and official National Audit Office data showing the high cost of New Labour's Academies with 'one in 20 of open academies ... forecasting debts' (Richardson, 2010).

The drawing in of approved private interests remains key, with celebrity experts drafted in to work on the curriculum, for example, Carol Vorderman (maths). 'Clubness' is evident through the award of £500,000 to the New Schools Network (NSN) headed up by Gove's former colleague, Rachel Wolf. The NSN has been contracted to provide advice to people on setting up a 'Free' School, and questions have been asked about why the SSAT has not been used (Syal, 2010) and the transparency regarding NSN and other interests has been challenged by Fiona Millar:

> the more serious question is whether this secretly funded outfit is in a position to provide parents with the objective advice they need. The NSN needs to say whether it has ever received funds from organizations with a vested interest in the drive to remove education from the maintained sector. They are well represented among its advisers and trustees. (Clark, 2010, p 5)

While disinvestment has led to BECTA, GTCE and the Qualifications and Curriculum Development Agency (QCDA)[0] being abolished, the National College has been retained:

> I want to reassure you and all of those working in the College that I am clear that the College is fulfilling a hugely important role, that you and everyone who works at the College are genuinely committed to improving the quality of leadership in our schools and that the College has been making a real difference in achieving this. I am truly appreciative of everything that the College has accomplished and believe that the College should be proud of its work. (Gove, 2010d, p 1)

The National College is explicitly onside as 'we stand ready to support the Government in a number of key challenges to the system' (Treves, 2010, p 1), and has been symbolically anointed through major policy speeches (Gove, 2010a, 2010b). A 10% reduction in the National College budget has been made (Gove, 2010c) and it is no longer an NDPB, but has been brought under the direct control of the Department by being designated an Executive Agency in order to deliver the policy agenda.[9] Steve Munby has welcomed the changes:

> School leadership has never been more important and I welcome the prominence the coalition government has given to it in the White Paper. The National College has been supporting outstanding heads as they support others since 2006. The expansion of our National and Local Leaders of Education programmes; the roll-out of teaching schools and the designation of specialist leaders of education will change the face of education in this country forever. In our new status as an Executive Agency, we will continue to operate in a way that retains our special relationship with leaders for children and young people. With value-for-money as our key priority, we look forward to supporting the next generation of leaders. (National College, 2010d)

It seems as if the National College remit continues to be politically controlled, with responsibilities being given and taken away. Since the 2010 White Paper (DfE, 2010a), the National College has moved into territory that previously the TDA and universities occupied regarding initial teacher training (National College, 2010e).

Clearly, there is *symbolic exchange of capital* taking place between the Department for Education and private interests, either directly through, for example, NSN, or indirectly through, for example, the National College. In addition, reports on the progress of Academies and 'Free' Schools shows that there are heads who are on board (Tickle, 2010), together with a range of organisations (Vasagar, 2010b, 2011). However, headship remains risky, with headteachers facing a difficult situation regarding cuts (Mansell, 2010), with reports that business autonomy can lead to school failure (Northern, 2010), and stories about how untrained people will be teaching in 'Free' Schools (Murray, 2010). There is emerging evidence that heads and parents have largely located themselves outside of this exchange process, with reports that while there had been 1,900 enquiries about Academy conversion (Gillard, 2011b, p 3), only 32 opened in September 2010 (Lightfoot, 2010), and while the 'Free' School policy had generated over 700 expressions of interest, only 62 applications had been made (Asthana, 2010, p 7), with an estimated 16 to be opened by September 2011 (Gillard, 2011b, p 6). A poll conducted by the NUT shows parental views on 'Free' Schools are varied: '31% were against ... 26% were in favour, and 29% were neither in favour nor against' (Vasagar, 2011, p 13). There are reports of resistance to 'Free' Schools regarding the way that advantaged parents are using the scheme to protect the education of their children (Davis, 2011), and how local Conservative and Liberal Democrat councillors around the country are 'claiming that they threaten to wreck social harmony by creating ethnic or religious enclaves and will disrupt efforts to improve the lives of all children' (Vasagar, 2010a). This is in addition to the ongoing campaign by the Anti-Academies Alliance (AAA),[10] which brings together parents, children, communities and researchers to both locally and nationally challenge the dominance of private interests in education services.

Making sense of unfolding policy projects is a challenge as teaching and learning continues to take place within this dynamic policy context. Whether the leadership of schools *game* remains useful to Gove in the delivery of his neoliberal project remains to be seen. New Labour played this *game* as a motivator for dealing with the contradiction of projects that were mainly neoliberal, but also had civic overtones and intentions. However, the redesign of the public as 'active users' of the public sector (Ozga, 2002, p 332) was interpreted and practised as consumers rather than citizens, and so modernisation was more about business than civic *dispositions*. The Conservative-led government is reaping the benefits of this through the 'Big Society', which is a neoliberal project designed to benefit markets and philanthropy:[11] 'Free schools are actually being constructed for political purposes, as a safety valve for the few irate advantaged, but at the cost of public education. The Coalition are vandals of the public sphere' (Ranson, 2010, p 157). It seems that the bigger-picture Thatcherite *game* of privatisation is revealed.

Old games, new games?

In May 2010, New Labour went into opposition and, while recognising a productive legacy, Giddens (2010, p 27) argued that 'New Labour as such is dead, and it is time to abandon the term', and policy development is under way following the election of Ed Miliband as party leader. In relation to education, this is taking place partly in response to the Conservative-led policies, with Hyman (2011) being critical of cuts and curriculum changes. However, his acceptance of 'Free' Schools and Academies, as long as there are 'safeguards' such as 'thorough accountability, fair funding and guarantees on admissions' (Hyman, 2011, p 27), illustrates how Blairites are finding opposition difficult as these policies flow from New Labour's concern to generate independence within publicly funded provision. While West and

Pennell (2002) give recognition to New Labour's emphasis on social inclusion as distinct from the Thatcherite promotion of competition, they conclude that this was little more than an attempt 'to soften the edges of the quasi-market ... [because] it has not tackled some of its major deficiencies such as the power that schools that are their own admission authorities have to distort it' (p 220). Indeed, researchers have shown that New Labour's claims for social justice are difficult to square with a policy that 'subjugates teachers and children, giving them neither autonomy nor scope for creativity, and which treats children as commodities, and segregates them into hierarchically-tiered groupings' (Gewirtz, 2000, p 367). Nevertheless, Andy Burnham, the Shadow Education Secretary, is drawing on and seeking to rehabilitate the 'comprehensive ideal' because there is evidence that it is already working across England, and 'it is about having a plan for everyone rather than just a few. But I also want to rethink it for new times – so that it speaks to a sense of achievement, quality and excellence as well as one of togetherness and fairness' (Burnham, 2010). It is early days as yet, and the question to be asked is whether the NLPR can and will reposition here and be joined by others who could sign up to this approach.

The NLPR can no longer play in the way that it did – it does not have a mandate. Repositioning is taking place. While history shows that the same advisers have served both Conservative and Labour governments, 2010 seems to be more of a watershed. Politicians are on the backbenches (or have retired), professors have gone back to their universities and private companies are trading in the marketplace. Anecdotal evidence indicates that the cutting of commissioned projects from the Department and National College is impacting on researchers, but how repositioning is taking place is unclear. However, the *disposition* to accept how neoliberal ideas frame a problem and provide answers is very strong within knowledge production in education. In the 1980s, the emphasis was on marketised 'cookery-book literature' (Raab, 1994, p 19) for professionals to restructure and reculture the school as a business, and from the 1990s, this shifted towards providing evidence and prescribed practice for how change could and should take place. It seems that while there remains SLR activity it is unlikely to be revitalised as a regime due to the repositioning (and retirements) of those who traditionally have been there. However, there is a space for the SESI community, though significant work needs to be done on knowledge claims in order to handle major critiques (eg Coe, 2009; Gorard, 2010) and dependence on the NLPR for investment. In particular, the relationship with government policymakers needs attention, with Goldstein and Woodhouse (2000) arguing over a decade ago that school effectiveness researchers had to break away from government influence and reposition around 'educational effectiveness' and that school improvement should rebrand as 'institutional change', and this would provide the opportunity to be 'critical' rather than 'committed friends' (p 361). Attractive for the CMR could be the repositioning of former NLPR members directly within the leadership industry, with Barber setting up the US Education Delivery Institute (http://www.deliveryinstitute.org) to design deliverology projects and bring about improved performance, and the former New Labour Innovation Unit being independent now of government, working across public-sector services and including people who were players in the NLPR leadership of schools *game* (http://www.innovationunit. org). A combination of both *field* watching and empirical research will be needed to see how former NLPR members handle the ongoing challenges to their knowledge claims, and how they stake their *capital* in relation to project funding and the market.

The PRR engages in *symbolic exchange* regarding the interplay between theory, research and professional practice, with activism around social justice. This regime has shown endurance over time as people have retired and new researchers have staked their claims there. Professionals have sought to relocate there both as serving teachers/headteachers, and by moving into higher education. So the PRR was in play pre-1997 and remains in play post-2010, with independently funded research and contributions to debates that are congenial to the Labour Party's reimagining of the comprehensive school; and academia is certainly not passive, with opportunities being taken by a range of educational researchers to fire back at current reforms (Bassey et al, 2010). For those who do focus in particular on critical leadership, there are resources and networks to connect with that are committed to democratic renewal, such as the New DEEL in the US (see Gross, 2008).

What seems to be central to the vibrancy of the territory that the PRR inhabits is reflexivity regarding the politics of the purposes and practices of knowledge production. This can be productive but, as Ranson (1995, p 442) has identified, there are 'fissiparous tendencies' amongst policy researchers, where the *field* can turn in on itself, or, as Apple (2006a, p 686) states: 'when the left organizes a firing squad, it lines up in a circle'. The relationship between public policy, knowledge and professional practice is central to these debates, and it could be that such research is 'conducted in the knowledge that the state is unlikely to be persuaded by, or to act on, any of ... [the] findings, however relevant' (Fitz et al, 1994, p 53). It seems that Young's (2008) conceptualising of change narratives as 'theoretical' (issues of knowledge claims) and 'political' (how change might take place) debates is helpful in enabling positioning and the staking of *capital* to be opened up to scrutiny and strategising. Young (2008, p 105) is clear that there are 'boundaries to be maintained and crossed but not blurred', and Whitty's (2002) analysis that crossing such boundaries by policy scholars is appropriate but not an imperative means that analysis of and for action is not automatically oppositional, but an essential and distinct contribution to educational change. However, the current threats to knowledge production in a publicly funded university are a challenge for all social science and humanities researchers, and so the PRR will go through tough times as public funds for teaching and research are cut and the business of higher education grows rapidly. Therefore, the politics of knowledge production is not just about the specifics of how a government draws on research evidence regarding a particular policy, but is located in the wider debates about the role of the state and in particular the role of education as a public service within a dynamic and increasingly marketised higher education.

The politics of knowledge production

Describing, understanding and explaining education policy requires an analysis of the relationship between the state, public policy and knowledge. Specifically, when public institutions of the state make policy, they do so through investing in particular types of knowledge production, and as a social practice, this process can be understood as a *game* in play. The type of play and players within institutionalised governance enables control of the process, and regimes of practice can be mapped to show how the *game* and other *games* may be in play, and how *dominance* and *domination* works in the staking of *capital*. So, while claims can be made that the process is rational and transparent, as Ranson (1995, p 432) states, 'transactions with the state are by definition likely to be unequal and as a last resort it will usually find the powers and resources to win most games'. New Labour did claim to operate evidence-informed policy and practice, with Blunkett arguing that 'the Government has given a clear commitment that we will be guided not by dogma but by an open-minded approach to understanding what works and why' (DfEE, 2000, p 2). But, as the analysis of New Labour's investment into the leadership of schools *game* shows, the framework of institutionalised governance combined with symbolic exchange within the NLPR predefined which types of research matter and how that research was to be used. It seems as if this is a denial of politics because of the way inclusion and exclusion of particular ideas, people and organisations operated. Symbolic exchange was with contracted and preferred knowledge producers and deliverers, and even though the NLPR was not hegemonic, it conducted itself as if it was. It is still early days for the Conservative-led symbolic exchange process, but it seems as if Gove is just as interested as his predecessors in expounding his belief systems and selecting evidence to make claims about national interventions into professional practice. For example, Gove's 'mythbuster' (DfE, 2010b) document outlines the positive impact of schools outside of local democratic control, while research evidence (eg Allen, 2010; Gunter, 2011) and investigative journalism (eg Evans, 2011) tell another story.

The politics (or rather the lack of politics) of knowledge production is located within the interplay between hierarchy, markets and civil society. Consequently, education policy needs to be related to wider public policy, where, as already noted, other and interlinked leadership *games* are being played as a means of securing neoliberal projects in social work, the police, local government and health. The all-embracing and suffocating nature of this *game* makes research difficult, but there are projects that have challenged the neoliberal position: first, the modernisation agenda across the public services is highly problematic, with Midwinter (2001, p 319) arguing that 'the public interest' is more likely to be delivered by public-sector professionals, and 'as in the USA, the case for bureaucracy is much stronger than its critics acknowledge'. Second, Newman and Clarke (2009) have argued that while the public wants better local services, they do not necessarily want marketised services. Third, Wilby (2008) reports on research by Gregg et al (2008) which shows that public-sector workforce investment into services is high, with 'an extra 120 million hours at no cost, equivalent to 60,000 employees (or 2.4 per cent of the public sector workforce in education, health and social care) working for nothing' (p 14). Consequently, research regarding how service provision can improve and be effective needs to have recognition of the professional who invests their expertise within civic projects, which Marquand (2004, p 1) identifies as 'the domain of citizenship, equity and service whose integrity is essential to democratic governance and social well-being', and where 'citizenship rights trump both market power and the bonds of clan or kinship' (p 1).

The recognition of the NLPR seeking to dominate, but not actually dominant, and the positioning of the PRR in relation to ongoing neoliberal projects and working for socially just civic projects both within and outside of public institutions, suggests the need for further work. The interdisciplinary nature of education as a *field* that draws on social science disciplines enables a dynamic approach to research and theorising, but, as Apple's (2005) and Connell's (2007) arguments show, knowledge production flows need to make the role of the South more visible 'by having the South teach the North about "what works" in powerful models of school reform' (Apple, 2005, p 394). So I am mindful that the analysis presented here has only begun to make a contribution and this needs ongoing research and theorising. There is sufficient evidence to show that the leadership of schools *game* is one that is not only in education or in England, but is also being played throughout the public sector and internationally, and there is a need to give attention to players I have acknowledged but not yet studied, such as the unions,[12] media[13] and publishing industry. Institutionalised governance again has possibilities for examining other parts of the public sector and for comparative analysis with other countries, particularly those that have more decentralised systems than the UK government of education in England. As already noted, Rowan's (2002) study of the school improvement industry in the US is an example of marketised governance, and, interestingly, an examination of the contribution made by school change and improvement knowledge workers in Canada by Hargreaves and Fink (2006) suggests a form of partnership governance through links between universities, provincial government and school districts. Regimes of practice need more fine-grained genealogical analysis, particularly through the examination of how people and projects are historically and organisationally located at a particular time and over time.

Such ongoing work can help with strategies for democratic renewal, particularly through research activism that makes the *game*, the players and the way power works more visible:

> Not many 'lay people' are likely to challenge the Chancellor of the Exchequer, the Secretary of the Treasury or their expert advisors in such matters. Were they to do so, they would be told – much as a medieval priest might have advised his flock – that these are questions with which they need not concern themselves. The liturgy must be chanted in an obscure tongue, accessible only to the initiated. For everyone else, faith will suffice. (Judt, 2010, p 161)

Research has a contribution to make towards challenging the faith, and hence accountability is less about data and more about social relations. Researching policy as a power process enables questions to be asked about knowledge, knowing and knowers in regard to decisions and investments. Speaking up and speaking out is difficult but not impossible,[14] and researchers in education can stake and have staked a claim for a *game* that includes learners as active players (eg Fielding, 2007a, 2007b). However, rehabilitating politics as an essential part of public life requires a shift from "'sloganization" and falsification of the adversary's thought' to a process of 'argument and refutation' (Bourdieu, 1998b, p 9). Following Richardson (1997), I am well aware that I play and I am a player in this research *game* and like all researchers I am deeply embedded in the politics of knowledge production: 'the "field" is also a battleground, a minefield, a war zone, as well as an open, inviting expanse' (p 4). I look forward to the debate and further research.

Notes

[1] Mansell (2009) notes that the 2000 PISA results are regarded as 'unofficial' because not enough students took the tests to meet the sampling requirements, but he argues that even in being cautious:

> when you compare the unofficial results of the 2000 and 2003 PISA tests with the PISA scores from 2006 and 2009, there is no evidence of the improvements registered particularly through the GCSE scores. And the England's PISA results are static between 2006 and 2009, while GCSE scores climbed.

Mansell (2010) also notes that the Trends in International Mathematics and Science Study (TIMSS) results shows 'England's performance in the four tested subjects of maths and science in primary and secondary consistently now well above the international average' (p 1).

[2] The Academies Programme has been extended to all schools, and those identified as 'outstanding' will be fast-tracked (see Gunter, 2011).

[3] 'Free' Schools are based on applications from parents, charities, teachers, businesses and universities to set up a school free from local authority control (see Gunter, 2011).

[4] There has been a shift regarding the funding of the pupil premium. Gillard (2011b) says that in October 2010, it was announced that £7bn had been found to fund the pupil premium, but a week later, Gove announced that 'he had had to make cuts elsewhere in the education budget to fund the premium' and so 'some schools would face a budget cut in order to make the extra payment to schools taking pupils from the poorest homes' (p 8).

[5] There is research from the right that challenges this emphasis on the headteacher, for example, O'Shaughnessy (2007).

[6] The English Baccalaureate is the government's attempt to redefine basic standards at the end of Key Stage 4. Previously, New Labour had used five A*–C grades at GCSE as the benchmark, and then they changed the five to include English and maths. The Conservative-led government has now defined the standard as: English, maths, one science, one foreign language and one humanity (Gillard, 2011b, p 9).

[7] Several New Labour projects have been terminated, bringing trouble for Gove. Following protests regarding the announcement that the school sports partnership scheme was to be ended (£162m per year), this was reviewed and 'money would be found to keep "key elements" of the scheme going until the 2012 London Olympics' (Gillard, 2011b, p 9). The abolition of *Creative Partnerships*, which has invested in musicians, artists and actors working in schools, has brought criticism from the profession as well as the arts (Thorpe, 2011). In July 2010, it was announced that 715 projects as part of the Building Schools for the Future (BSF) programme would be cancelled, but Gove was forced to apologise when errors regarding the identification of particular projects came to light. Gove was defeated in the courts after a challenge by six local authorities was upheld because he had failed to consult on the axing of BSF projects (Richardson, 2011).

[8] BECTA was set up in 1997 with the remit to improve the role of technology in learning and it closed in 2011. The GTCE was set up in 1998 with the remit to regulate the profession; it will close in March 2012. The QCDA was set up in 1997 with the remit to oversee the national curriculum and testing; its closure in early 2012 has been announced.

[9] The Conservative-led government is using the Executive Agency status to bring the TDA under closer control. The TDA (formerly the Teacher Training Agency [TTA]) was set up in 2005 to oversee the training of the school workforce; it will close and then reopen as an Executive Agency in April 2012.

[10] The Anti-Academies Alliance is a campaign against Academies and 'Free' Schools including parents, pupils, teachers, unions, councillors, MPs and researchers, see http://www.antiacademies.org.uk

[11] Prime Minister Cameron has declared the 'Big Society' as the means by which the state provision of services is replaced by private and voluntary interests. This is highly controversial and questions are being raised about

whether this shift is in reality a cover for major public spending cuts (BBC, 2011).

[12] Thomson (2008) has shown how the headteacher unions are policy actors who not only oppose or accept, but are working on alternatives, and rightly argues that the collective positioning and activity of headteachers through their associations needs detailed research.

[13] Millar and Benn (2009) have examined the relationship between negative press stories regarding publicly funded education and the personal views of journalists and editors.

[14] At the time of writing, there are social protests in England regarding disinvestment in public services and changes to the funding of higher education, and targeted protests at retail entrepreneurs who, it is argued, have tax arrangements that mean the exchequer is losing revenue.

Knowledge Production in Educational Leadership Project

The Knowledge Production in Educational Leadership (KPEL) project was funded by the Economic and Social Research Council (ESRC) (RES-000-23-1192) and began in January 2006 and was completed in December 2007. The project explored the relationship between the state, public policy and knowledge by focusing on New Labour's investment in the leadership of schools as a central strategy for delivering reform. The project examined the first decade of New Labour education policy with a specific focus on: the antecedence of leadership; the assumptions and strategising of policymakers; centralised interventions in local professional practice; and the responses of practitioners. The study was designed:

- to map the field of educational leadership: types of knowledge produced, ways of knowing being used and who are regarded as knowledgeable, and why;
- to examine and chart New Labour policies regarding educational leadership;
- to identify those who position themselves as New Labour policymakers or close to New Labour policymaking, and those who are outside. Particular emphasis was on how practitioners position themselves in regard to New Labour reforms; and
- to conceptualise positioning within policymaking using Bourdieu's theory of practice as a framework for describing and explaining the dynamics of the policy process.

A qualitative survey was undertaken: first, primary documentary sources were analysed – over 200 government documents (including documents released under the Freedom of Information Act) and over 30 websites – and secondary sources were read – over 300 published articles and books on leadership and policy. Second, interviews and biographical work about professional practice with a sample of 116 policymakers including ministers, civil servants, advisers (appointed to role), private-sector consultants (contracted to provide a service), headteachers, local government, unions and researchers in higher education:

- eight from government (three former Secretaries of State for Education and five civil servants);
- ten from NDPBs/agencies/local government/unions;
- sixty-three researchers in universities;
- twenty-five headteachers; and
- ten private-sector consultants.

The data was coded and, following Bourdieu (2005), professional practice was mapped based on indicators of capital in their biography, professional practice and *dispositions*. Figure 5.1 in Chapter 5 presents the map where positions are taken in relation to proximity to and distance from the state as power and economy:

Economy + Power + : space is occupied by those who have direct access to public 'government' institutions, and are using leadership as a means of extending private-sector practices and cultures into public-sector services.

Economy − Power + : space is occupied by those who have direct access to public 'government' institutions and who want to engage with leadership to develop public-sector services.

Economy − Power − : space is occupied by those outside of public 'government' institutions who undertake critical policy analysis of leadership, and its place in policymaking. The aim is to develop alternative approaches to leadership within the public sector.

Economy + Power − : space is occupied by those who do not have direct access to public 'government' institutions, but who are using leadership as a means to make public-sector services work more efficiently and effectively as a business.

References

Abra, J., Hunter, M., Smith, R. and Kempster, R. (2003) *What Leaders Read 1, Key Texts from the Business World*. Nottingham: NCSL.

Addison, B. (2009) 'A feel for the game – a Bourdieuian analysis of principal leadership: a study of Queensland secondary school principals'. *Journal of Educational Administration and History*, 41(4), pp 327–41.

Adonis, A. (2010) 'Eyes on the Prize'. *New Statesman*, 11 October, pp 53–4.

Ainscow, M., Fox, S. and Coupe O'Kane, J. (2003) *Leadership and Management in Special Schools*. Nottingham: NCSL.

Alexander, R.J. (2009) *Towards a New Primary Curriculum: A Report from the Cambridge Primary Review. Part 2: The Future*. Cambridge: University of Cambridge Faculty of Education.

Alexander, R.J. and Flutter, J. (2009) *Towards a New Primary Curriculum: A Report from the Cambridge Primary Review. Part 1: Past and Present*. Cambridge: University of Cambridge.

Alexiadou, N. and Ozga, J. (2002) 'Modernising education governance in England and Scotland: devolution and control'. *European Educational Research Journal*, 1(4), pp 676–91.

Allen, R. (2010) 'Replicating Swedish "free school" reforms in England'. *Research in Public Policy*, 10, Summer issue, pp 4–7.

Alton, S. (2006) *National Standards for Headteachers in Focus: Extended Schools*. Nottingham: NCSL.

Alvesson, M. and Sveningsson, S. (2003) 'The great disappearing act: difficulties in doing "leadership"'. *The Leadership Quarterly*, 14(3), pp 359–81.

Anderson, G. (2009) *Advocacy Leadership*. New York: Routledge.

Anderson, G. and Herr, K. (1999) 'The new paradigm wars: is there room for rigorous practitioner knowledge in schools and universities?'. *Educational Researcher*, 28(5), pp 12–21.

Appadurai, A. (2006) 'The right to research'. *Globalisation, Societies and Education*, 4(2), pp 167–77.

Apple, M.W. (2005) 'Audit cultures, commodification, and class and race strategies in education'. *Policy Futures in Education*, 3(4), pp 379–99.

Apple, M.W. (2006a) 'Rhetoric and reality in critical educational studies in the United States'. *British Journal of Sociology of Education*, 27(5), pp 679–87.

Apple, M.W. (2006b) 'Interrupting the Right: on doing critical educational work in conservative times'. In G. Ladson-Billings and W.F.Tate (eds) *Education Research in the Public Interest*. NewYork, NY: Teachers College Press, pp 27–45.

Apple, M.W. (ed) (2010) *Global Crises, Social Justice, and Education*. New York: Routledge.

Apple, M.W. and Beane, J.A. (1999) *Democratic Schools*. Buckingham: OUP.

Arrowsmith, R. (2001) 'A right performance'. In D. Gleeson and C. Husbands (eds) *The Performing School*. London: RoutledgeFalmer, pp 33–43.

Asthana, A. (2010) 'Gove under fire after poor take-up of free schools offer'. *The Observer*, 1 August, p 7.

Astle, J. and Ryan, C. (eds) (2008) *Academies and the Future of State Education*. London: CentreForum.

Bacchi, C. (2009) *Analysing Policy:What's the Problem Represented to Be?* Frenchs Forrester, NSW: Pearson Australia.

Baker, K. and Blunkett, D. (2009) 'Foreward by Lord Baker and the Right Honourable David Blunkett MP'. In C.Taylor (ed) *A Good School for Every Child*. Abingdon: Routledge, pp xiv–xv.

Ball, S.J. (1990) *Politics and Policymaking in Education*. London: Routledge.

Ball, S.J. (1993) 'Education policy, power relations and teachers' work'. *British Journal of Educational Studies*, 41(2), pp 106–21.

Ball, S.J. (1994a) *Education Reform:A Critical and Post-Structural Approach*. Buckingham: OUP.

Ball, S.J. (1994b) 'Some reflections on policy theory: a brief response to Hatcher and Troyna'. *Journal of Education Policy*, 9(2), pp 171–82.

Ball, S.J. (1995) 'Intellectuals or technicians? Urgent role of theory in educational studies'. *British Journal of Educational Studies*, 43(3), pp 255–71.

Ball, S.J. (1997) 'Policy sociology and critical social research: a personal review of recent education policy and policy research'. *British Educational Research Journal*, 23(3), pp 257–74.

Ball, S.J. (2003) 'The teacher's soul and the terrors of performativity'. *Journal of Education Policy*, 18(2), pp 215–28.

Ball, S.J. (2007a) *Education PLC*. London: Routledge.

Ball, S.J. (2007b) 'Policy sociology and critical social research: a personal view of recent education policy and policy research'. *British Education Research Journal*, 23(3), pp 257–74.

Ball, S.J. (2008a) *The Education Debate*. Bristol:The Policy Press.

Ball, S.J. (2008b) 'New philanthropy, new networks and new governance in education'. *Political Studies*, 56(4), pp 747–65.

Ball, S.J. (2009) 'Beyond networks? A brief response to "which networks matter in education governance"'. *Political Studies*, 57(3), pp 688–91.

Ball, S.J. (2010) 'New voices, new knowledges and the new politics of education research: the gathering of the perfect storm?'. *European Educational Research Journal*, 9(2), pp 124–37.

Ball, S.J. and Exley, S. (2010) 'Making policy with "good ideas": policy networks and the "intellectuals" of New Labour'. *Journal of Education Policy*, 25(2), pp 151–69.

Balls, E. (2007) *Response to Advice on Primary Leadership*. London: DCSF.

Balls, E. (2008) *National College for School Leadership (NCSL) Priorities: 2008–09*. London: DCSF.

Balls, E. (2010) *The National College Priorities: 2010–11*. London: DCSF.

Barber, M. (1996) *The Learning Game: Arguments for a Learning Revolution*. London: Victor Gollancz.

Barber, M. (1997) 'Reengineering the political/educational system'. *School Leadership and Management*, 17(2), pp 187–99.

Barber, M. (2001) 'High expectations and standards for all, no matter what'. In M. Fielding (ed) *Taking Education Really Seriously*. London: RoutledgeFalmer, pp 17–41.

Barber, M. (2007) *Instruction to Deliver*. London: Politico's Publishing.

Barber, M., Moffit, A. and Kihn, P. (2011) *Deliverology 101, A Field Guide for Educational Leaders*. London: Sage.

Barker, B. (1999) 'Double vision: 40 years on'. In H. Tomlinson, H. Gunter and P. Smith (eds) *Living Headship: Voices, Values and Vision*. London: PCP, pp 73–85.

Barker, B. (2005) *Transforming Schools: Illusion or Reality*. Stoke-on-Trent: Trentham Books.

Barker, B. (2007) 'The leadership paradox: can school leaders transform student outcomes?'. *School Effectiveness and School Improvement*, 18(1), pp 21–43.

Barker, B. (2009) 'Public service reform in education: why is progress so slow?'. *Journal of Educational Administration and History*, 41(1), pp 57–72.

Barker, B. (2010a) 'The five assumptions that ensure we fail'. *Times Educational Supplement*, 26 February. Available at: www.tes.co.uk/article.aspx?storycode=6037036 (accessed 25 June 2010).

Barker, B. (2010b) *The Pendulum Swings*. Stoke-on-Trent: Trentham Books.

Barker, I. (2009) 'The executive head's unique role'. *TES Connect*, 10 December. Available at: http://www.tes.co.uk/article.aspx?storycode=6000092 (accessed 7 February 2011).

Barkham, P. and Curtis, P. (2010) 'Gove has no "ideological objection" to firms making profits by running academy schools'. *The Guardian*, 1 June, p 6.

Barry, C.H. and Tye, F. (1972) *Running a School*. London: Temple Smith.

Bassey, M., Brown, M., Boyle, B., Barker, B., Coffield, F., Elliott, J., Edwards, T., Glatter, R., Kushner, S., Pollard, A., Pring, R. and Richards, C. (2010) 'Gove should delay creating more academies and free schools. Letters and Emails'. *The Guardian*, 14 September, p 31.

Bates, R. (2006) 'Educational administration and social justice'. *Education, Citizenship and Social Justice*, 1(2), pp 171–87.

Bates, Y. (1999) 'A vision for Lilian Baylis'. In H. Tomlinson, H. Gunter and P. Smith (eds) *Living Headship, Voices, Values and Vision*. London: PCP, pp 86–95.

BBC (British Broadcasting Corporation) (2008) 'Deadline for school "rescue plan"'. Available at: http://news.bbc.co.uk/1/hi/education/7442361.stm (accessed 10 June 2008).

BBC (2011) 'Prime Minister Cameron defends big society policy'. Available at: http://www.bbc.co.uk/news/uk-politics-12441972 (accessed 22 February 2011).

Beckett, F. (2000) 'Which of these two men is the real education secretary? (Not the one you think)'. *New Statesman*, 16 October, pp 11–12.

Beckett, F. (2007) *The Great City Academy Fraud*. London: Continuum.

Beckett, F. (2009) 'From head of geography to whistleblower'. *EducationGuardian*, 7 July, p 3.

Beckett, F. and Hencke, D. (2004) *The Survivor: Tony Blair in Peace and War*. London: Aurum Press Ltd.

Béland, D. (2005) 'Ideas and social policy: an institutionalist perspective'. *Social Policy and Administration*, 39(1), pp 1–18.

Bell, L. and Bolam, R. (2004) 'A systematic review of the impact of headteachers on student outcomes'. Paper presented to the Researching the Impact of School Leadership DfES Seminar, 8 March, London.

Bell, L., Bolam, R. and Cubillo, L. (2002) *A Systematic Review of the Impact of School Leadership and Management on Student Outcomes*. London: EPPI-Centre, Social Science Research Unit, Institute of Education.

BELMAS (British Educational Leadership Management and Administration Society) (2011) 'Welcome to BELMAS'. Available at: http://www.belmas.org.uk/belmas/home.eb (accessed 12 February 2011).

Bennett, N., Wise, C., Woods, P. and Harvey, J. (2003a) *Distributed Leadership*. Nottingham: NCSL.

Bennett, N., Newton, W., Wise, C., Woods, P.A. and Economou, A. (2003b) *The Role and Purpose of Middle Leaders in Schools*. Nottingham: NCSL.

Benson, S. (undated) *Leading Learning: Instructional Leadership in Infant Schools*. Nottingham: NCSL.

Bentham, J. (2006) 'The IPPR and Demos: Think Tanks of the New Social Democracy'. *The Political Quarterly*, 77(2), pp 166–74.

Berkhout, S. (2007) 'Democratization and the remaking of teachers in South Africa'. In G. Butt and H.M. Gunter (eds) *Modernizing Schools*. London: Continuum, pp 149–62.

Biott, C. and Spindler, J. (2005) 'Sustained motivation embedded in place: living with accountability and mandated change'. In C. Sugrue (ed) *Passionate Principalship*. London: RoutledgeFalmer, pp 29–41.

Blackler, F. (2006) 'Chief executives and the modernization of the English National Health Service'. *Leadership*, 2(1), pp 5–30.

Blackmore, J. (1999) *Troubling Women*. Buckingham: OUP.

Blair, T. (1998) *Speech to the New Heads Conference*. London: DfEE.

Blair, T. (1999a) 'A message from the Prime Minister, Modernising Government White Paper'. Available at: www.dfee.gov.uk/modgov/pmmg.html (accessed 19 November 1999).

Blair, T. (1999b) 'Speech to the National Association of Headteachers'. Available at: www.pm.gov.uk/output/Page1446.asp (accessed 11 December 2006).

Blair, T. (1999c) *Speech to the New Headteachers Conference*. London: DfEE.

Blair, T. (2006) '21st century public services speech'. Available at: http://www.number10.gov.uk/output/page9564.asp (accessed 17 January 2008).

Blunkett, D. (1998) *New National College for Headteachers*. DfEE Press Notice 1998/0477. Available at: www.dfes.gov.uk/pns/DisplayPNcgi?pn_id=1998_0477 (accessed 11 December 2006).

Blunkett, D. (2000) *National College for School Leadership*. London: DfEE.

Blunkett, D. (2001a) 'The challenges of improving schools'. Speech to the IPPR Seminar, 1 May. Available at: www.dfee.gov.uk/dfee_speeches/01_05_01/index.shtml (accessed 20 January 2003).

Blunkett, D. (2001b) *National College for School Leadership: Further Remit*. London: DfEE.

Blunkett, D. (2006) *The Blunkett Tapes: My Life in the Bear Pit*. London: Bloomsbury Publishing PLC.

Bobbitt, P. (2002) *The Shield of Achilles*. London: Penguin.

Bogdanor, V. (1979) 'Power and participation'. *Oxford Review of Education*, 5(2), pp 157–68.

Bogotch, I., Beachum, F., Blount, J., Brooks, J. and English, F., with Jansen, J. (2008) *Radicalizing Educational Leadership*. Rotterdam: Sense Publishers.

Bolam, R. (1986) 'The National Development Centre for School Management Training'. In E. Hoyle and A. McMahon (eds) *World Yearbook of Education 1986, The Management of Schools*. London: Kogan Page.

Bolam, R. (2003) 'The changing roles and training of headteachers: recent experience in England and Wales'. In P. Hallinger (ed) *Reshaping the Landscape of School Leadership Development*. Lisse, The Netherlands: Swets and Zeitlinger, pp 41–52.

Bolam, R. (2004) 'Reflections on the NCSL from a historical perspective'. *Educational Management Administration and Leadership*, 32(3), pp 251–67.

Bottery, M. (2004) *The Challenges of Educational Leadership*. London: PCP.

Bottery, M. (2007a) 'Reports from the front line: English headteachers' work in an era of practice centralisation'. *Educational Management, Administration and Leadership*, 35(1), pp 89–110.

Bottery, M. (2007b) 'New Labour policy and school leadership in England: room for manoeuvre?'. *Cambridge Journal of Education*, 37(2), pp 153–72.

Bourdieu, P. (1990) *In Other Words*. Cambridge: Polity Press.

Bourdieu, P. (1992) *The Logic of Practice*. Cambridge: Polity Press.

Bourdieu, P. (1998a) *Homo Academicus*. Cambridge: Polity Press.

Bourdieu, P. (1998b) *Acts of Resistance*. Cambridge: Polity Press.

Bourdieu, P. (1999) 'Postscript'. In P. Bourdieu, A. Accardo, G. Balazs, S. Beaud, R. Bonvin, E. Bourdieu, P. Bourgois, S. Broccolichi, P. Champagne, R. Christin, J. Faguer, S. Garcia, R. Lenoir, F. Œuvrard, M. Pialoux, L. Pinto, Podalydès, A. Sayad, C. Soulié and L. Wacquant (eds) *The Weight of the World*. Cambridge: Polity Press, pp 627–9.

Bourdieu, P. (2000) *Pascalian Meditations*. Cambridge: Polity Press.

Bourdieu, P. (2003) *Firing Back*. London: Verso.

Bourdieu, P. (2005) *The Social Structures of the Economy*. Cambridge: Polity.

Bourdieu, P. and Wacquant, L.J.D. (1992) *An Invitation to Reflexive Sociology*. Cambridge: Polity Press.

Bowe, R. and Ball, S.J., with Gold, A. (1992) *Reforming Education and Changing Schools*. London: Routledge.

Boyne, G., Jenkins, G. and Poole, M. (1999) 'Human resource management in the public and private sectors: an empirical comparison'. *Public Administration*, 77(2), pp 406–20.

Bristow, G., Ireson, G. and Coleman, A. (2007) *A Life in the Day of a Headteacher*. Nottingham: NCSL.

Brown, G. (2007) 'Speech at the University of Greenwich', 31 October.

Brundrett, M., Fitzgerald, T. and Sommefeldt, D. (2006) 'The creation of national programmes of school leadership development in England and New Zealand: a comparative study'. *International Studies in Educational Administration*, 34(1), pp 89–105.

Burch, P. (2009) *Hidden Markets*. New York: Routledge.

Burnham, A. (2010) 'Speech to the National Children and Adult Services Conference', 4 November.

Burns, J.M. (1978) *Leadership*. New York: Harper and Row.

Bush, T. (2004) 'Editorial: The National College for School Leadership'. *Educational Management Administration and Leadership*, 32(3), pp 243–9.

Bush, T. and Glover, D. (2003) *School Leadership: Concepts and Evidence*. Nottingham: NCSL.

Bush, T. and Glover, D. (2004) *Leadership Development: Evidence and Beliefs*. Nottingham: NCSL.

Bush, T., Bell, L., Bolam, R., Glatter, R. and Ribbins, P. (eds) (1999) *Educational Management: Redefining Theory, Policy and Practice*. London: PCP.

Butt, G. and Gunter, H.M. (eds) (2007) *Modernizing Schools: People, Learning and Organizations*. London: Continuum.

Byrne, D. and Ozga, J. (2008) 'BERA review 2006: education research and policy'. *Research Papers in Education*, 23(4), pp 377–405.

Caldwell, B.J. (1999) 'The world is watching, Tony'. *Times Educational Supplement*, 11 June, Opinion Page.

Caldwell, B.J. (2006) *Re-imagining Educational Leadership*. London: Sage.

Caldwell, B.J. (undated) *Leadership and Innovation in the Transformation of Schools*. Nottingham: NCSL.

Callahan, R.E. (1962) *Education and the Cult of Efficiency*. Chicago: University of Chicago Press.

Cambell, P., Nash, K., Molyneux, L., Partington, S., Groves, N. and Stubbs, S. (2006a) *National Standards for Headteachers in Focus: Rural Schools*. Nottingham: NCSL.

Cambell, P., Nash, K., Molyneux, L., Partington, S., Groves, N. and Stubbs, S. (2006b) *National Standards for Headteachers in Focus: Small Schools*. Nottingham: NCSL.

Cammarota, J. and Fine, M. (2008) *Revolutionizing Education*. New York: Routledge.

CfBT (undated a) 'The London leadership strategy workstreams overview'. Available at: www.cfbt.com (accessed 17 October 2007).

CfBT (undated b) 'Leading the way in leadership development and talent management'. Available at: www.cfbt.com (accessed 17 October 2007).

Chapman, C. (2005) *Improving Schools through External Intervention*. London: Continuum.

Chapman, C. and Gunter, H.M. (2009) *Radical Reforms, Perspectives on an Era of Educational Change*. Abingdon: Routledge.

Chapman, C., Ainscow, M., Bragg, J., Gunter, H.M., Hull, J., Mongon, D., Muijs, D. and West, M. (2008) *Emerging Patterns of School Leadership*. Nottingham: NCSL.

Christopoulos, D.C. (2006) 'Relational attributes of political entrepreneurs: a network perspective'. *Journal of European Public Policy*, 13(5), pp 757–78.

Christopoulos, D.C. (2008) 'The governance of networks: heuristic or formal analysis? A reply to Rachel Parker'. *Political Studies*, 56(4), pp 475–81.

Chubb, J.E. and Moe, T.M. (1990) *Politics, Markets and America's Schools*. Washington, DC: The Brookings Institute.

Clark, L. (2010) 'After 13 years of New Labour, one in three primary pupils are still failing the 3Rs'. *Mail Online*. Available at: http://www.dailymail.co.uk/news/article-1299943/After-13-years-Labour-1-3-primary-pupils-failing-3Rs.html (accessed 10 August 2010).

Clark, P. (1998) *Back from the Brink*. London: Metro Books.

Clark, T. (2010) 'We have donors who wish to remain anonymous'. *EducationGuardian*, 6 July, p 5.

Clarke, C. (2004) *Transforming Secondary Education*. London: DfES.

Coburn, C.E. (2005) 'The role of nonsystem actors in the relationship between policy and practice: the case of reading instruction in California'. *Educational Evaluation and Policy Analysis*, 27(1), pp 23–52.

Cocentra (undated) 'School leadership and management, the buck stops here'. Available at: www.cocentra.com/cocentra/advisory/schoolsupport/schoolLM/ (accessed 29 October 2007).

Codd, J. (2005) 'Teachers as "managed professionals" in the global education industry: the New Zealand experience'. *Educational Review*, 57(2), pp 193–206.

Coe, R. (2009) 'School improvement: reality and illusion'. *British Journal of Educational Studies*, 57(4), pp 363–79.

Coleman, M. (2005) *Gender and Headship in the 21st Century*. Nottingham: NCSL.

Coles, M.J. and Southworth, G. (eds) (2005) *Developing Leadership*. Maidenhead: OUP.

Collarbone, P. (1999) 'The oxygen mask: an investigation into the establishment of the National College for School Leadership'. Unpublished EdD thesis, University of Lincolnshire and Humberside.

Collarbone, P. (2005) 'Touching tomorrow: remodelling in English Schools'. *The Australian Economic Review*, 38(1), pp 75–82.

Collarbone, P. (undated) *Reflections on Headship: Grounded Leadership – Lessons from the Field*. Nottingham: NCSL.

Collinson, M. and Collinson, D. (2005) *The Nature of Leadership*. Lancaster: Centre for Excellence in Leadership, Lancaster University Management School.

Connell, R. (2007) *Southern Theory: The Global Dynamics of Knowledge in Social Science*. Cambridge: Polity Press.

Connell, R., Fawcett, B. and Meagher, G. (2009) 'Neoliberalism, New Public management and the human service professions'. *Journal of Sociology*, 45(4), pp 331–8.

Coopers and Lybrand (1988) *Local Management of Schools. A Report to the Department of Education and Science*. London: DES.

Corson, D. (2000) 'Emancipatory leadership'. *International Journal of Leadership in Education*, 3(2), pp 93–120.

Coupland, C., Currie, G. and Boyett, I. (2008) 'New public management and a modernization agenda: implications for school leadership'. *International Journal of Public Administration*, 31(9), pp 1079–94.

Court, M. (2003a) *Different Approaches to Sharing School Leadership*. Nottingham: NCSL.

Court, M. (2003b) 'Towards democratic leadership: co-principal initiatives'. *International Journal of Leadership in Education*, 6(2), pp 161–83.

Crace, J. (2006) 'Children are less able than they used to be'. *The Guardian*. Available at: http://www.guardian.co.uk/education/2006/jan/24/schools.uk (accessed 22 August 2011).

Craig, I. (ed) (1989) *Primary Headship in the 1990s*. Harlow: Longman.

Cresswell, L., Morrisey, P. and Soles, G. (2006) *Personalising the Curriculum at 14–19*. Nottingham: NCSL.

Crow, G.M. (2004) 'The National College for School Leadership: a North American perspective on opportunities and challenges'. *Educational Management Administration and Leadership*, 32(3), pp 289–307.

Crow, G.M. and Weindling, D. (2010) 'Learning to be political: new English headteachers' roles'. *Educational Policy*, 24(1), pp 137–58.

CSE (undated) 'Brief biographical note on A. D. Mackay'. Available at: http://www.cse.edu.au (accessed 11 December 2010).

Cummings, A.J. (2002) 'NPQH: the making of a curriculum for headship'. Unpublished EdD thesis, Institution of Education, University of London.

Currie, G. and Lockett, A. (2007) 'A critique of transformational leadership: moral, professional and contingent dimensions of leadership within public services organizations'. *Human Relations*, 60(2), pp 341–70.

Currie, G., Boyett, G. and Suhomlinova, O. (2005) 'Transformational leadership within secondary schools in England. A panacea for organizational ills'. *Public Administration*, 83(2), pp 265–96.

Dale, R. (1989) *The State and Education Policy*. Milton Keynes: OUP.

Daniels, D. (2011) 'From reality to vision: the "birth" of the Petchey Academy in Hackney'. In H.M. Gunter (ed) *The State and Education Policy: The Academies Programme*. London: Continuum, pp 92–104.

Davies, L. (1997) 'The case for leaderless schools'. In K. Watson, C. Modgil and S. Modgil (eds) *Educational Dilemmas: Debate and Diversity, Volume Three, Power and Responsibility in Education*. London: Cassell, pp 304–15.

Davis, B. (2001) 'The Australian Principals Centre: a model for the accreditation and professional development of the principalship'. *International Studies in Educational Administration*, 29(2), pp 20–9.

Davis, R. (2011) 'Parents divided by city bankers' backing for "free school"'. *The Observer*, 16 January, p 11.

Day, C. and Harris, A. (undated) *Effective School Leadership*. Nottingham: NCSL.

Day, C., Harris. A., Hadfield, M., Tolley, H. and Beresford, J. (2000) *Leading Schools in Times of Change*. Buckingham: OUP.

Day, C., Sammons, P., Stobart, G., Kington, A. and Gu, Q. (2007) *Teachers Matter*. Maidenhead: OUP.

Day, C., Sammons, P., Hopkins, D., Harris, A., Leithwood, K., Gu, Q., Brown, E., Ahtaridou, E. and Kington, A. (2009) *The Impact of School Leadership on Pupil Outcomes*. London: DCSF/NCSL.

Denham, A. and Garnett, M. (2006) '"What works"? British think tanks and the "end of ideology"'. *The Political Quarterly*, 77(2), pp 156–65.

DES (Department of Education and Science) (1985) *Better Schools*. London: DES.

DfE (Department for Education) (2010a) *The Importance of Teaching: Schools White Paper*. London: DfE.

DfE (2010b) 'The case for school freedom: national and international evidence (Gove mythbuster 2)'. Available at: http://teachers.org.uk/files/mythbusters-busted.doc (accessed 2 July 2010).

DfE (2010c) *School Teachers' Pay and Conditions Document 2010 and Guidance on School Teachers' Pay and Conditions*. London: DfE.

DfE (2011a) 'School Improvement Partner (SIP) programme'. Available at: http://nationalstrategies.standards.dcsf.gov.uk/node/186547 (accessed 7 February 2011).

DfE (2011b) 'Specialist schools – overview'. Available at: http://www.education.gov.uk/schools/pupilsupport/sen/supportinglearners/a0011046/specialist-schools-overview (accessed 7 February 2011).

DfEE (Department for Education and Employment) (1997) *Excellence in Schools*. Cm 3681. London: DfEE.

DfEE (1998a) *teachers: meeting the challenge of change*. London: DfEE.

DfEE (1998b) *teachers: meeting the challenge of change, Technical Consultation Document on Pay and Performance Management*. London: DfEE.

DfEE (1998c) *teachers: meeting the challenge of change, Summary*. London: DfEE.

DfEE (1998d) *teachers: meeting the challenge of change, Response Form*. London: DfEE.

DfEE (2000) *Influence or Irrelevance: Can Social Science Improve Government?* London: DfEE.

DfES (Department for Education and Skills) (2002a) *Time for Standards, Reforming the School Workforce*. London: DfES.

DfES (2002b) *Developing the Role of School Support Staff.* London: DfES.

DfES (2002c) *Developing the Role of School Support Staff, Consultation Response Form.* London: DfES.

DfES (2002d) *Planning Guidance for Primary Teachers.* London: DfES.

DfES (2003) *Special Report, the Government's Proposals to Reduce Teacher Workload and Raise Standards.* London: DfES.

DfES (2004a) *Smoking Out Underachievement, Guidance and Advice to Help Secondary Schools Use Value Added Approaches with Data.* London: DfES.

DfES (2004b) *National Standards for Headteachers.* London: DfES.

DfES (2004c) *Every Child Matters: Change for Children in Schools.* London: DfES.

DfES (2004d) *Five Year Strategy for Children and Learners.* Cm 6272, White Paper, July. London: DfES.

DfES (2005) *Higher Standards, Better Schools for All, More Choice for Parents and Pupils.* Cm 6677, White Paper. London: HM Government.

DfES and Ofsted (Office for Standards in Education) (2004) *A New Relationship with Schools.* London: DfES.

DfES and PwC (PricewaterhouseCoopers) (2007) *Independent Study into School Leadership.* London: DfES.

Domhoff, G.W. (2006) 'The limitations of regime theory'. *City and Community*, 5(1), pp 47–51.

Du Quesnay, H. (2004) *Speech to the Primary Strategy Conference 2004.* Nottingham: NCSL.

Eacott, S. (2011) 'Preparing "educational" leaders in managerialist times: an Australian story'. *Journal of Educational Administration and History*, 43(1), pp 43–59.

Earl, L., Watson, N., Levin, B., Leithwood, K., Fullan, M., Torrance, N., Jantzi, D., Mascall, B. and Volante, L. (2003) *Watching and Learning 3. Executive Summary. Final Report of the External Evaluation of England's National Literacy and Numeracy Strategies.* Toronto: Ontario Institute for Studies in Education, University of Toronto.

Earley, P. and Evans, J. (2004) 'Making a difference?'. *Educational Management Administration and Leadership*, 32(3), pp 325–38.

Earley, P., Evans, J., Collarbone, P., Gold, A. and Halpin, D. (2002) *Establishing the Current State of School Leadership in England.* London: DfES.

Evans, R. (2011) 'What Gove forgot to say?'. *EducationGuardian*, 4 January, p 1.

Fairclough, N. (2000) *New Labour, New Language?* London: Routledge.

Fielding, M. (2000) 'Community, philosophy and education policy: against effectiveness ideology and the immiseration of contemporary schooling'. *Journal of Education Policy*, 15(4), pp 397–415.

Fielding, M. (2006) 'Leadership, radical student engagement and the necessity of person-centred education'. *International Journal of Leadership in Education*, 9(4), pp 299–313.

Fielding, M. (2007a) 'On the necessity of radical state education: democracy and the common school'. *Journal of Philosophy of Education*, 41(4), pp 539–57.

Fielding, M. (2007b) 'Beyond "voice": new roles, relations, and contexts in researching with young people'. *Discourse*, 28(3), pp 301–10.

Fielding, M. and Moss, P. (2011) *Radical Education and the Common School*. Abingdon: Routledge.

Fincham, R. (1999) 'The consultant–client relationship: critical perspectives on the management of organizational change'. *Journal of Management Studies*, 36(3), pp 335–51.

Fink, D. and Hargreaves, A. (2006) *Sustainable Leadership*. San Francisco, CA: Jossey-Bass.

Fitz, J. and Hafid, T. (2007) 'Perspectives on the privatisation of schooling in England and Wales'. *Educational Policy*, 21(1), pp 273–96.

Fitz, J. and Halpin, D. (1991) 'From a "sketchy policy" to a "workable scheme": the DES and grant-maintained schools'. *International Studies in the Sociology of Education*, 1(1), pp 129–51.

Fitz, J., Halpin, D. and Power, S. (1994) 'Implementation research and education policy: practice and prospects'. *British Journal of Educational Studies*, 42(1), pp 53–69.

Fitzgerald, T. (2007) 'Remodelling schools and schooling, teachers and teaching: a New Zealand perspective'. In G. Butt and H.M. Gunter (eds) *Modernizing Schools*. London: Continuum, pp 163–76.

Forde, R., Hobby, R. and Lees, A. (2000) *The Lessons of Leadership*. London: Hay Management Consultants Ltd.

Foster, W. (1986) *Paradigms and Promises*. Amherst, NY: Prometheus Books.

Foster, W. (1989) 'Towards a critical practice of leadership'. In J. Smyth (ed) *Critical Perspectives on Educational Leadership*. London: Falmer Press, pp 39–62.

Frankham, J. (2006) 'Network utopias and alternative entanglements for educational research and practice'. *Journal of Educational Policy*, 21(6), pp 661–77.

Fraser, N. (2007) 'Feminist politics in the age of recognition: a two-dimensional approach to gender justice'. *Studies in Social Justice*, 1(1), pp 23–35.

Fullan, M. (1999) *Change Forces: The Sequel*. London: Falmer.

Fullan, M. (undated) *The Role of the Head in School Improvement*. Nottingham: NCSL.

Galton, M. (2007) 'New Labour and education: an evidence-based analysis'. *Forum*, 49(1/2), pp 157–77.

Gewirtz, S. (2000) 'Bringing the politics back in: a critical analysis of quality discourses in education'. *British Journal of Educational Studies*, 48(4), pp 352–70.

Gewirtz, S. (2001) 'Cloning the Blairs: New Labour's programme for the re-socialization on working-class parents'. *Journal of Education Policy*, 16(4), pp 365–78.

Gewirtz, S. (2002) *The Managerial School.* London: Routledge.

Gewirtz, S. and Ball, S.J. (2000) 'From "welfarism" to "new managerialism": shifting discourses of school headship in the education marketplace'. *Discourse: Studies in the Cultural Politics of Education*, 21(3), pp 253–68.

Gewirtz, S. and Ozga, J. (1990) 'Partnership, pluralism and education policy: a reassessment'. *Journal of Education Policy*, 5(1), pp 37–48.

Gibbons, M., Limoges, C., Nowotny, H., Schwartzman, S., Scott, P. and Trow, M. (2007) *The New Production of Knowledge.* London: Sage.

Giddens, A. (2000) *The Third Way and Its Critics.* Cambridge: Polity Press.

Giddens, A. (2010) 'The rise and fall of New Labour'. *New Statesman*, 17 May, pp 25–7.

Gillard, D. (2011a) 'The history of education in England, Chapter 10: 1997–2007, the Blair decade: selection, privatisation and faith'. Available at: http://www.educationengland.org.uk/history/chapter10.html (accessed 5 February 2011).

Gillard, D. (2011b) 'The history of education in England, Chapter 12: 2010, what future for education in England?'. Available at: http://www.educationengland.org.uk/history/chapter12.html (accessed 5 February 2011).

Gillborn, D. (1994) 'The micro-politics of macro reform'. *British Journal of Sociology of Education*, 15(2), pp 147–64.

Glatter, R. and Harvey, J.A. (2006) *Varieties of Shared Headship: A Preliminary Exploration.* Nottingham: NCSL.

Gleeson, D. (2011) 'Academies and the myth of evidence-based policy: limits and possibilities'. In H.M. Gunter (ed) *The State and Education Policy: The Academies Programme.* London: Continuum, pp 199–211.

Gleeson, D. and Husbands, C. (eds) (2001) *The Performing School.* London: RoutledgeFalmer.

Glickman, C. (1998) 'Educational leadership for democratic purpose: what do we mean?'. *International Journal of Leadership in Education*, 1(1), pp 47–53.

Gold, A., Evans, J., Earley, P., Halpin, D. and Collarbone, P. (2003) 'Principled principals? Values-driven leadership: evidence from ten case studies of "outstanding" school leaders'. *Educational Management and Administration*, 31(2), pp 127–38.

Goldring, E. and Mavrogordato, M. (2011) 'International perspectives on academies: lessons learned from charter schools and choice options around the globe'. In H.M. Gunter (ed) *The State and Education Policy: The Academies Programme*. London: Continuum, pp 185–98.

Goldstein, H. and Woodhouse, G. (2000) 'School effectiveness research and education policy'. *Oxford Review of Education*, 26(3/4), pp 353–63.

Goodwin, M. (2009) 'Which networks matter in education governance? A reply to Ball's "New Philanthropy, New Networks and New Governance in Education"'. *Political Studies*, 57(3), pp 680–7.

Gorard, S. (2010) 'Serious doubts about school effectiveness'. *British Educational Research Journal*, 36(5), pp 645–766.

Goss, P. (2008) *An Investigation into the Possible Pressures on Headteachers – Particularly the Current School Inspection Arrangements in England and Wales – and the Potential Impact on Recruitment*. London: NAHT.

Goulden, R. and Robinson, L. (2006) *National Standards for Headteachers in Focus: Schools with a Religious Foundation*. Nottingham: NCSL.

Gove, M. (2009) 'A comprehensive programme for state education'. Speech, 6 October. Available at: http://www.michaelgove.com/content/comprehensive_programme_state_education (accessed 29 September 2010).

Gove, M. (2010a) Speech to the National College Annual Conference, 17 June 2010. Available at: http://www.michaelgove.com/content/national_college_annual_conference (accessed 29 September 2010).

Gove, M. (2010b) 'New leadership for children in need'. Press Notice. Available at: http://www.education.gov.uk/inthenews/pressnotices/a0067808/new-leadership-for-children-in-need (accessed 20 November 2010).

Gove, M. (2010c) 'Letter to Ed Balls'. Department for Education, 7 June.

Gove, M. (2010d) 'Public bodies reform. Letter to Vanni Treves', 24 November. Available at: http://www.nationalcollege.org.uk/docinfo?id=141051&filename=sos-gove-letter-nov10.pdf (accessed 10 January 2011).

Government of New Zealand (1988) *Tomorrow's Schools: The Reform of Education Administration in New Zealand*. Wellington: Government Printer.

Grace, G. (1995) *School Leadership: Beyond Educational Management*. London: The Falmer Press.

Grace, G. (2000) 'Research and the challenges of contemporary school leadership: the contribution of critical scholarship'. *British Journal of Educational Studies*, 48(3), pp 231–47.

Gray, J. (2010) 'The nanny diaries'. *New Statesman*, 11 January, pp 52–3.

Gregg, P., Grout, P., Ratciffe, A., Smith, S. and Windmeijer, F. (2008) 'How important is pro-social behaviour in the delivery of public services?'. CMPO Working Paper Series No 08/197. Available at: http://www.bris.ac.uk/Depts/CMPO/workingpapers/wp197.pdf (accessed 10 June 2008).

Griffiths, M. (1998) *Educational Research for Social Justice*. Buckingham: OUP.

Gronn, P. (2003) *The New Work of Educational Leaders*. London: Sage.

Gronn, P. (2010) 'Leadership: its genealogy, configuration and trajectory'. *Journal of Educational Administration and History*, 42(4), pp 405–35.

Gross, S.J. (2008) '(Re-)Constructing a movement for social justice in our profession'. In A.H. Normore (ed) *Leadership for Social Justice*. Charlotte, NC: IAP, pp 257–66.

Grubb, W.N. and Flessa, J.J. (2006) '"A job too big for one": multiple principals and other non-traditional approaches to school leadership'. *Educational Administration Quarterly*, 42(4), pp 518–50.

Guldberg, H. (2009) *Reclaiming Childhood*. Abingdon: Routledge.

Gunter, H.M. (1997) *Rethinking Education: The Consequences of Jurassic Management*. London: Cassell.

Gunter, H.M. (1999) 'An intellectual history of the field of educational management from 1960'. Unpublished PhD thesis, Keele University.

Gunter, H.M. (2001a) *Leaders and Leadership in Education*. London: PCP.

Gunter, H.M. (2001b) 'Modernising headteachers as leaders: an analysis of the NPQH'. In M. Fielding (ed) (2001) *Taking Education Really Seriously: Three Years Hard Labour*. London: Routledge/Falmer, pp 155–68.

Gunter, H.M. (2004) 'Labels and labelling in the field of educational leadership'. *Discourse*, 25(1), pp 21–42.

Gunter, H.M. (2005) 'Putting education back into leadership'. *Forum* (Special double issue: Reclaiming the Radical Agenda), 47(2/3), pp 181–7.

Gunter, H.M. (2009) 'The "C" word in educational research: an appreciative response'. *Critical Studies in Education*, 50(1), pp 93–102.

Gunter, H.M. (ed) (2011) *The State and Education Policy: The Academies Programme*. London: Continuum.

Gunter, H.M. and Fitzgerald, T. (2008) 'The future of leadership research'. *School Leadership and Management*, 28(3), pp 263–80.

Gunter, H.M. and Forrester, G. (2008) 'New Labour and school leadership 1997–2007'. *British Journal of Educational Studies*, 55(2), pp 144–62.

Gunter, H.M. and Forrester, G. (2009a) 'Institutionalised governance: the case of the National College for School Leadership'. *International Journal of Public Administration*, 32(5), pp 349–69.

Gunter, H.M. and Forrester, G. (2009b) 'School leadership and policymaking in England'. *Policy Studies*, 31(5), pp 495–511.

Gunter, H.M. and Thomson, P. (2009) 'The makeover: a new logic in leadership development in England?'. *Educational Review*, 61(4), pp 469–83.

Gunter, H.M. and Thomson, P. (2010) 'Life on Mars: headteachers before the National College'. *Journal of Educational Administration and History*, 42(3), pp 203–22.

Gunter, H.M., Hall, D. and Bragg, J. (forthcoming) *Distributed Leadership: A Study of Knowledge Production*.

Gunter, H.M., Raffo, C., Hall, D., Dyson, A., Jones, L. and Kalambouka, A. (2010) 'Policy and the policy process'. In C. Raffo, A. Dyson, H.M Gunter, D. Hall, L. Jones and A. Kalambouka (eds) *Education and Poverty in Affluent Countries*. London: Routledge, pp 163–76.

Hall, I. (undated) 'The new school leader'. Available at: www.nationaleducationtrust.net (accessed 19 October 2007).

Hall, V. and Southworth, G. (1997) 'Headship'. *School Leadership and Management*, 17(2), pp 151–69.

Hall, V., MacKay, H. and Morgan, C. (1986) *Headteachers at Work*. Milton Keynes: OUP.

Hallinger, P. and Heck, R.H. (1996) 'Reassessing the principal's role in school effectiveness: a review of empirical research, 1980–1995'. *Educational Administration Quarterly*, 32(1), pp 5–44.

Hallinger, P. and Snidvongs, K. (2005) *Adding Value to School Leadership and Management*. Nottingham: NCSL.

Hamilton, D. (1999) 'Peddling feel-good fictions'. In P. Sammons (ed) *School Effectiveness, Coming of Age in the Twenty-First Century*. Lisse, The Netherlands: Swets and Zeitlinger Publishers, pp 219–22.

Harding, A. (2000) 'Regime formation in Manchester and Edinburgh'. In G. Stoker (2000) *The New Politics of British Local Governance*. Basingstoke: MacMillan, pp 54–71.

Hargreaves, A. and Fink, D. (2006) 'Canadian approaches to school improvement and educational change'. In J.C. Lee and M. Williams (eds) *School Improvement: International Perspectives*. New York: Nova Science Publishers Inc, pp 257–80.

Hargreaves, D.H. (2003) *Education Epidemic, Transforming Secondary Schools through Innovation Networks*. London: Demos.

Hargreaves, D.H. (2004) *Personalising Learning: Next Steps in Working Laterally*. London: Specialist Schools and Academies Trust.

Hargreaves, D.H. (2006) '*Personalising Learning*'. *In Booklets 1–6*. London: Specialist Schools and Academies Trust.

Hargreaves, D.H. (2010) *Creating a Self-Improving School*. Nottingham: National College.

Harris, A. (2005) 'Leading from the chalk-face: an overview of school leadership'. *Leadership*, 1(1), pp 73–87.

Harris, A. (2008) *Distributed School Leadership*. London: Routledge.

Harris, A. and Chapman, C. (2002) *Effective Leadership in Schools Facing Challenging Circumstances*. Nottingham: NCSL.

Harris, A. and Muijs, D. (2003) *Teacher Leadership: Principals and Practice*. Nottingham: NCSL.

Harris, A., Day, C., Hadfield, M., Hopkins, D., Hargreaves, A. and Chapman, C. (2003) *Effective Leadership for School Improvement*. London: RoutledgeFalmer.

Harris, A., James, S., Gunraj, J., Clarke, P. and Harris, B. (2006a) *Improving Schools in Exceptionally Challenging Circumstances*. London: Continuum.

Harris, A., Moos, L., Møller, J., Robertson, J. and Spillane, J. (2006b) *Challenging Leadership Practice*. Nottingham: NCSL.

Harrison, A. (2010) 'Truancy in schools in England reaches record high'. BBC News, 25 March. Available at: http://news.bbc.co.uk/1/hi/education/8586770.stm (accessed 25 March 2010).

Hartle, F. (undated) *Shaping Up To The Future*, Nottingham: NCSL. Available at: www.ncsl.org.uk (accessed 10/07/2007).

Hartle, F. and Thomas, K. (2003) *Growing Tomorrow's School Leaders: The Challenge*. Nottingham: NCSL.

Hartley, D. (2007) 'The emergence of distributed leadership in education; why now?'. *British Journal of Educational Studies*, 55(2), pp 202–14.

Hartley, D. (2010) 'The management of education and the social theory of the firm: from distributed leadership to collaborative community'. *Journal of Educational Administration and History*, 42(4), pp 345–61.

Hasenclever, A., Mayer, P. and Rittberger, V. (1997) *Theories of International Regimes*. Cambridge: Cambridge University Press.

Hatcher, R. (1998) 'Social justice and the politics of school effectiveness and improvement'. *Race Ethnicity and Education*, 1(2), pp 267–89.

Hatcher, R. (2001) 'Getting down to business: schooling in the globalised economy'. *Education and Social Justice*, 3(2), pp 45–59.

Hatcher, R. (2005) 'The distribution of leadership and power in schools'. *British Journal of Sociology of Education*, 26(2), pp 253–67.

Hatcher, R. (2006) 'Privatisation and sponsorship: the re-agenting of the school system in England'. *Journal of Education Policy*, 21(5), pp 599–619.

Hatcher, R. (2008) 'Academies and diplomas: two strategies for shaping the future workforce'. *Oxford Review of Education*, 34(6), pp 665–76.

Hatcher, R. and Troyna, B. (1994) 'The "policy cycle"; a ball by ball account'. *Journal of Education Policy*, 9(2), pp 155–70.

Hattersley, R. (2010) 'The long morning after'. *New Statesman*, 15 November, pp 24–7.

Hay Group (undated) 'Education'. Available at: www.haygroup.com (accessed 17 October 2007).

Hay McBer (2000) *Research into Teacher Effectiveness.* Available at: www. education.gov.uk/rsgateway/DB/RRP/u012734/index/shtml (accessed 16 October 2000).

Hayes, D. (1995) 'The primary head's tale: collaborative relationships in a time of rapid change'. *Educational Management and Administration,* 23(4), pp 233–44.

Helsby, G. (1999) *Changing Teachers' Work.* Buckingham: OUP.

Hill, R. (2010) *Chain Reactions: A Think Piece on the Development of Chains of Schools in the English School System.* Nottingham: National College.

HM Government (2010) *The Coalition: Our Programme of Government.* London: Cabinet Office.

Hodge, G. and Bowman, D. (2006) 'The "consultocracy": the business of reforming government'. In G. Hodge (ed) *Privatisation and Market Development.* Cheltenham: Edward Elgar, pp 97–126.

Hodgson, P. (2006) 'The rise and rise of the regulatory state'. *The Political Quarterly,* 77(2), pp 247–54.

Holliday, I. (2000) 'Is the British state hollowing out?'. *The Political Quarterly,* 71(2), pp 167–76.

Hollins, K., Gunter, H.M. and Thomson, P. (2006) 'Living Improvement: a case study of a secondary school in England'. *Improving Schools,* 9(2), pp 141–52.

Hood, C. (2007) 'Intellectual obsolescence and intellectual makeovers: reflections on the tools of government after two decades'. *Governance: An International Journal of Policy, Administration, and Institutions,* 20(10), pp 127–44.

Hood, C. and Jackson, M. (1991) *Administrative Argument.* Aldershot: Dartmouth Publishing Company Limited.

Hood, C., Rothstein, H. and Baldwin, R. (2004) *The Government of Risk.* Oxford: Oxford University Press.

Hopkins, D. (2001) *'Think Tank' Report to Governing Council.* Nottingham: NCSL.

Hopkins, D. (2007) *Every School a Great School.* Maidenhead: OUP.

House of Commons (1998) *The Role of Headteachers. Ninth Report, Volume 1, Education and Employment Committee.* London: The Stationery Office.

Hoyle, E. (1982) 'Micropolitics of educational organisations'. *Educational Management and Administration,* 10(2), pp 87–98.

Hoyle, E. and Wallace, M. (2005) *Educational Leadership: Ambiguity, Professionals and Managerialism.* London: Sage.

HTI (Headteachers into Industry) (2007) 'Stretch, interim assignments for lasting change'. Available at: www.hti.org.uk (accessed 17 October 2007).

Huber, S., Moorman, H. and Pont, B. (2007) *School Leadership for Systemic Improvement in England. A Case Study Report for the OECD Activity Improving School Leadership.* Paris: OECD.

Hyman, P. (2005) *One Out Of Ten: From Downing Street Vision to Classroom Reality.* London: Vintage.

Hyman, P. (2011) 'The Tories want to send schools back by 50 years'. *New Statesman,* 24 January, pp 25–7.

Iedema, R., Degeling, P., Braithwaite, J. and White, L. (2003) '"It's an interesting conversation I'm hearing": the doctor as manager'. *Organization Studies,* 25(1), pp 15–33.

Innovative Schools (2010) 'Welcome to Innovative Schools'. Available at: http://www.innovativeschools.co.uk (accessed 12 February 2010).

Ireson, J. (2007) *A Study of Hard Federations of Small Primary Schools.* Nottingham: NCSL.

Jackson, D.S. (2000) 'The school improvement journey: perspectives on leadership'. *School Leadership and Management,* 20(1), pp 61–78.

Jackson, D.S. (2001) 'The research section: further information'. Unpublished job application pack. Nottingham: NCSL.

Jenkins, S. (2010) 'Another middle-class escape tunnel parents don't want'. *The Guardian,* 21 September. Available at: http://www.guardian. co.uk/commentisfree/2010/sep/21/middle-class-escape-free-schools (accessed 21 September 2010).

Jessop, B. (2002) *The Future of the Capitalist State.* Cambridge: Polity Press.

Johnson, A. (2003) 'Centre for Excellence in Leadership launch London Studios', 8 October. Available at: www.dcsf.gov.uk/speeches/ search_detail.cfm?ID=90,(accessed 20 November 2009) (Document is now located at the National Archives (http:nationalarchives.gov.uk).)

Johnson, A. (2007) *National College for School Leadership (NCSL) Priorities: 2007–08.* London: DfES.

Johnson, G.C., Møller, J. and Portin, B.S. (2009) 'Special issue: researching leadership for learning'. *International Journal of Leadership in Education,* 12(3), pp 217–318.

Joseph, K. (1984) 'Speech by the Rt Hon Sir Keith Joseph, Secretary of State for Education and Science, at the North of England Education Conference, Sheffield, on Friday 6th January 1984'. *Oxford Review of Education,* 10(2), pp 137–46.

Judt, T. (2010) *Ill Fares the Land.* New York: The Penguin Press.

Kelly, R. (2004) *National College for School Leadership Priorities: 2005–06.* London: DfES.

Kelly, R. (2005a) *National College for School Leadership Priorities: 2006–07.* London: DfES.

Kelly, R. (2005b) 'New heads conference', 17 November. Available at: www.dcsf.gov.uk/speeches/search_detail.cfm?ID=288 (accessed 20 November 2009). (Document is now located at the National Archives (http:nationalarchives.gov.uk).)

Kerr, K. and West, M. (eds) (2010) *BERA Insight: Schools and Social Inequality*, London: BERA.

Kimber, M. (undated) *Does Size Matter?* Nottingham: NCSL.

King, A. (1976) 'The problem of overload'. In A. King (ed) *Why is Britain Becoming Harder to Govern?* London: BBC, pp 8–30.

Kingdon, J. W. (2003) *Agendas, Alternatives, and Public Policies.* New York: Longman.

Knight, J. (2006) 'Perspectives on Leadership for Systemic Improvements'. Speech to the OECD International Conference. Available at: www.dcsf.gov.uk/speeches/search_detail.cfm?ID=370 (accessed 20 November 2009). (Document is now located at the National Archives (http:nationalarchives.gov.uk).)

Knight, J. (2007) 'Address to the National Governors Association', 27 January. Available at: www.dcsf.gov.uk/speeches/search_detail.cfm?ID=503 (accessed 20 November 2009). (Document is now located at the National Archives (http:nationalarchives.gov.uk).)

Lapsley, I. and Oldfield, R. (2001) 'Transforming the public sector: management consultants as agents of change'. *The European Accounting Review*, 10(3), pp 523–43.

Lather, P. (1991) *Feminist Research in Education: Within/Against.* Geelong, Vic: Deakin University.

Law, J. and Hassard, J. (1999) *Actor Network Theory and After.* Oxford: Blackwell.

Law, S. (2006) *The War for Children's Minds.* Abingdon: Routledge.

Lawn, M. and Lingard, B. (2002) 'Constructing a European policy space in educational governance: the role of transnational policy actors'. *European Educational Research Journal*, 1(2), pp 290–307.

Learmonth, M. (2005) 'Doing things with words: the case of "management" and "administration"'. *Public Administration*, 83(3), pp 617–37.

Lee, K. (2006) *More Than a Feeling: Developing the Emotionally Literate Secondary School.* Nottingham: NCSL.

Leggett, B.M. (1997) 'Pressures of managerialism and its implications: perspectives from the centre and the secondary school'. *Australian Journal of Education*, 41(3), pp 276–88.

Leithwood, K. (2001) 'School leadership in the context of accountability'. *International Journal of Leadership in Education*, 4(3), pp 217–35.

Leithwood, K. and Levin, B. (2004) 'Assessing school leader and leadership programme effects on pupil learning'. Paper presented to the Researching the Impact of School Leadership DfES Seminar, 8 March, London.

Leithwood, K. and Levin, B. (2005) *Assessing School Leader and Leadership Programme Effects on Pupil Learning.* London: DfES.

Leithwood, K.A. and Riehl, C. (2003) *What We Know About Successful School Leadership.* Nottingham: NCSL.

Leithwood, K., Jantzi, D. and Steinbach, R. (1999) *Changing Leadership for Changing Times.* Buckingham: OUP.

Leithwood, K., Day, C., Sammons, P., Harris, A. and Hopkins, D. (2006a) *Seven Strong Claims about Successful School Leadership.* Nottingham: NCSL.

Leithwood, K., Day, C., Sammons, P., Harris, A. and Hopkins, D. (2006b) *Successful School Leadership, What It Is and How It Influences Pupil Learning.* London: DfES/NCSL.

Leo, E., Galloway, D. and Hearne, P. (2010) *Academies and Educational Reform, Governance, Leadership and Strategy.* Bristol: Multilingual Matters.

Lightfoot, L. (1991) 'Back to the blackboard'. *The Mail on Sunday,* 10 November, p 1.

Lightfoot, L. (2010) 'Schools are lining up to be free. But not enough for Mr Gove'. *The Observer,* 5 September, p 34.

Lindsay, G., Muijs, D., Harris, A., Chapman, C., Arweck, E. and Goodall, J. (2007) *Evaluation of the Federations Programme.* London: DfES.

Lingard, B. and Ozga, J. (2007) 'Introduction, reading education policy and politics'. In B. Lingard and J. Ozga (eds) *The RoutledgeFalmer Reader in Education Policy and Politics.* London: Routledge.

Lingard, B., Hayes, D., Mills, M. and Christie, P. (2003) *Leading Learning.* Maidenhead: OUP.

Lloyd, S. (2005) *Distributed Leadership: The Rhetoric and the Reality.* Nottingham: NCSL.

Lumby, J., Crow, G. and Pashiardis, P. (eds) (2008) *International Handbook of the Preparation and Development of School Leaders.* New York: Routledge.

Lyons, G., Jirasinghe, D., Ewers, C. and Edwards, S. (1993) 'The development of a Headteachers' Assessment Centre'. *Educational Management and Administration,* 21(4), pp 245–8.

Macaulay, H. (2008) *Under the Microscope.* Nottingham: NCSL.

MacBeath, J. (1998) *Effective School Leadership.* London: PCP.

MacBeath, J. and Moos, L. (2004) *Democratic Learning.* London: RoutledgeFalmer.

MacBeath, J. and Mortimore, P. (eds) (2001) *Improving School Effectiveness.* Buckingham: OUP.

MacBeath, J., Oduro, G.K.T. and Waterhouse, J. (2004) *Distributed Leadership in Action: Full Report.* Nottingham: NCSL.

MacKay, T. (2011) 'President's welcome'. Available at: http://www.icsei.net/index.php?id=542 (accessed 12 February 2011).

Maguire, M., Perryman, J., Ball, S.J. and Braun, A. (2009) 'The Ordinary School – what is it?'. Paper presented to the British Educational Research Association Conference, Manchester, September.

Mahony, P., Hextall, I. and Menter, I. (2004) 'Building dams in Jordan, assessing teachers in England: a case study in edu-business'. *Globalisation, Societies and Education,* 2(2), pp 277–96.

Maloney, R.J. (2009) 'Contextualising headship: a qualitative analysis of the situated experiences of five headteachers'. Unpublished PhD thesis, King's College, London.

Mandelson, P. and Liddle, R. (1996) *The Blair Revolution, Can New Labour Deliver?* London: Faber and Faber.

Mansell, W. (2009) 'PISA tests: don't rush to judgement but these scores do raise serious questions'. Available at: http://www.naht.org.uk/welcome/resources/blogs/warwick-mansell's-blog/?blogpost=, Document is now located at the National Archives (http:nationalarchives.gov.uk) (accessed 5 February 2011).

Mansell, W. (2010) 'Redundant promises'. *EducationGuardian,* 12 October, pp 1–2.

Marinetto, M. (2003) 'Governing beyond the centre: a critique of the Anglo-Governance School'. *Political Studies,* 51, pp 592–608.

Marley, D. (2009) 'Five-fold leap in number of heads sacked'. *Times Educational Supplement,* 6 March, p 1.

Marquand, D. (1981) 'Club government – the crisis of the Labour Party in the national perspective'. *Government and Opposition,* 16(1), pp 19–36.

Marquand, D. (2004) *Decline of the Public.* Cambridge: Polity Press.

Marquand, D. (2009) 'The warrior woman'. *New Statesman,* 2 March, pp 16–19.

Mayers, B. (2010) 'Letter in reply to freedom of information request', 1 November.

McCrone, T., Rudd, P., Blenkinsop, S., Wade, P., Rutt, S. and Yeshanew, T. (2007) *Evaluation of the Impact of Section 5 Inspections.* Slough: NFER.

McEwen, A. and Salters, M. (1997) 'Values and management: the role of the primary school headteacher'. *School Leadership and Management,* 17(1), pp 69–79.

McGaw, B. (undated) *Some Research Issues for the National College for School Leadership.* Nottingham: NCSL.

McNamara, O., Howson, J., Gunter, H.M. and Fryers, A. (2009) *The Leadership Aspirations and Careers of Black and Ethnic Minority Teachers.* Birmingham: NASUWT.

McNamara, O., Howson, J., Gunter, H.M. and Fryers, A. (2010) *No Job for a Woman. The Impact of Gender in School Leadership.* Birmingham: NASUWT.

Menter, I., Holligan, C. and Mthenjwa, V. (2005) 'Reaching the parts that need to be reached? The impact of the Scottish Qualification for Headship'. *School Leadership and Management,* 25(1), pp 7–23.

Mercer, D. (1996) '"Can they walk on water?": professional isolation and the secondary headteacher'. *School Organisation,* 16(2), pp 165–78.

Merrick, N. (1992) 'How to win top prize in the lottery'. *Times Educational Supplement,* 8 May, p 4.

Midwinter, A. (2001) 'New Labour and the modernisation of British local government: a critique'. *Financial Accountability and Management,* 17(4), pp 311–20.

Miliband, D. (2003a) 'Challenges for school leadership'. Speech to the SHA Conference On Leadership, London, 1 July. Available at: www.dcsf.gov.uk/speeches/search_detail.cfm?ID=81(accessed 20 November 2009). (Document is now located at the National Archives (http:nationalarchives.gov.uk).)

Miliband, D. (2003b) 'School leadership: the productivity challenge'. Speech to the National College for School Leadership, 22 October. Available at: www.dcsf.gov.uk/speeches/search_detail.cfm?ID=91 (accessed 20 November 2009). (Document is now located at the National Archives (http:nationalarchives.gov.uk).)

Miliband, D. (2004a) 'Building success for the Blair generation'. Speech to the Annual Meeting of the Secondary Heads Association, 26 March. Available at: www.dfes.gov.uk/speeches/latest.cfm (accessed 30 March 2004). (Document is now located at the National Archives (http:nationalarchives.gov.uk).)

Miliband, D. (2004b) 'Personalised learning: building a new relationship with schools'. Speech to the North of England Conference, Belfast, 8 January.

Millar, F. (2011) 'The bribes to schools aren't looking quite so shiny now'. *Education Guardian,* 11 January, p 2.

Millar, F. and Benn, M. (2009) 'Bury the good news'. *New Statesman,* 23 March, pp 36–40.

Miller, P. and Rose, N. (2008) *Governing the Present.* Cambridge: Polity Press.

Molnar, A. (2006) 'The commercial transformation of public education'. *Journal of Education Policy,* 21(5), pp 621–40.

Moore, A., George, R. and Halpin, D. (2002) 'The developing role of the headteacher in English Schools: management, leadership and pragmatism'. *Educational Management and Administration,* 30(2), pp 175–88.

Moran, M. (2007) *The British Regulatory State*. Oxford: Oxford University Press.

Morley, L. and Rassool, N. (1999) *School Effectiveness: Fracturing the Discourse*. London: Falmer Press.

Morris, E. (2001) *Professionalism and Trust, Social Market Foundation Speech*. London: DfES.

Morrison, N. (2009) 'Heads who can't teach'. *TES Magazine*, 6 March, pp 11–17.

Mortimore, P. (2009) 'Ignoring bad news is politically naïve'. *EducationGuardian*, 6 January.

Mossberger, K. and Stoker, G. (2001) 'The evolution of urban regime theory: the challenge of conceptualisation'. *Urban Affairs Review*, 36(6), pp 810–35.

Mulderrig, J. (2003) 'Consuming education: a critical discourse analysis of social actors in New Labour's education policy'. *The Journal for Critical Education Policy Studies*. Available at: www.jceps.com/index.php?pageeID=homes&issueID=1 (accessed 21 November 2008).

Mulford, B. (2004) 'Organizational life cycles and the development of the National College for School Leadership: an Antipodean view'. *Educational Management Administration and Leadership*, 32(3), pp 309–24.

Mulgan, G. (2006) 'Thinking in tanks: the changing ecology of political ideas'. *The Political Quarterly*, 77(2), pp 147–55.

Munby, S. (2006) *The School Leadership Challenges for the 21st Century*. Nottingham: NCSL.

Munby, S. (2007) *Primary Leadership: Advice to the Secretary of State*. Nottingham: NCSL.

Munby, S. (2008) *Steve Munby's Speech to the National Conference for Sure Start Children's Centre Leaders*. Nottingham: NCSL.

Munby, S. (2010) *Seizing Success 2010: Annual Leadership Conference, Steve Munby – Chief Executive*. Nottingham: NCSL.

Murray, J. (2010) 'A question of status'. *EducationGuardian*, 28 September, p 3.

National College (2010a) *A National College Guide to Federations*. Nottingham: NCLSCS.

National College (2010b) *A National College Guide to Partnerships and Collaborations*. Nottingham: NCLSCS.

National College (2010c) *Making a Difference*. Nottingham: National College.

National College (2010d) 'What is an executive agency?'. Available at: http://www.nationalcollege.org.uk/index/about-us/national-college-role/national-college-whitepaper2010/executive-agency.htm (accessed 31 January 2011).

National College (2010e) *Teaching Schools*. Nottingham: NCSL.

National Commission on Education (1996) *Success Against the Odds.* London: Routledge.

National Commission on Excellence in Education (1983) *A Nation at Risk,* Washington DC: US Department of Education.

NCSL (National College for School Leadership) (1999) 'Every new head to get a free lap top as government reveals plans for new headship college', NCSL press release. Available at: http://www.dfes.gov.uk/pns/DisplayPN.cgi?pn_id+1999_0461 (accessed 23 October 2006).(Document is now located at the National Archives (http:nationalarchives.gov.uk).)

NCSL (2000) *Leading and Learning.* Nottingham: NCSL.

NCSL (2001) *Leadership Development Framework.* Nottingham: NCSL.

NCSL (2002) *The Future Started Here.* Nottingham: NCSL.

NCSL (2006a) *Leadership Succession: an Overview.* Nottingham: NCSL.

NCSL (2006b) *Narrowing the Gap, Reducing Within-School Variation in Pupil Outcomes.* Nottingham: NCSL.

NCSL (2006c) *Succession Planning, Formal Advice to the Secretary of State.* Nottingham: NCSL.

NCSL (2007) *What We Know About School Leadership.* Nottingham: NCSL.

NCSL (2008) 'Heads up'. *EducationGuardian,* 4 November.

NCSL (undated a) *Prospectus 2002–2003.* Nottingham: NCSL.

NCSL (undated b) *Annual Review of Research 2002–2003.* Nottingham: NCSL.

NCSL (undated c) *Annual Review of Research 2003–2004.* Nottingham: NCSL.

NCSL (undated d) *School Leadership 2004.* Nottingham: NCSL.

NCSL (undated e) *Annual Review of Research 2004–2005.* Nottingham: NCSL.

NCSL (undated f) *School Leadership 2005.* Nottingham: NCSL.

NCSL (undated g) *Prospectus 2005.* Nottingham: NCSL.

NCSL (undated h) *Corporate Plan 2005–2008.* Nottingham: NCSL.

NCSL (undated i) *Corporate Plan 2006–2009.* Nottingham: NCSL.

NCSL (undated j) *Corporate Plan 2007–2008.* Nottingham: NCSL.

NCSL (undated k) *Corporate Plan 2008–2009.* Nottingham: NCSL.

NCSL (undated l) *Shaping Up To the Future.* Nottingham: NCSL.

NCSL (undated m) *talk2learn.* Nottingham: NCSL.

NCSL (undated n) *NCSL's Extended Remit – Advice to the Secretary of State.* Nottingham: NCSL.

NCSL (undated p) *Making the Difference: Successful Leadership in Challenging Circumstances,* Nottingham: NCSL.

NESSRT (National Evaluation of Sure Start Research Team) (2008) *The Impact of Sure Start Local Programmes on Three Year Olds and Their Families.* London: DfES.

Newman, J. (2001) *Modernising Governance*. London: Sage, pp 90–100.

Newman, J. and Clarke, J. (2009) *Publics, Politics and Power*. London: Sage.

Newton, P. (2003) 'The National College for School Leadership: its role in developing leaders'. In M. Brundrett, N. Burton and R. Smith (eds) *Leadership in Education*. London: Sage.

Ng, H. and Wong, K. (2001) 'Special Issue: professional development for school leaders: international perspectives'. *International Studies in Educational Administration*, 29(2), pp 1–87.

NHS Modernisation Agency Leadership Centre (2003) *An Introduction to the NHS Leadership Centre*. London: NHS Leadership Centre.

Normore, A.H. (ed) (2008) *Leadership for Social Justice*. Charlotte, NC: IAP.

Northern, S. (2010) 'Flying solo … and crashing'. *EducationGuardian*, 12 October, p 3.

NRT (National Remodelling Team) (2001) *Touching Tomorrow*. Nottingham: NCSL.

OECD (Organisation for Economic Co-operation and Development) (2001) *Public Sector Leadership for the 21st Century*. Paris: OECD.

Ofsted (Office for Standards in Education) (1998) *School Evaluation Matters*. London: Ofsted.

Ofsted (2002) *Performance Management of Teachers*. London: Ofsted.

Ofsted (2003a) *Excellence in Cities and Education Action Zones: Management and Impact*. London: Ofsted.

Ofsted (2003b) *Leadership and Management, What Inspection Evidence Tells Us*. London: Ofsted.

Ofsted (2004) *Remodelling the School Workforce, Phase 1*. London: HNI 2298.

O'Hara, M. (2010) 'The naughty specialist'. *EducationGuardian*, 24 August, p 3.

O'Reilly, D. and Reed, M. (2010) '"Leaderism": an evolution of managerialism in UK public service reform'. *Public Administration*, 88(4), pp 960–78.

Osborne, D. and Gaebler, T. (1993) *Reinventing Government*. New York: Plume.

O'Shaughnessy, J. (ed) (2007) *The Leadership Effect*. London: Policy Exchange.

Ozga, J. (1987) 'Studying education policy through the lives of the policymakers: an attempt to close the macro–micro gap'. In S. Walker and L. Barton (eds) *Changing Policies, Changing Teachers: New Directions for Schooling?* Milton Keynes: OUP.

Ozga, J. (2000a) *Policy Research in Educational Settings*. Buckingham: OUP.

Ozga, J. (2000b) 'Leadership in education: the problem, not the solution?'. *Discourse: Studies in the Cultural Politics of Education*, 21(3), pp 355–61.

Ozga, J. (2002) 'Education governance in the United Kingdom: the modernisation project'. *European Educational Research Journal*, 1(2), pp 331–41.

Ozga, J. (2005) 'Modernizing the education workforce: a perspective from Scotland'. *Educational Review*, 57(2), pp 207–19.

Ozga, J. (2009) 'Governing education through data in England: from regulation to self-evaluation'. *Journal of Education Policy*, 24(2), pp 149–62.

Ozga, J. and Jones, R. (2006) 'Travelling and embedded policy: the case of knowledge transfer'. *Journal of Education Policy*, 21(1), pp 1–17.

Pascal, C. and Ribbins, P. (1998) *Understanding Primary Headteachers*. London: Cassell.

Peters, T. and Waterman, R. (1982) *In Search of Excellence*. London: HarperCollins.

Pierre, J. and Peters, B.G. (2000) *Governance, Politics and the State*. Basingstoke: Macmillan Press Ltd.

PIU (Performance and Innovation Unit) (2001) 'Strengthening leadership in the public sector'. Available at: http://www.number-10. gov.uk/su/leadership/00/content01/htm, Document is now located at the National Archives (http:nationalarchives.gov.uk) (accessed 23 March 2004).

Plant, R. (2010) *The Neo-Liberal State*. Oxford: Oxford University Press.

Pollitt, C. (2007) 'New Labour's re-disorganisation'. *Public Management Review*, 9(4), pp 529–43.

Pont, B., Nusche, D. and Hopkins, D. (eds) (2008a) *Improving School Leadership, Volume 2: Case Studies on System Leadership*. Paris: OECD.

Pont, B., Nusche, D. and Moorman, H. (2008b) *Improving School Leadership, Volume 1: Policy and Practice*. Paris: OECD.

Popkewitz, T. and Lindblad, S. (2004) 'Historicizing the future: educational reform, systems of reason, and the making of children who are future citizens'. *Journal of Educational Change*, 5(3), pp 229–47.

Power, S., Halpin, D. and Whitty, G. (1997) 'School managers, the state and the market'. Paper presented to the ESRC Seminar Redefining Educational Management, Leicester, June.

PwC (PricewaterhouseCoopers) (2008) *Academies Evaluation: Fifth Annual Report*. London: DCSF.

Raab, C. (1994) 'Theorising the governance of education'. *British Journal of Educational Studies*, 42(1), pp 6–21.

Raffo, C. and Gunter, H.M. (2008) 'Leading schools to promote social inclusion: developing a conceptual framework for analysing research, policy and practice'. *Journal of Education Policy*, 23(4), pp 397–414.

Ranson, S. (1994) 'Towards a tertiary tripartism: new codes of social control and the 17 plus'. In P. Broadfoot (ed) *Selection, Certification, and Control: Social Issues in Educational Assessment.* Lewes: Falmer Press, pp 221–44.

Ranson, S. (1995) 'Theorising education policy'. *Journal of Education Policy*, 10(4), pp 427–48.

Ranson, S. (2010) 'Returning education to layered horizons'. *Forum*, 52(2), pp 155–8.

Ravitch, D. (2010) *The Death and Life of the Great American School System.* New York: Basic Books.

Rayner, S. and Ribbins, P. (1999) *Headteachers and Leadership in Special Education.* London: Cassell.

Reynolds, D. (undated) 'How can recent research in school effectiveness, teacher effectiveness and school improvement inform our thinking about educational policies?' Available at: www.highreliability.co.uk (accessed 9 October 2007).

Reynolds, D., Sammons, P., Stoll, L., Barber, M. and Hillman, J. (1996) 'School effectiveness and school improvement in the United Kingdom'. *School Effectiveness and School Improvement*, 7(2), pp 133–58.

Reynolds, D. and Teddlie, C., with Hopkins, D. and Stringfield, S. (2000) 'Linking school effectiveness and school improvement'. In C. Teddlie and D. Reynolds (eds) *The International Handbook of School Effectiveness Research.* London: RoutledgeFalmer, pp 206–31.

Rhodes, R.A.W. (1994) 'The hollowing out of the state: the changing nature of the public service in Britain'. *The Political Quarterly*, 65(2), pp 138–51.

Rhodes, R.A.W. (1996) 'The new governance: governing without government'. *Political Studies*, 44(4), pp 652–67.

Ribbins, P. (ed) (1997) *Leaders and Leadership in the School, College and University.* London: Cassell.

Richardson, H. (2010) 'Spending watchdog warns over academies' finances', BBC News. Available at: http://www.bbc.co.uk/news/education-11229213 (accessed 15 September 2010).

Richardson, H. (2011) 'Councils defeat government over school buildings', BBC News. Available at: http://www.bbc.co.uk/news/education-12429152 (accessed 14 February 2011).

Richardson, L. (1997) *Fields of Play (Constructing an Academic Life).* New Brunswick, NJ: Rutgers University Press.

Riley, D. and Mulford, B. (2007) 'England's National College for School Leadership: a model for leadership education?'. *Journal of Educational Administration*, 45(1), pp 80–98.

Rizvi, F. (2006) 'Imagination and the globalisation of educational policy research'. *Globalisation, Societies and Education*, 4(2), pp 193–205.

Rizvi, F. and Lingard, B. (2010) *Globalizing Education Policy*. London: Routledge.

Robinson, S. (2011) 'Primary headteachers: new leadership roles inside and outside of schools'. *Educational Management and Leadership*, 39(1), pp 63–83.

Rodger, I. (2006) *National Standards for Headteachers in Focus: Urban Primary Schools*. Nottingham: NCSL.

Rowan, B. (2002) 'The ecology of school improvement: notes on the school improvement industry in the United States'. *Journal of Educational Change*, 3(3/4), pp 283–314.

Rudduck, J. and Fielding, M. (2006) 'Student voice and the perils of popularity'. *Educational Review*, 58(2), pp 219–31.

Rudduck, J. and Flutter, J. (2003) *How to Improve Your School: Giving Pupils a Voice*. London: Continuum.

Rusch, E.A. and Marshall, C. (2006) 'Gender filters and leadership: plotting a course to equity'. *International Journal of Leadership in Education*, 9(3), pp 229–50.

Russell, B. (2000) 'Ministers admit defeat in "fresh start" policy for failing schools'. *The Independent*, 2 December. Available at: http://www.independent.co.uk/news/education/education-news/ministers-admit-defeat-in-fresh-start-policy-for-failing-schools-626379.html (accessed 7 February 2011).

Ryan, J. (1998) 'Critical leadership for education in a postmodern world: emancipation, resistance and communal action'. *International Journal of Leadership in Education*, 1(3), pp 257–78.

Ryan, J. (2010) 'Promoting social justice in schools: principals' political strategies'. *International Journal of Leadership in Education*, 13(4), pp 357–76.

Saint-Martin, D. (2000) *Building the New Managerialist State*. Oxford: Oxford University Press.

Saint-Martin, D. (2001) 'How the reinventing government movement in public administration was exported from the U.S. to other countries'. *International Journal of Public Administration*, 24(6), pp 573–604.

Salt, T. (2009) *Toby Salt's Speech to the National New Heads Conference 2009*. Nottingham: NCSL.

Sammons, P. (1999) *School Effectiveness: Coming of Age in the Twenty-First Century*. Lisse, The Netherlands: Swets and Zeitlinger Publishers.

Sammons, P. (2008) 'Zero tolerance of failure and New Labour approaches to school improvement in England'. *Oxford Review of Education*, 34(6), pp 651–64.

Sammons, P., Hillman, J. and Mortimore, P. (1995) *Key Characteristics of Effective Schools: A Review of School Effectiveness Research*. London: Ofsted.

Sammons, P., Mortimore, P. and Hillman, J. (1999) 'Key characteristics of effective schools: a response to peddling feel-good fictions'. In P. Sammons (ed) *School Effectiveness, Coming of Age in the Twenty-First Century*. Lisse, The Netherlands: Swets and Zeitlinger Publishers, pp 223–6.

Sammons, P., Chapman, C., Muijs, D., Day, C., Gu, Q., Harris, A., Kelly, A. and Reynolds, D. (2010) 'Evidence shows we can effect change'. *Times Educational Supplement*, 12 March. Available at: www.tes.co.uk/article.aspx?storycode=6038668 (accessed 25 June 2010).

Scott, J. (2009) 'The politics of venture philanthropy in Charter School policy and advocacy'. *Educational Policy*, 23(1), pp 106–36.

Scott, W., Riddell, B., Rees-Jones, S., de Keller, L., Roberts, C., Robson, T., Donnelly, J. and Morrow, J. (2006) *National Standards for Headteachers in Focus: Nursery Schools*. Nottingham: NCSL.

Seddon, T. (1996) 'The principle of choice in policy research'. *Journal of Education Policy*, 11(2), pp 197–214.

SEU (Standards and Effectiveness Unit) and DfEE (Department for Education and Employment) (1997) *From Targets to Action*. London: DfEE.

Shamir, R. (2008) 'The age of responsibilization: on market-embedded morality'. *Economy and Society*, 37(1), pp 1–19.

Sharp, C., Eames, A., Sanders, D. and Tomlinson, K. (2006) *Leading a Research-Engaged School*. Nottingham: NCSL.

Shaw, E. (2007) *Losing Labour's Soul?* Abingdon: Routledge.

Shayer, M., Ginsburg, D. and Coe, R. (2007) 'Thirty years on – a large anti-Flynn effect? The Piagetion test *Volume & Heaviness* norms 1975–2003', *British Journal of Educational Psychology*, 77(1) pp 25–41.

Shields, C.M. (1999) 'Learning from students about representation, identity, and community'. *Educational Administration Quarterly*, 35(1), pp 106–29.

Shields, C.M. (2004) 'Dialogic leadership for social justice: overcoming pathologies of silence'. *Educational Administration Quarterly*, 40(1), pp 109–32.

Shields, C.M. (2010) 'Transformative leadership: working for equity in diverse contexts'. *Educational Administration Quarterly*, 46(4), pp 559–89.

Shulman, L. (2005) 'Signature pedagogies in the professions'. *Daedalus*, Summer, pp 52–9.

Skelcher, C. (1998) *The Appointed State*. Buckingham: OUP.

Slee, R. and Weiner, G., with Tomlinson, S. (eds) (1998) *School Effectiveness for Whom? Challenges to the School Effectiveness and School Improvement Movements*. London: Falmer Press.

Smith, M. (2002) 'The school leadership initiative: an ethically flawed project?'. *Journal of Philosophy of Education*, 36(1), pp 21–39.

SMTF (School Management Task Force) (1990) *Developing School Management, The Way Forward*. London: HMSO.

Smyth, J. (ed) (1989) *Critical Perspectives on Educational Leadership*. London: Falmer Press.

Smyth, J. (ed) (1993) *A Socially Critical View of the Self Managing School*. London: The Falmer Press.

Smyth, J. (1998) 'Reprofessionalising teaching: a university research institute engages teachers in creating dialogic space in schools'. *Teacher Development*, 2(3), pp 339–49.

Smyth, J. (2005) 'An argument for new understandings and explanations of early school leaving that go beyond the conventional'. *London Review of Education*, 3(2), pp 117–30.

Smyth, J. (2006a) 'Researching teachers working with young adolescents: implications for ethnographic research'. *Ethnography and Education*, 1(1), pp 31–51.

Smyth, J. (2006b) 'Educational leadership that fosters "student voice"'. *International Journal of Leadership in Education*, 9(4), pp 279–84.

Smyth, J. (2006c) '"When students have power": student engagement, student voice, and the possibilities for school reform around "dropping out" of school'. *International Journal of Leadership in Education*, 9(4), pp 285–98.

Smyth, J. and Hattam, R., with Cannon, J., Edwards, J., Wilson, N. and Wurst, S. (2004) *Dropping Out, Drifting Off, Being Excluded*. New York, NY: Peter Lang.

Smyth, J. and McInerney, P. (2007) *Teachers in the Middle*. New York, NY: Peter Lang.

Smyth, J., Angus, L., Down, B. and McInerney, P. (2008) *Critically Engaged Learning*. New York, NY: Peter Lang.

Smyth, W.J. (1985) 'An educative and empowering notion of leadership'. *Educational Management and Administration*, 13(3), pp 179–86.

Southworth, G.W. (1995) *Looking into Primary Headship*. London: Falmer Press.

Southworth, G. (1999) 'Continuities and changes in primary headship'. In T. Bush, L. Bell, R. Bolam, R. Glatter and P. Ribbins (eds) *Educational Management: Redefining Theory, Policy and Practice*. pp 43–58.

Southworth, G. (2002) 'Instructional leadership in schools: reflections and empirical evidence'. *School Leadership and Management*, 22(1), pp 73–91.

Southworth, G. (2004) 'A response from the National College for School Leadership'. *Educational Management Administration and Leadership*, 32(3), pp 339–54.

Squires, P. (ed) (2008) *Asbo Nation*. Bristol: The Policy Press.

Stevens, J., Brown, J., Knibbs, S. and Smith, J. (2005) *Follow-up Research into the State of School Leadership in England*. London: DfES.

Steward, R. (2007) *A Better Way?* Nottingham: NCSL.

Stewart, W. (2003) 'Storm out of blue skies'. *Times Educational Supplement*, 5 December.

Stoll, L. (undated) *Enhancing Internal Capacity: Leadership for Learning.* Nottingham: NCSL.

Stoll, L. and Fink, D. (1996) *Changing Our Schools*. Buckingham: OUP.

Stoll, L. and Myers, K. (eds) (1998a) *No Quick Fixes: Perspectives on Schools in Difficulty*. London: Falmer Press.

Stoll, L. and Myers, K. (1998b) 'No quick fixes: an introduction'. In L. Stoll and K. Myers (eds) *No Quick Fixes: Perspectives on Schools in Difficulty*. London: Falmer Press, pp 1–14.

Stubbs, M. (2003) *A Head of the Class*. London: John Murray.

Sturdy, A., Handley, K., Clark, T. and Fincham, R. (2009) *Management Consultancy*. Oxford: Oxford University Press.

Swidenbank, H. (2007) *The Challenges and Opportunities of Leading and Managing an All-Age School*. Nottingham: NCSL.

Syal, R. (2010) 'Michael Gove's 25-year-old ex-adviser given £500,000 free schools contract'. *The Guardian*. Available at: http://www.guardian.co.uk/education/2010/oct27/michael-gove-adviser-free-schools (accessed 28 October 2010).(Document is now located at the National Archives (http:nationalarchives.gov.uk).)

Taylor, C. (2009) *A Good School for Every Child*. Abingdon: Routledge.

Taylor, C. and Ryan, C. (2005) *Excellence in Education: The Making of Great Schools*. London: David Fulton Publishers.

Taylor, W. (1976) 'The head as manager: some criticisms'. In R.S. Peters (ed) *The Role of the Head*. London: Routledge & Kegan Paul, pp 37–49.

Taysum, A. and Gunter, H.M. (2008) 'A critical approach to researching social justice and school leadership in England'. *Education, Citizenship and Social Justice*, 3(2), pp 211–27.

Thomas, H., Butt, G., Fielding, A., Foster, J., Gunter, H.M., Lance, A., Pilkington, R., Potts, E., Powers, S., Rayner, S., Rutherford, D., Selwood, I. and Szwed, C. (2004) *The Evaluation of the Transforming the School Workforce Pathfinder Project. Research Report 541*. London: DfES.

Thompson, K., with Davies, B. and Ellison, L. (2004) *Can Private Companies Successfully Turn Around a Failing School?* Nottingham: NCSL.

Thomson, P. (2001) 'How principals lose "face": a disciplinary tale of educational administration and modern managerialism'. *Discourse: Studies in the Cultural Politics of Education*, 22(1), pp 5–22.

Thomson, P. (2005) 'Bringing Bourdieu to policy sociology: codification, misrecognition and exchange value in the UK context'. *Journal of Education Policy*, 20(6), pp 741–58.

Thomson, P. (2007) 'Leading schools in high poverty neighbourhoods: the National College for School Leadership and beyond'. In T. W. Pink and G. W. Noblit (eds) *The International Handbook of Urban Education.* pp 1049–78.

Thomson, P. (2008) 'Headteacher critique and resistance: a challenge for policy, and for leadership/management scholars'. *Journal of Educational Administration and History*, 40(2), pp 85–100.

Thomson, P. (2009) *School Leadership, Heads on the Block?* London: Routledge.

Thomson, P. (2010a) 'Headteacher autonomy: a sketch of a Bourdieuian field analysis of position and practice'. *Critical Studies in Education*, 51(1), pp 5–20.

Thomson, P. (2010b) 'A critical pedagogy of global place: regeneration in and as action'. In C. Raffo, A. Dyson, H. Gunter, D. Hall, L. Jones and A. Kalambouka (eds) *Education and Poverty in Affluent Countries.* New York: Routledge, pp 124–34.

Thomson, P. and Blackmore, J. (2006) 'Beyond the power of one: redesigning the work of school principals'. *Journal of Educational Change*, 7(3), pp 161–77.

Thomson, P. and Gunter, H.M. (2006) 'From "consulting pupils" to "pupils as researchers": a situated case narrative'. *British Educational Research Journal*, 32(6), pp 839–56.

Thorpe, V. (2011) 'Outrage over scrapping of arts projects in schools'. *The Observer*, 9 January, p 4.

Thrupp, M. (1999) *Schools Making a Difference: Let's be Realistic!* Buckingham: OUP.

Thrupp, M. (2005a) *School Improvement: An Unofficial Approach.* London: Continuum.

Thrupp, M. (2005b) 'The National College for School Leadership: a critique'. *Management in Education*, 19(2), pp 13–19.

Thrupp, M. and Willmott, R. (2003) *Education Management in Managerialist Times.* Maidenhead: OUP.

Tickle, L. (2010) 'We are still a part of a family of schools'. *EducationGuardian*, 5 October, p 5.

Tilly, C. (2005) *Trust and Rule.* New York, NY: Cambridge University Press.

Tobin, L. (2009) 'The kind of help you can do without'. *EducationGuardian*, 24 November, p 3.

Tomlinson, H. (2003) 'Supporting school leaders in an era of accountability: the National College for School Leadership in England'. In P. Hallinger (ed) *Reshaping the Landscape of School Leadership Development.* Lisse, The Netherlands: Swets and Zeitlinger, pp 217–33.

Tomlinson, H., Gunter, H. and Smith, P. (eds) (1999) *Living Headship: Voices, Values and Vision*. London: PCP.

Tomlinson, S. (2003) 'New Labour and education'. *Children and Society*, 17(3), pp 195–204.

Townsend, T. (2001) 'Satan or saviour? An analysis of two decades of school effectiveness research'. *School Effectiveness and School Improvement*, 12(1), pp 115–29.

Treves, V. (2010) *Seizing Success 2010: Annual Leadership Conference, Vanni Treves – Chair, National College's Governing Council Speech highlights*. Nottingham: National College.

TTA (Teacher Training Agency) (1997) *Report on the Outcomes of the NPQH Trials 1996–1997*. London: TTA.

TTA (1998) *National Standards for Qualified Teacher Status, Subject Leaders, Special Educational Needs Co-ordinators, Headteachers*. London: TTA.

Tucker, M. and Codding, J. (undated) *School Headship in the United States: A Situation Report*. Nottingham: NCSL.

Vasagar, J. (2010a) 'Councils revolt against free schools'. *The Guardian*. Available at: http://www.guardian.co.uk/education/2010/oct.25/free-schools-revolt/print (accessed 28 October 2010). (Document is now located at the National Archives (http:nationalarchives.gov.uk).)

Vasagar, J. (2010b) 'Gove to approve plans for four more free schools in England'. *The Guardian*, 5 November, p 20.

Vasagar, J. (2011) 'More maths, longer days … Gove's school vision takes shape'. *The Guardian*, 4 January, p 13.

Vasagar, J. and Shepherd, J. (2011) 'Ministers to get more powers to intervene in failing schools'. *The Guardian*, 28 January, p 13.

Vidovich, L. (2007) 'Navigating "global" modernization policies in education: responses from Australia'. In G. Butt and H.M. Gunter (eds) *Modernizing Schools*. London: Continuum, pp 189–202.

Wacquant, L. (2009) *Punishing the Poor*. Durham, NC: Duke University Press.

Walford, G. (2005) 'Introduction: education and the Labour government'. *Oxford Review of Education*, 31(1), pp 3–9.

Walker, A. and Dimmock, C. (2004) 'The international role of the NCSL: tourist, colporteur or confrere'. *Educational Management Administration and Leadership*, 32(3), pp 269–87.

Watt, N. (2009) 'Friends in need'. *The Guardian*, 13 January, pp 4–7.

Weindling, D. (1992) 'Marathon running on a sand dune: the changing role of the headteacher in England and Wales'. *Journal of Educational Administration*, 30(3), pp 63–76.

Weindling, D. (2004) *Funding for Research on School Leadership*. Nottingham: NCSL.

West, A. and Pennell, H. (2002) 'How new is New Labour? The quasi-market and English schools 1997–2001'. *British Journal of Educational Studies*, 50(2), pp 206–24.

West, M., Ainscow, M. and Notman, H. (2003) *What Leaders Read 2, Key Texts from Education and Beyond*. Nottingham: NCSL.

Western, S. (2008) *Leadership: A Critical Text*. London: Sage.

Whitty, G. (2002) *Making Sense of Education Policy*. London: PCP.

Whitty, G., Edwards, T. and Gewirtz, S. (1993) *Specialisation and Choice in Urban Education: The City Technology College Experiment*. London: Routledge.

Whitty, G., Power, S. and Halpin, D. (1998) *Devolution and Choice in Education*. Buckingham: OUP.

Wilby, P. (2008) 'For the good of others'. *New Statesman*, 2 June, p 14.

Wilby, P. (2009) 'Practising what he preaches'. *EducationGuardian*, 7 September, p 1.

Wilkinson, R. and Pickett, K. (2009) *The Spirit Level*. London: Allen Lane.

Williams, V. (1995) 'The context of development'. In V. Williams (ed) *Towards Self-Managing Schools*. London: Cassell, pp 3–23.

Winkley, D., with Pascal, C. (1998) 'Developing a radical agenda'. In C. Pascal and P. Ribbins (eds) *Understanding Primary Headteachers*. London: Cassell, pp 230–51.

Winkley, D. (2002) *Handsworth Revolution*. London: Giles de la Mare Publishers Limited.

Wong, S. (2006) *Perceptions of the Impact of Leadership Training on Newly Appointed Female Principals in Middle and Secondary Schools in England and Hong Kong*. Nottingham: NCSL.

Wood, A.D. (1983) 'A training college for headteachers of secondary schools; some thoughts and considerations'. *School Organization*, 3(3), pp 287–95.

Wright, N. (2001) 'Leadership, "bastard leadership" and managerialism'. *Educational Management and Administration*, 29(3), pp 275–90.

Wright, N. (2003) 'Principled "bastard" leadership? A rejoinder to Gold, Evans, Earley, Halpin and Collarbone'. *Educational Management and Administration*, 31(2), pp 139–43.

Wrigley, T. (2008) 'School improvement in a neo-liberal world'. *Journal of Educational Administration and History*, 40(2), pp 129–48.

Wrigley, T. (2011) '"Rapidly improving results": penetrating the hype of policy-based evidence'. In H.M. Gunter (ed) *The State and Education Policy: The Academies Programme*. London: Continuum, pp 133–45.

Yarker, P. (2005) 'On not being a teacher: the professional and the personal costs of workforce remodelling'. *Forum*, 47(2/3), pp 169–74.

Young, M.F.D. (2008) *Bringing Knowledge Back In*. Abingdon: Routledge.

Index

Note: Page numbers in italics indicate an illustration, those followed by *n* refer to information in a note and those followed by *fig* and *tab* refer to information in a figure or a table.

A

Absolute Return for Kids (ARK) 57
Academies Programme 4, 22, 23-4, 25, 46, 127, 138
  and coalition 139, 141, 142, 143
accountability 12, 49, 61, 62, 135, 149
  headteachers and delivery 99, 106
Adonis, Andrew 56-7, 67*n*
'advocacy coalitions' 46
agency issues 98-100, 125-6
Alexander, R.J. 138
Alexiadou, N. 68*n*
Alvesson, M. 129
Anderson, G. 124
Anti-Academies Alliance (AAA) 144
Appadurai, A. 13
Apple, M.W. 14, 126, 128, 146, 149
Arrowsmith, R. 97, 98, 106-7
Atkinson, Sir William 101

B

Bacchi, C. 1
Baker, Kenneth 11, 56
Ball, S.J. 5-6, 18, 23, 26, 98
  knowledge production 46
    and networks 75, 76-7
  policies and professionals 95, 96, 105
  policy research 129-30
Balls, Ed 15*n*, 65-6, 67
Barber, Michael 12, 37, 61, 71*n*
  on characteristics of failing schools 41
  and 'deliverology' 4, 49, 54-5, 56
  global influence 136, 146
  and National College 66-7, 72*n*
  and research-based investment 38, 40-1
  and SESI intellectuals 43
  and urgency for reform 24-5
Barker, Bernard 102, 122-3
Bates, R. 127
Bates, Y. 108
Beane, J.A. 126
Beckett, F. 25-6, 34*n*, 67*n*, 69*n*
Béland, D. 56, 58
beliefs and assertions 38, 41-2, 47, 133, 148
BELMAS 63, 90
Benn, M. 152*n*
Bentham, J. 69*n*
bespoke leadership programmes 44-5

Bichard, Michael 71*n*, 72*n*
Big Society 144
Blackler, F. 116
Blackmore, J. 112
Blair, Tony 17, 35*n*, 56, 67*n*, 69*n*, 80, 115, 138
  see also New Labour
Bloomberg, Michael 72*n*
Blunkett, David 15*n*, 17, 25, 69*n*, 107, 147
  and interventionist approach 11, 12, 22-3
  and National College 64-5, 66-7
Bobbitt, P. 60
Bolam, R. 63
Bottery, M. 104-5
Bourdieu, Pierre 2, 3, 6-7, 13, 14, 75
  on bureaucratic field 42
  on habitus and practice 78
  and regime practices 117-21
  and regimes of practice 77-8
  on responsibility of research 130
  on strategies 46
  see also capital; cultural capital; doxa; field; game; habitus; illusio; logic of practice; misrecognition; social capital; symbolic capital
Bowe, R. 96
branding 22, 26, 44
Brighouse, Tim 61
British Educational Communications and Technology Agency (BECTA) 142
Brown, Gordon 18, 56-7
Brundrett, M. 51*n*
Building Schools for the Future (BSF) 151*n*
Burch, P. 134
bureaucratic field 42
Burnham, Andy 145
Bush, T. 61
business approaches 4, 6, 11, 33, 138-9
  Conservative market regime 139-40, 146
  demands on headteachers 103-4
  impact on standards 134-6
  leadership industry 7-8, 44-6
  research view of 86, 121
  see also consultants; effectiveness of schools
Byrne, D. 13

C

Caldwell, Brian 29*tab*, 35*n*, 136
Callahan, R.E. 134, 136-7
Cambridge Primary Review 138
capital 3
  investment and regimes of practice 78, 81, 85
  and leadership game 42-3, 44, 81, 133
  and regime practices 117, 118, 119
central government
  and governance 58-62, 147
  and public institutions 55-6
centralisation
  cult of standards 136-9
  and foundation of National College 63-6
  and institutionalised governance 55-6
  and neoliberalist policies 11
  see also interventionist approach; managerialism
CfBT 45
change
  in critical policy context 13, 91
  frequent change and delivery 4-5
    demands on headteachers 97-8, 99, 103-4, 106-7
  in governance 60-1
  resistance to change 41, 66, 102
  see also educational reform
charismatic headteachers 20, 80, 89, 123-4, 138-9
charter schools in US 135-6
children in research and policy 122-3, 125, 128
Children's Services and National College 67
Christopoulos, D.C. 76
Chubb, J.E. 60
City Technology Colleges (CTCs) 7, 138
civil servants and leadership doxa 80
civil society 53, 55-6, 148
Clark, Peter 101
Clarke, Charles 15*n*, 17
Clarke, J. 148
Clarke, Kenneth 1
'club rule' and governance 60-1, 142
coalition government 1, 139-44, 148
  Conservative Market Regime 139-40, 146
  and New Labour policies 140-2
Coburn, C.E. 59
Cocentra 45
Codd, J. 1
codification of leadership 2, 18, 121
Collarbone, Dame Pat 37, 61, 71*n*, 101
Commonwealth Council for Educational Administration and Management (CCEAM) 90
communities and research and policy 127-9

comprehensive school rehabilitation 145, 146
Connell, R. 51, 149
Conservative Market Regime (CMR) 139-40, 146
Conservatives 1, 7-8, 9-10, 43, 70-1*n*
  New Labour and Thatcher legacy 9-12, 60-1
  see also coalition government
Consultant Leaders' Programme 66
consultants
  and institutionalised governance 59, 61-2
  and leadership industry 6, 8, 44-6
  National College and knowledge production 47-8
  and regimes of practice 75-6, 81-2
    and New Labour policy regime 83-4
Contextual Value Added (CVA) 6, 22
control *see* centralisation; institutionalised governance; interventionist approach of New Labour
Coopers and Lybrand 8
Crace, J. 137-8
creative partnerships 151*n*
critical policy scholarship 13, 53-5, 130, 149-50
  headteachers' positioning 95-6, 108
  and National College 88-9, 110-15
  and policy research regime 84-5, 86-7, 88-9, 146-7
Crow, G.M. 106
cultural capital 42, 81, 85
culture of schools *see* reculturing
Cummings, A.J. 68*n*, 70-1*n*
curriculum 79, 138
  'place-based curriculum' 128
Currie, G. 114

D

data generation and performance 4, 67, 103, 137
  and risk management 21-2, 58
Davies, Sir Alan 34*n*
Day, Chris 49-50
de Quesnay, Heather 31, 61, 65
delivery disposition 10
  b(r)ought-in delivery 46, 81-2
  headteachers' role 91, 114-15, 139
    demands of 97-8, 99, 103-4, 106-7
  and leadership game 19, 26, 81-2, 115, 119, 139
  National College remit 57, 64, 65-6, 121
  and public institutions 56-7
democratic nature of schools 126-7
Demos 48, 69*n*
Denham, A. 68-9*n*
Department
  changing titles 14-15*n*
  criticism of National College training material 66-7

prescriptive curriculum 138
Remit letters and National College
  64-6
and symbolic exchange of capital 143
Department for Children, Schools and
  Families (DCSF) 15*n*
Department for Education (DfE) 15*n*
Department for Education and
  Employment (DfEE) 14*n*
  Excellence in Schools 1, 17, 38
  Teachers (Green Paper) 20, 35n
Department for Education and Skills
  (DfES) 14-15*n*, 21
  Higher Standards, Better Schools for
  All 17
  A New Relationship with Schools
  16n, 22
Department for Innovation, Universities
  and Skills (DIUS) 15*n*
deprofessionalisation 23, 137
deregulation and Thatcher legacy 10
devolution of power and governance 57
Directors of Children's Services 67
disadvantage 122-3, 138
disposition *see* habitus (disposition)
distributed leadership 2, 121, 127, 139, 141
  critiques 88
  and demands on headteachers 103-4
  National College promotion 32-3,
  47, 50-1
dominant power relations 123, 147
doxa 13, 133
  and leadership approaches 3, 19, 42,
  80, 81, 117, 118, 119
  neoliberalism as 14, 33

E

Earley, P. 108-9
economic capital 42, 81
economic deregulation and Thatcher
  legacy 10
Economic and Social Research Council
  (ESRC) 88, 91, 153
  see also Knowledge Production in
  Educational Leadership (KPEL)
  project
education as focus of research 86-7, 123
Education Reform Act (1988) 7, 68*n*, 102,
  105, 136
educational reform
  centralised control 55-6, 106-7, 113
  and coalition government 139-44
  cult of standards 136-9
  and teaching to tests 137-8
  demands on headteachers 98, 99, 103-
  4, 106-7
  headteachers and delivery 91, 114-15,
  139
  and knowledge production 134, 148
  leadership as key 3-6, 80-1
  changes and delivery 4-5, 57, 97-8
  and public institutions 56-7

strategic pragmatism of headteachers
  104-8
  see also New Labour Policy Regime;
  policymaking and regimes of
  practice
effectiveness of schools
  business approach 6, 7, 33, 86, 103,
  138-9
  negative effect 134-6
  and intellectual work 37-51, 133
  and characteristics of effective schools
  38-41
  critiques of knowledge base 122-3
  headteacher and student outcomes link
  49-51, 67
  see also performance management;
  School Effectiveness, School
  Improvement (SESI) studies; testing
elites
  and 'club' government 60-1, 118, 142
  see also policy elite and intellectual
  work
English Baccalaureate 141
entrepreneurialism 10-11, 59, 138-9
ESRC *see* Economic and Social Research
  Council
Evans, J. 108-9
Every Child Matters agenda 21, 88
evidence-based practice 31, 40, 47-51, 147
exclusion and leadership of schools game
  24-6, 60, 118
  and National College approach 112
  research divisions 91-2
Executive Heads 4, 24
Exley, S. 26, 76
expectations and effectiveness 39*tab*, 40, 41
experts
  and coalition policy 142, 148
  and institutionalised governance 59,
  61-2
  and leadership industry 6, 44-6
  National College and knowledge
  production 47-8, 112
  New Labour's selective approach 24-6,
  29, 30-1, 41-6, 81-2
  see also consultants; knowledge
  production

F

failing schools
  characteristics 41
  demands on headteachers 99-100, 104
  headteachers and capacity for change
  20, 24
  and intellectual work 41-6
  interventionist approach 12, 38, 101
  restructuring and closure 24, 141
Federations 4, 22, 24
feminism and research 88
field 3
  bureaucratic field 42
  and intellectual work 43-4, 119, 123,
  124

rethinking the field 128-9
and privatisation of education 6-7
and regimes of practice 78, 79*fig*
  New Labour policy regime 82-3, 91,
    119, 146
Fielding, M. 122, 125, 126-7
Fink, D. 149
Fitz, J. 59, 68*n*
Foster, W. 123-4
Fraser, N. 127
Free Schools programme 139, 141, 142,
  143-4
Fresh Start Schools 4, 24
Fullan, Michael 29*tab*, 35*n*, 41
Future Leaders 57, 58

G

Gaebler, T. 60
Galton, M. 138
game 7
  Conservatives and neoliberal position
    9-10, 144
  and disposition 2, 3, 42, 81-2, 114-15,
    117, 118-19
  and intellectual work 37-51, 61-2, 133
    National College 46-51, 112, 114
  and policy research regime 88-9, 91-2,
    120
  and politics of knowledge production
    147-50
  see also leadership of schools policy:
    leadership of schools game
Garnett, M. 68-9*n*
gender and leadership approach 51
General Teaching Council for England
  (GTCE) 72*n*, 142
Gewirtz, S. 10, 60, 95, 145
Gibb, Nick 139
Gibbons, Michael 43
Giddens, Anthony 144
Gillard, D. 67*n*, 139, 150*n*
Gleeson, D. 11, 97
globalisation 13, 140
Gold, A. 107
Goldring, E. 135
Goldstein, H. 38, 146
good practice 29
  and distributed leadership 32-3, 47,
    121, 139
  and National College 47-51, 112-13
Goodwin, M. 76
Gorard, S. 6
Goss, P. 100
Gove, Michael 139-43, 144, 148
governance *see* central government;
  institutionalised governance
Grace, G. 7, 101, 102, 105, 112
Grant Maintained Status (GMS) 7-8, 68*n*,
  138
Gray, J. 10
Gregg, P. 148
Gronn, P. 112

Guldberg, H. 125
Guyte, George 68*n*

H

habitus (disposition) 3, 78, 90, 119, 133
  and game-playing 2, 3, 42, 114-15,
    117, 118-19
  and leadership game 19, 26, 81-2
  and intellectual work 38, 59, 117, 133
    policy research regime 85
  requirements of headteachers 113-14
  and risk management 58
  see also delivery disposition
Hafid, T. 59
Hall, Sir Iain 43, 101
Hall, V. 97
Hallinger, P. 49
Halpin, D. 68*n*
Harding, A. 77
Hargreaves, Andy 41, 149
Harris, Alma 36*n*, 49
Hartley, D. 51
Hatcher, R. 6, 51, 57, 127
Hattersley, Roy 35*n*
Hay Group 44, 45
Hay McBer 45
headteacher unions 63, 152*n*
headteachers
  and coalition policy 140-1, 143
  complexity of role 103
  delivery role
    demands of 97-8, 99, 103-4, 106-7
    mediation and strategic pragmatism
      104-8
    and New Labour Policy Regime 91,
      114-15, 139
  and dominant power relations 123
  Executive Heads 4, 24
  'heroic' headteachers 20, 88, 89
  identity of headteachers 97-8, 103
  and leadership industry 8, 44-6
  leadership and reform 5, 23, 80-1
  and leadership of schools game 114-
    15, 138-9
  and National College 63-7, 102, 103,
    109-10
  and New Labour policy regime 100-
    2, 107-8
  and policy research regime 85, 88-9,
    102-4, 107-8
  as policymakers and advisors 101, 102
  positioning and professional practice
    95, 96-100
  and regimes of practice 100-8, 114
  and qualifications 8, 34*n*, 70*n*, 100,
    109, 110, 111
  and research on student outcomes
    49-51, 67
  resistance to leadership game and
    remodelling 20-1, 66, 102
  supply problems 100, 110

see also leadership of schools policy; professional knowledge; professional practice
Headteachers into Industry (HTI) 44
Heck, R.H. 49
Hencke, D. 67*n*
Herr, K. 124
heterarchic governance and networks 76-7
hierarchies 57, 123-4, 128-9
higher education institutions (HEIs)
    marketisation 147
    and New Labour policy regime 82-4, 91, 121
    and professional practitioners 89-90
    see also research and scholarship
Hillman, Josh 43
Hodgson, P. 70*n*
Holliday, I. 57
Hood, C. 24, 55, 118
Hopkins, David 32, 43, 49, 61, 65
Hopkins, Sir Michael 26
Hoyle, E. 129
human capital 9-10
Husbands, C. 97
Hutt, Sir Dexter 101
Hyman, Peter 22, 25, 107, 144

I

Iedema, R. 115
illusio and leadership game 42, 117, 119
Improving the Quality of Education for All (IQEA) 44
independent schools as model 138
Innovation Unit 57, 146
inspection and leadership game 22, 100
institutionalised governance 3, 53-73
    and coalition policy 141
    comparative analysis 149
    and National College 53, 62-7, 113
    and politics of knowledge production 147, 149
    see also National College; regimes of practice
intellectual work and New Labour 37-51
    critiques of knowledge base 122-3, 146-7
    network and interconnections 43-4, 59, 117
        inclusion and exclusion 75-6, 91-2, 112, 118, 133, 147-8
        policy elite 37-8, 61-2, 76-7, 81-2, 118
    see also knowledge production; New Labour Policy Regime; Policy Research Regime; research and scholarship
International Congress for School Effectiveness and Improvement (ICSEI) 82
interventionist approach of New Labour 4, 12, 38, 57, 60, 79

conflict with educational values 107, 138
    lack of professional autonomy 22, 98-100
    see also New Labour Policy Regime
investment for results 26, 54-5, 59, 78, 81
    coalition cuts 139
    research and practice 38-41, 47-51

J

Jackson, David 61, 101
Jackson, M. 24, 118
Jessop, B. 76
Johnson, Alan 15*n*, 18, 65, 67
Jones, R. 96
Joseph, Sir Keith 11-12
Judt, T. 149

K

Kelly, Ruth 15*n*, 18, 65, 66, 67
Kingdon, J.W. 59
Knight, Jim 15*n*, 43
knowledge production 134, 136
    New Labour's functional approaches 2, 3, 37-51
        and colonisation of practice 5-6, 9, 37-8, 47, 91, 121
        critiques of knowledge base 122-3, 146-7
        exclusion of critique and debate 24-6, 89, 91-2, 106-7, 118, 147-8
        National College approach 26, 28-9, 30-3, 46-51, 112-13
    politics of 133, 147-50
    see also experts; professional knowledge; regimes of practice; research and scholarship
Knowledge Production in Educational Leadership (KPEL) project 3, 18, 62, 98-102, 103-4, 105-6, 109-14, 153-4

L

Lacey, Ron 123
Lawn, M. 37, 76
leadership approaches and New Labour 1-2, 3-9, 80-1
    and delivery of change 4-5, 57, 97-8, 114-15, 121, 139
    and research 39, 49-51, 67, 86-7
    see also leadership of schools policy
Leadership Development Framework 29
Leadership Incentive Grant (LIG) 21
leadership industry 5-9, 44-6
Leadership Programme for Serving Headteachers (LPSH) 109, 110
leadership of schools policy 2-3, 13, 17-36, 80-1
    alternative approaches 123-30
    leadership of schools game 19-26, 133, 138-9
        coalition continuation 140-1, 144

global legitimacy 95
institutionalised governance 53-67,
   149
and intellectual work 41-6, 133
objects of 120, 125
positioning of heads 95-115
and regime practices 118-21
and regimes of practice 77-8, 81
resistance and policy research regime
   88-9, 102-4, 120
and National College 26-33, 113
and potential school leadership regime
   activity 75, 104-8, 120-1
Leggett, B.M. 100
Leithwood, Ken 49, 50
Liddle, R. 12
Lingard, B. 14, 37, 76, 95, 125-6
literacy strategy 1, 4, 79, 137
local authorities 7-8, 55, 57-8, 61
Local Leaders of Education (LLEs) 141,
   143
Local Management of Schools (LMS) 7, 8
Lockett, A. 114
logic of practice 3, 7, 13, 42, 81, 117, 119
London Leadership Centre 63

M

Mackay, Tony 43, 44-5, 61, 92*n*
McKinsey and Company 48
MacMillan, Harold 70*n*
Maguire, M. 126
Maloney, R.J. 138
managerialism 1, 56, 86, 98, 100-1, 103,
   107
   see also new public management
Mandelson, Peter 12
Mansell, W. 137
market approach *see* business approaches
marketised knowledge production 84, 147
markets in education 134-5, 149
Marquand, D. 12, 60, 148
Mavrogordato, M. 135
media 149
Menter, I. 111
Midwinter, A. 148
Miliband, David 15*n*, 17, 22, 25
Miliband, Ed 144
Millar, Fiona 142, 152*n*
Millet, Anthea 70-1*n*, 136
misrecognition 7, 81-2, 87, 114, 119
modelling 19-21, 29-30, 35*n*
modernisation agenda 56-7, 62, 98, 101,
   148
Moe, T.M. 60
Molnar, A. 134
Monk, Heath 57
Moore, A. 105
Moran, M. 59-60
Morris, Estelle 15*n*, 69*n*, 107, 136
Moss, P. 126-7
Mulderrig, J. 56

Munby, Steve 61, 65, 143

N

'naming and shaming' schools 12, 135
National Audit Office 142
National Challenge Schools 99-100
National College 3, 5, 9, 25
   architecture and building 26, *27*
   and centralised control 63-6
   coalition government and Executive
      Agency status 142-3
   and cult of standards 138
   and delivery remit 57, 64, 65-6, 121
   document review 67
   foundation 53, 62-7
   headteachers' experiences 108-15
   headteachers' involvement 102, 103,
      109-10
   interconnectedness of intellectuals 43,
      112
   and leadership of schools 26-33
      and critical policy scholarship 88-9,
         110-15
      criticism of training materials 66-7,
         113-14
   and professional preparation 108-15
   positive evaluation 108-9
   publications and outreach 36*n*
   regional outposts 62, 112
   research and knowledge production
      26, 28-9, 30-3, 46-51, 112
      academic ambivalence 91
      marketisation 84
National College for Leadership of
   Schools and Children's Services
   (NCLSCS) 15*n*, 26
   see also National College
National College for School Leadership
   (NCSL) 15*n*, 26
   see also National College
National Development Centre (NDC)
   8, 63
National Leaders of Education (NLEs)
   141, 143
National Literacy Strategy 1, 4, 79, 137
National Numeracy Strategy 1, 4, 79, 137
National Professional Qualification for
   Headship (NPQH) 8, 70*n*, 109, 110,
   111, 113
National Remodelling Team (NRT) 37
National Standards 19
neoliberalism
   challenges to 148
   and Conservative policy 9-10, 139-40,
      144
   as doxa 14, 33
   New Labour and Thatcher legacy
      9-11, 12
   and 'policy entrepreneurs' 59
   research view 86, 121
   and standards problem 134-6

networks and institutionalised governance 57
  intellectuals and government 43-4, 59, 117
  inclusion and exclusion 75-6, 91-2, 112, 118, 133, 147-8
New Labour
  leadership approaches 1-2
  policy in opposition 144-7
  and Thatcher legacy 9-12, 60-1
New Labour Policy Regime (NLPR) 3, 75, 78-84, 90, 91, 133
  approach to leadership of schools game 121, 147-8
  and coalition succession 139, 141-2, 146, 148
  and headteachers' positioning 100-2, 107-8
  position in opposition 145-6
  and regime practices 117, 118, 119
  scrutiny and critique 120
new public management 57, 60
  see also managerialism
New Relationship with Schools policy 16*n*, 22
New Schools Network (NSN) 142
Newman, J. 10, 53-4, 56, 57, 148
NHS Leadership Centre 16*n*
NHS and New Labour reforms 116*n*
No Child Left Behind Act (2001)(US) 135
Non-Departmental Public Bodies (NDPBs) 55
  National College as 63-4
numeracy strategy 1, 4, 79, 137

O

Office for Standards in Education (Ofsted) 4, 38, 56, 69*n*, 104
O'Reilly, D. 2
Organisation for Economic Co-operation and Development (OECD) 108
Osborne, D. 60
Ozga, J. 13, 58-9, 60, 68*n*, 95, 96, 108, 124

P

Pennell, H. 144-5
performance management 4, 11, 21-2, 103, 107, 139
  and NHS 116*n*
  see also data generation and performance; effectiveness of schools; managerialism
Peters, T. 8
'place-based curriculum' 128
Plant, R. 10
policy elite and intellectual work 37-8, 61-2, 81-2, 118, 133
  academics and government 82-4
  and heterarchic power relations 76-7
  see also New Labour Policy Regime; Policy Research Regime

'policy entrepreneurs' 59
Policy Research Regime (PRR) 3, 75, 84-9, 117
  and coalition succession 146-7
  disciplinary divisions 91-2
  and headteachers' positioning 102-4, 107-8
  and scrutiny of New Labour Policy Regime 120
policymaking and regimes of practice 75-93, 133
  and headteachers 104-8
  policy and professional practice 95-6
  see also educational reform
politics of knowledge production 133, 147-50
Pollitt, C. 61
power
  and leadership approach 51, 57, 121, 123-4
  and networks 76-7, 117
  and New Labour policy regime 78-9, 117, 120, 147
  power flows and governance 59-61
  as research subject 87-8
  see also hierarchies
practice *see* professional practice; regime practices; regimes of practice
pragmatism and professional practice 104-8
PricewaterhouseCoopers 45, 46
private sector and education 3, 4, 137
  and coalition policy 139-40, 144
  game and regime practices 118-19
  and institutionalised governance 57, 58, 61
  and leadership industry 6-7, 20, 44-6
  and restructuring 23-4, 61, 127
'productive pedagogies' 125-6
professional knowledge
  constraints on 22, 103
  and National College 91, 108-15
  selective appropriation 31, 112
  and New Labour policy regime 82, 90, 91, 120, 146
  and policy research regime 85-7, 102-4, 120, 146
  and potential school leadership regime research 89-92, 104-8, 120-1
  see also experts; training
professional practice 95-116
  control through interventions 4, 12, 38, 57
  cult of standards 137-8
  and headteachers 100-2, 104-5
  and lack of autonomy 22, 98-100
  deprofessionalisation 23, 137
  functional knowledge and colonisation of practice 5-6, 9, 37-8, 91, 121
  and National College 31-3, 47, 112
  and policy implementation 4, 95-6
  strategic pragmatism approach 104-5

and policy research regime 84-9, 102-4, 107-8, 120, 146
and potential school leadership regime activity 89-92, 104-8, 120-1
remodelling and reculturing 22-3, 35*n*, 56-7, 79-80
role of National College 29-30
see also good practice; headteachers; regimes of practice; teachers
Programme for International Student Assessment (PISA) 137
public institutions 53, 55-8
publishing industry 8, 149
pupil premium funding 140
Putnam, David 72*n*

Q

Qualifications and Curriculum Authority (QCA) 138
Qualifications and Curriculum Development Agency (QCDA) 142
Qualified Teacher Status (QTS) 34*n*, 100

R

Ranson, S. 9, 18, 53, 144, 146, 147
Ravitch, D. 72*n*, 129, 135-6
rebranding 22, 121
reculturing 22-3, 29-30, 80-1, 113
Reed, M. 2
reform *see* educational reform
regime practices 117-31, 133
regimes of practice 75-93, 133, 149
headteachers' positioning 100-8, 114
and New Labour in opposition 145-6
New Labour policy regime 3, 75, 78-84, 90, 91, 100-2, 107-8, 120, 146
policy research regime 3, 75, 84-9, 91-2, 102-4, 107-8, 120, 146-7
potential school leadership regime activity 89-92, 104-8, 120-1
see also professional practice; regime practices
regulation 11, 22, 100, 137
remodelling
and reculturing 22-3, 35*n*, 56-7, 79-80
see also modelling
research and scholarship
and coalition government 147, 148
and National College 26, 28-9, 30-3, 46-51
and neoliberal doxa 14, 33, 59, 86, 121
New Labour's selective approach 24-6, 29, 30-1, 37-51, 147-8
bought-in and brought-in research 45-6, 81-4
critiques of knowledge base 122-3, 146-7
policy research regime 3, 75, 84-9, 91-2, 120, 146-7
headteachers and professional practice 102-4, 107-8
politics of 147-50

potential school leadership regime research 89-92, 104-8, 120-1
see also knowledge production; School Effectiveness, School Improvement (SESI) studies
responsibility and Thatcher legacy 10-11
restructuring 23-4, 56-7, 61, 127
Reynolds, David 41, 43, 44
Rhodes, R.A.W. 57
Ribbins, Peter 102
Richardson, L. 150
risk management 21-2, 58
Rizvi, F. 10, 14, 95
Roberts, Hank 34*n*
Rowan, B. 6, 55, 149
Rudduck, J. 125
Ryan, Conor 46

S

Saint-Martin, D. 16*n*, 58-9
Salt, Toby 43
Sammons, Pam 38-40, 43, 49, 50, 122-3
Satchwell, Sir Kevin 61, 101
School Effectiveness, School Improvement (SESI) studies 13, 30, 145-6
and New Labour knowledge production 38-41, 43-4, 48, 82-4, 91
critiques of limitations 89, 122-3
School Evaluation Form (SEF) 22
'school improvement industry' in US 6, 55, 149
School Improvement Partners (SIPs) 4, 22
school leadership *see* leadership of schools
School Leadership Regime (SLR)
research 75, 89-92, 123
and New Labour in opposition 145-6
problems on fringe 91-2, 120-1
and professional practice 104-8
and regime practices 120-1
schools 126-7
systems reform and leadership 4, 23, 141
see also effectiveness of schools; School Leadership Regime (SLR) research
Scotland 57, 111
Scott, J. 68*n*
Scottish Qualification for Headship (SQH) 111
self-evaluation of schools 22
senior leadership teams 22-3, 45
Shamir, R. 10
Shaw, E. 16*n*
Shaw, Rowie 71*n*
Shields, C.M. 128
Shulman, L. 5
site-based management of schools 7-8
Skelcher, C. 71*n*
Smith, Des 25-6
Smyth, J. 124, 125, 126, 134
social capital 42-3, 81
social class and achievement 138

social cohesion and Conservative policy 9-10

social justice 100, 103, 107, 121, 145
  as research subject 88, 92, 127-8, 130

social partnership and unions 58

Southworth, Geoff 61, 98, 123-4

specialist curriculum status 23

Specialist Schools and Academies Trust (SSAT) 57, 142

sports partnerships 151*n*

Standards and Effectiveness Unit (SEU) 57, 136

standards problem 134-9
  coalition and standards agenda 139-44
  as global problem 1, 13, 136
  New Labour solutions 1-2
    cult of standards 136-9
    and fall in standards 137-8
    and intellectual work 41-6
    interventions 12, 38, 79, 137-8
    leadership of schools 26-33, 138-9
    New Labour policy regime 78-84
    performance management 21-2
  see also effectiveness of schools; testing

state and institutionalised governance 53, 147

Stoll, Louise 43

Story of England (TV series) 130-1*n*

strategic initiatives and National College 29-30

strategic pragmatism of headteachers 104-8

'Stretch Programme' for headteachers 44

structural changes 23-4

structure and regime practices 117, 118

Stubbs, Lady Marie 101

student outcomes and leadership 49-51, 67

Sturdy, A. 61

succession planning 32

'Super-Heads' 20, 24

Sveningsson, S. 129

Swift, Peter 72*n*

symbolic capital 43, 81, 85, 121
  symbolic exchange 7, 117, 118, 119, 120, 121, 143, 146
    and politics of knowledge production 147-8

systems reform and leadership 4, 23, 141

T

talk2learn online system 29, 112

target setting and workforce 11, 21

Taylor, Cyril 61

Taylor, W. 124

Teacher Training Agency (TTA) 33*n*, 68*n*, 70-1*n*, 72*n*
  see also Training and Development Agency (TDA)

teachers
  as 'absent presence' 18-19, 22-3
  and dominant power relations 123
  and failing and effective schools 41
  as focus of research and policy 125-6
  quality of teaching and effectiveness 39, 40, 89
  reform and deprofessionalisation 23, 137
  see also headteachers; workforce reform

teaching assistants 23

testing 1, 99, 134, 135, 137-8, 139

Thatcher, Margaret 9-12, 35*n*, 60-1, 138
  see also Conservatives

think tanks 68-9*n*

Thomson, P. 6-7, 95, 100, 108, 112, 113, 114, 115, 128, 152*n*

Thrupp, M. 25, 113

training 4, 80, 109
  alternative approaches 123-30
  and leadership industry 8, 44-6
  and National College 108-15
    critical assessments 88-9, 110-15
    government criticism 66-7
    headteachers and development 63-7
    positive evaluation 108-9
  pre-leadership path 124
  requirements for teaching 23
  see also National College

Training and Development Agency (TDA) 143, 151*n*

'transformational' leaders 2, 19-20, 47, 98, 121, 123-4, 138-9
  critiques 88, 89

Transforming the School Workforce Pathfinder Project 35*n*, 51*n*

Trends in International Mathematics and Science Study (TIMSS) 150*n*

U

unions 58, 60-1, 63, 149

United States
  charter school 135-6
  'school improvement industry' 6, 55, 149
  and standards 1, 134-6

universities *see* higher education institutions

University Council for Educational Administration (UCEA) 90

University Partnership Group (UPG) 91

V

Vasagar, J. 143-4

virtual college at National College 28, 29, 112

Vorderman, Carol 142

W

Wacquant, L. 11, 14

Waterman, R. 8

Weindling, D. 65, 106

welfare state devolution as Thatcher legacy
   10
West, A. 144-5
Western, S. 130
what works approach 31, 147
   see also evidence-based practice
Whitty, G. 97-8, 120, 147
Wilby, P. 148
Willmott, R. 25
Winkley, D. 102-3
Wolf, Rachel 142
women researchers 92
Woodhead, Chris 61, 72*n*
Woodhouse, G. 38, 146
workforce reform 4, 11, 79-80
   deprofessionalisation 23, 137
   governance and power flows 60-1
   involvement in research 87
   and leadership game 18-19, 22-3, 81,
      139
   National College role 29-30
   Transforming the School Workforce
      Pathfinder Project 35*n*, 51*n*
   see also headteachers; teachers; training
Wright, N. 107

Y

Young, M.F.D. 146-7